TRAVELLING TOWARDS HOME

Articulating Journeys: Festivals, Memorials, and Homecomings
General Editors:
Tom Selwyn, SOAS University of London
Nicola Frost, Devon Community Foundation

The landscape of contemporary mobility stresses ideas of home, return, commemoration and celebration. Groups seek to mark changing elements of historical and cultural importance through architecture, narrative and festivity. Migrants and their descendants frequently travel between 'homes', reinventing and reshaping as they go. Such events can themselves attract travellers and pilgrims with their own stories to tell. Engaging with more substantive ethnographic features and linking back to classical anthropological and philosophical concerns, this series contributes to a new understanding of the Other encountered away from home but also of the Self and home.

TRAVELLING TOWARDS HOME

Mobilities and Homemaking

═══════════

Edited by

Nicola Frost and Tom Selwyn

Foreword to the Paperback Edition by
Safet HadžiMuhamedović

berghahn
NEW YORK • OXFORD
www.berghahnbooks.com

First published in 2018 by

Berghahn Books

www.berghahnbooks.com

© 2018, 2023 Nicola Frost and Tom Selwyn
First paperback edition published in 2023

Library of Congress Cataloging-in-Publication Data

Names: Frost, Nicola, 1974– editor. | Selwyn, Tom, 1944– editor.
Title: Travelling towards Home: Mobilities and Homemaking / edited by Nicola Frost
and Tom Selwyn.
Description: First edition. | New York: Berghahn Books, 2018. | Series: Articulating
Journeys: Festivals, Memorials, and Homecomings; 3 | Includes bibliographical
references and index.
Identifiers: LCCN 2018024656 (print) | LCCN 2018035339 (ebook) |
ISBN 9781785339561 (Ebook) | ISBN 9781785339554 (hardback: alk. paper)
Subjects: LCSH: Home—Social aspects—Case studies. | Emigration and immigration—
Social aspects—Case studies. | Migration, Internal—Social aspects—Case studies. |
Return migration—Social aspects—Case studies.
Classification: LCC GT2420 (ebook) | LCC GT2420 .T73 2018 (print) |
DDC 392.3/6—dc23
LC record available at https://lccn.loc.gov/2018024656

British Library Cataloguing in Publication Data

A catalogue record for this book is available from the British Library

ISBN 978-1-78533-955-4 hardback
ISBN 978-1-80073-949-9 paperback
ISBN 978-1-78533-956-1 ebook

https://doi.org/10.3167/9781785339554

*We dedicate this book to the memory of Colin Murray who inspired us
and many generations of anthropology students and scholars*

CONTENTS

Illustrations

Figures

Tables

FOREWORD TO THE PAPERBACK EDITION

We need this book to start to heal from the anxious safety of home, which produces terror as it appeals to its own defence. To have such a home – determined, bounded, inflexible, explicit – is to commit to a narrow inward orientation, to live in perpetual, precarious unhomeliness of the fearful Self and its frightful shadow of the Other. As the cornerstones of modern ideologies, the reified tropes of belonging, anchored in race, nationality, territory, class, and other entitled imaginations of the Self, conceal a deep alienation from the lifeworlds of home. The volume before you – aptly ending with John Donne's famous poem – turns the tables on such insular regimes by carefully attending to the different ways home gets caught up between the personal, the communal, and the large-scale political. Home is observed as it travels from public discourse and historiography to the intimacy of sexuality, dwelling or meditations on the place of one's own burial. In all cases, home appears as a verb, as an active process of communication with place and identity, never lending itself to easy definitions.[1] There is thus no home as such, free of negotiation and change, to be found in this volume. Yet, with each new chapter, we are able to find something powerful in home as a process of travelling towards oneself and others, which reiterates the importance of retaining the concept not only as a heuristic, but perhaps also as a window to our shared (more-than-)human condition.[2]

As Tom Selwyn reminds us in his Afterword, the result of home's reification and confinement (with the proliferation of walls and hard borders) is unhomely isolation. It rips through the relational fabric to produce fragments and absences, so that home steadily comes to be expressed in the left-over lacunas of memory, landscape, dreams and the supernatural. Like all spectral hauntings, these ways of holding on to or rediscovering the past, purposefully occupy the present until such time as some sort of resolution arrives. Strategies of homing, against various unhoming ruptures, sometimes require the piecing together of disarticulated stories and relations, and other times distil specific images, objects and stories as more instrumental in the process of perseverance.[3] These strategies appear throughout the book, whether as the Sydney Moluccans sing about 'coral-ringed islands, support for harmonious family and community life' (Chapter 6), or as an anthropologist does archival work on the reconstruction of family histories after apartheid (Chapter 7), as the Chinese migrant workers dwell on the everyday absences of home in Shantou city (Chapter 2), or as Jewish people return from Israel to (pre-war) Odessa after protracted absence (Chapter 3).[4] Encapsulating and fixing the desired past of home, or normativising the direction of resistance (Chapter 5), may be the outcome of deep changes to the fabric of the community. However, such efforts to freeze moments of social relations, imagined as harmonious or at least better than the present, and transplant them into the horizons of the future are more imaginative than insular regimes.

To observe the inherent relationality of home, and with such fine-tuned anthropological sensibilities for the voices of others as the contributors demonstrate, is then a globally relevant critique of unhoming ideologies. For, as we journey with the authors' interlocutors, we shift not just geo-graphically, but within and across the scales of homewardness, beginning to understand how home's diverse registers are dynamically negotiated: re-sisted, lived up to, co-orchestrated, dreamed, despaired, sung... These sto-ries are imbued with temporal, spatial and emotional movement, so that home is never abstract, even if each contribution shows how actual people live with and against abstractions. Travel, forced displacement and return are revealed as forms of disorientation, in which one's world is shifted from its axis, but also moments when many assumptions about home are recon-sidered and thus put into motion. For all its inherent movement, home is perceived in relation to orientational devices (kinship, landscape, commu-nity, architecture, calendar...), the habitual qualities of which are embraced, resisted and revised.

We learn that home may indeed be unhomely – exerting normative pres-sures or becoming the rationale for violence – yet continue to be called for, even longed for. This apparent paradox, of homing home, is expressed in the book's title as 'travelling towards home', which is not about destination or arrival, but a negotiation of orientations, meanings, and ideals, which is never one-directional, but cyclical, oscillating, spiralling, moving back and forth, or simultaneously moving along and against the grain of expectations.

These enthralling and often painful stories of homeward journeys are not clustered simply through the conceptual apparatus. Read together, the chap-ters cautiously venture to ask something more extensive about the patterns of tangible and intangible interactions of living beings with each other and their environments, about our increasingly shared task 'to deliver spaces and places where sociality and conviviality can flourish' (172). This question, as the book suggests through its grounded ethnographic approach, is not to be answered in any one way, but one to travel with, and often to travail with, as homing requires continual effort, albeit one that does not seem to have an alternative except total isolation. Therefore, homing appears in the chapters as a matter of reconfiguration of home to provide access to those for various reasons excluded from it. Desires and longings, for example, chip away at the confined structures of home and exclusionary articulations of belonging. The 'homeawayness', to use Shuhua Chen's term (Chapter 2), in these contributions reads as a critically productive, if precarious, position from which to think accessibility.

Working against isolation is not easy. Homing entails physical and emotional work, sometimes of the kind testing the far edges of human capacities. One of the catalysts for this book and the renewed attention to the questions of home and belonging is the global resurrection of unhoming ideologies and technologies (epitomised by the UK Home Office's anti-immigrant policy of 'hostile environment', announced in 2012).[5] These powerful unhoming programmes, linked together by the reification of home through the fictional possibility of defending pure identities, have been emboldened through each other's outspokenness and increased levels of violence exercised on defenceless populations. In particular, people seeking refuge from various forms of harm, essentialised in policy and public rhetoric as 'the migrants', have been exploited to consolidate the body politic. The advocates of the 'hostile environment' have co-opted the intimate domains of religion, kinship, and community to stoke fear that home will be lost or changed forever by the arrival of dangerous foreigners, or by propagating the return of some mythical national greatness.[6]

This book shows us that, when faced with repeated violence, or nesting forms of inequity, home becomes an insistent exercise in creativity, an art of reappropriation and alteration of injurious social matrices and material contexts into more hospitable ones. The investment into the 'creative reconstruction of home' (170) is imaginative. It involves the work of memory and adaptation, of resistance and endurance, of crafting alliances and nurturing communities, of trust and discovery. Homing is about active orientations, whether it appears as 'bodily contortions' whilst shifting between spaces of normative masculinity and queerness (Chapter 1), adopting a different narrative register of home for an immigration tribunal hearing (Chapter 6), or visiting home for holidays whilst performing emotional distance from the nonhomely everyday (Chapter 2). It is this surprising creativity that best captures the active entanglements of people, places, and times in the chapters before you. An equally creative anthropology of home – as the reader will find here – with adapting methods and conceptual apparatuses, is needed.

This book is thus of medicinal use in a 'fragmenting world' (172).[7] Its contributors are keenly aware of the need to avoid the 'danger of [home studies] becoming unmoored to specific lived realities' (2). Their anthropological sensibilities produce observations of homemaking not in static locations but in dynamic and diverse relations, which is why we are never asked to accede to the terms and conditions set out by the ideological co-optations of home.

Safet HadžiMuhamedović
London, 21 February 2023

NOTES

1. In Tom Selwyn's scholarship, home, and hospitality are not only the key words, but also indispensable questions of responsibility in what he has recognised as a 'fragmenting world'. I am lucky to be part of an ever-expanding group of researchers, artists, museum workers, students, and activists who have been guided by Tom into these questions. It is not surprising to me, then, that Tom has offered a set of *invitational endnotes* to this text, in the form of links to new communal initiatives, inclusive conversations, creative repositories, and collaborative learning programmes.

2. In the first two weeks of February 2023, an exhibition was held at the wildlife conservation charity, the Zoological Society of London (ZSL), displaying the artwork produced during the project *Refugia*, a co-produced project creatively exploring wildlife conservation with asylum seekers and refugees. It was jointly organised and managed by ZSL and The New Arts Studio, a therapeutic arts group for asylum seekers and refugees. Based in Islington, the latter holds weekly art therapy sessions for asylum seekers and refugees thus providing a safe space for some of the most dispossessed members of our society. Its overall aim is, in its own words, 'to enable our members to express experiences and feelings that can't always be put into words'. More information about the collaborative programme and the *Refugia* exhibition may be obtained from Lucy Brown (lucy.brown@zsl.org), ZSL's Public Engagement with Science Manager, or from the *Refugia* website (https://www.zsl.org/refugia).

3. London's Migration Museum (www.migrationmuseum.org) is the primary centre for the articulation of stories, artwork, exhibitions, discussions/discourses, and school/university/extra mural education about the contribution of migration to the cultural and economic life of the UK. On 21 February 2023, after a ten year journey from wonderful spaces in the old fire station in Battersea and, more recently in Lewisham Shopping Mall, the Migration Museum announced that it has been given the green light for a permanent home in the City of London – a stone's throw from Fenchurch Street – where it will continue, in its own words, 'to explore how the movement of people to and from these shores have shaped who we all are – as individuals, as communities, and as nations'.

4. Since Russia's invasion of Ukraine, Marina (m.sapritsky@lse.ac.uk) has been writing about the effects of war on the everyday lives of Ukrainian Jews who remain in the country, and of those who have fled to Europe and the UK, as well as the fragmentation and remaking of historical narratives.

5. The Xenia Series (from Greek *Xenia*: hospitality) is a multi-disciplinary network of scholars from various universities in the UK and beyond who organise and manage monthly presentations and discussions on the nature of identity, together with such interrelated topics as home, hospitality, hostility, exclusion, inclusion, and migration. Further information about the series may be obtained from Tom Selwyn (t.selwyn@soas.ac.uk) and at www.xeniaseries.com.

6. 'Shared Sacred', an exhibition of anthropological photography organised by Safet HadžiMuhamedović at the University of Cambridge, delves into the proximities, relations and encounters between persons and communities of 'different' faiths. It introduces diverse examples of co-orchestrated rituals, feasts and holy spaces testifying to rich historical and present-day coexistences in polities increasingly partitioned along the lines of religious identity. Its contributors from across the world search for ways out of simple, one-dimensional narratives of religion by pointing out the travels and negotiations of meaning between the political and the everyday. Further details are available at www.sharedsacred.com.

7. In the academic year 2021/2, colleagues from Al-Quds Bard, Jerusalem, SOAS University of London, and the University of the Arts (artEZ), the Netherlands, assembled and taught the course 'Dislocated Identities in a Fragmenting World' for the Open Society University Network (opensocietyuniversitynetwork.org). Taking the main inspiration from the work on socio-cultural identity by Amin Ma'aluf, the course covered topics from dislocation, shared sacred spaces, refugee return, cities of refuge, mediascapes, intergenerational trauma, and nationalism. The follow up course is presently in preparation. Further information is available from Carin Rustema (c.rustema@artEZ.nl), Jens Haendeler (jhaendeler@staff.alquds.edu), or Tom Selwyn (tsl4@soas.ac.uk).

INTRODUCTION

Home and Homemaking in a Time of Crisis

TOM SELWYN AND NICOLA FROST

Introduction

A decade ago, the question of homemaking within a mobile global population was an important one. Today, as we grapple with a growing refugee
crisis, alongside a hardening of anti-immigration feeling and deepening
communal segregation in many parts of the developed world, the issue of the
nature of home and homemaking is critical, and is becoming daily more so.
Media reports tumble over each other telling of refugees who, whilst seeking
home and hospitality in Europe, drown in the sea passages between North
Africa and Italy. Such news jostles with reports of a rising tide of political
rhetoric about building walls between 'us' and 'them' at a time when cities
in the Western world, including Europe and the United Kingdom, are wit-
nessing racist abuse, some of it deadly. For example, following the murder
in the marketplace of Harlow, Essex, United Kingdom in September 2016
of Arek Jozwik, a Polish resident of the town, his friend, Eric Hind, told the
journalist Jill Lawless (27 October 2016): 'It's just not nice to live in a country where you don't know where you stand . . . if you don't know what will
happen tomorrow, if someone will come to your door and say "OK, time for
you to pack your bags and go home".'

Such testimony reveals a variety of assumptions that our collection seeks
critically to scrutinize: *inter alia,* that home is associated inexorably with
place of birth, that homes made and/or remade by people on the move are
thought to be in some way less than fully rightful or authentic, and that migration is inherently destabilizing. These assumptions appear to render hostility legitimate (thus making it possible for hostility towards 'migrants' to
make regular appearances in tabloids) in a way that subverts the founda-
tional principles of hospitality.

Consideration of these and comparable claims is not made easier, either at an academic or policy level, not so much by the fact that the idea of home has been under-discussed and/or under-theorized, but rather that it has been the subject of reflection by such a wide body of different and disparate writers and thinkers across disciplines and genres of social thought. One of the consequences of this is that the concept has come to appear rather like a loose holding company for a diverse range of ideas, scales and registers used in a broad expanse of conceptual ground. The problem here is that the term is in danger of becoming unmoored to specific lived realities. As anthropologists concerned with the subject from the point of view (in the main) of travellers, we ground our thinking in this volume in closely observed and particular ethnography.

Within such a diverse literary and theoretical landscape, then, how do our authors help to focus our thinking? First, they point us towards using the idea of home to encompass attachments to spaces and places (seldom singular in the case of the ethnographies presented in this volume) by both individuals and collectivities. Second, they invite approaches that enable the term to cope both with the fixity that the idea of home seems to promote and the necessary fluidity of a notion positioned within a contemporary global system with movement, including movement of labour, at its heart. Third, since many of the chapters are haunted by notions of the 'unhomely' (a term used by a number of authors including Prakash (2015) and Sugars (2004) writing in 'postcolonial' modes used and personified by Homi Bhabha (2012)), we need to ensure that, whatever else we do with it, the definition of home emerging from this book needs to include attention to experiences of those categories of migrants in 'unhomely' states of being. Indeed, reporting of the shameful treatment in 2016/2017 of asylum seekers by U.K. authorities (Travis 2017) should increase our determination to search for definitions of home that encompass lessons to be learnt from the homeless. Fourth, the idea of home derives much of its potency by being one of those rare terms in the social sciences that finds a place in both external and internal worlds. In brief, studies of home and homecoming, exemplified by the chapters in this volume, allow and encourage analysis to move between inner feelings and emotions, on the one hand, and spaces and places in the outer world, on the other. In this sense we can find the term nestling on the threshold between the two.

The remainder of this Introduction, the aim of which is to draw out further the thematic framework of the volume as a whole, is grouped under subtitles that have been chosen to follow the concerns of our authors, each grouping opening with short references to previously published work.

The section that follows these opening paragraphs, 'Regular Doings versus the Migrancy of Identity', addresses a theme underlying all the chapters, namely the relation between fixity and fluidity in our definition of home. Is home, as Douglas had it, a notion that speaks of routine, comfortable familiarity, and fixed patterns of thought and action over generations? Is it, as Rapport and Overing have argued, a notion that is carved out of the movement of everyday contemporary life? Or does it encompass both?

The section that follows the above, 'Family Histories and Materials of the Everyday', takes inspiration from Colin Murray's assertion in this volume that family history is a stimulating route into history. Movements of families through generations, and sometimes territories, provide us with a rich source of indications on how best analytically to use the term 'home'. Reference to 'materials of the everyday' partly follows Shuhua Chen's distinction between the 'everyday life' of her Chinese migrant interlocutors, for whom 'home' is the place visited for an annual holiday, whilst 'everyday life' – with its 'everyday materials' (houses, land, objects, physical bodies and so on) – applies to times, places and things lived in throughout the working year.

'The Political Economy of Homemaking in the Contemporary World' draws particularly on the chapters by Nicola Frost and Marina Sapritsky, as well as every other chapter, in insisting that understanding home involves global, regional and local politico-economic contextualization. Thus, Frost's portrait of families belonging to a diaspora of migrants from Maluku, Indonesia begins with a description of their feelings of desire for a homeland and despair at the violent political upheavals in that homeland, both of which are set within a framework of Indonesian and Australian immigration policies as well as the violent political upheavals in Maluku itself. Homemaking in Odessa by Jewish families returning from Israel, as described by Sapritsky, requires us to consider how these activities are interwoven with and shaped by states, the relevant economies through which migrating families pass, as well as personal fortunes and misfortunes along the way.

Consideration of 'Symbols and Connotations' of home is a rich field for anthropological enquiry. Thus, Yuko Shioji's eyes light upon saucepans and other cooking utensils, tea services, gardens and examples of noteworthy architecture as aspects of complex symbolic worlds that enable residents of Chipping Camden to shape their notions of home and its landscapes, populated as this is by long-term residents, incomers, developers and others.

'Self as Mirror of Home',[1] the penultimate section, responds to Chand Starin Basi and Kaveri Qureshi's poignant interpretation of the feelings of young gay men they worked with whose families have close links to the Indian subcontinent. The issue they are concerned with is how to resolve or articulate allegiances to sexual orientation, on the one hand, and territory that parents view as 'homeland', on the other. The pain of split and fractured identity is also the subject of Ilana Webster-Kogen's reading and listening to the Palestinian rap group DAM. Criticized on social media for focusing in one of their songs on an honour killing within a Palestinian family, the group, well known for their political work opposing Israeli occupation, was accused at the time (November 2012) of releasing their song 'If I Could Go Back in Time' of watering down resistance by looking inwards at features of Palestinian society and culture as well as outwards towards Israeli occupiers. There are echoes here, that we will touch on below, of contemporary European experiences that render the Palestinian dilemma familiar: is resistance necessarily circumscribed by exclusive focus on occupation or are there also moments in which resistance engages both the other and ourselves?

Finally 'Home, Language and Meanings' acknowledges that our work in this volume involves thinking through the place of the English word 'home' in anthropological discussion, whilst terms in other languages make us consistently aware that the idea of home has multiple connotative variations. However, Chen's tender and historically framed examination of Chinese ideographs for home shows how approaches to the meanings of our subject need not necessarily be lost in translation.

We end this chapter by 'Thinking Ahead'.

'Regular Doings' versus 'the Migrancy of Identity'

Rapport and Overing (2007: 156–62) observe that the term 'home' did not figure greatly in traditional anthropological work, except as a synonym for 'house' or 'household'. They report on Mary Douglas' (1991: 289) attempt to understand the notion of home in terms of the routinization of time and space and thus of 'pattern(s) of regular doings, furnishings and appurtenances, and a physical space in which certain communitarian practices were realised' (1991: 157).

One classic ethnography (much praised by Douglas, incidentally) of home composed in terms of 'pattern(s) of regular doings' is Bourdieu's (1979) 'Kabyle House or the World Reversed'. Bourdieu's essay tells of the daily comings and goings of the people in an Algerian peasant house and relates these everyday routines to such monthly, annual and lifetime rhythms as sleeping and waking, menstruation and lovemaking, cooking and eating, giving birth, marrying and dying, with all their associated rituals, relating all these, in turn, to the coming and going of light and shade as days begin and end.

In the present book there is one ethnographic example – very different from Bourdieu's masterpiece to be sure – within which we can recognize Douglas' conceptions at work. In several senses all sexual activities are periodically grounded in 'pattern(s) of regular doings'. Thus, Starin Basi and Qureshi place home within the dynamics of sexual and cultural dispositions worked out by twentysomething gay men with South Asian family backgrounds in the United Kingdom. These tell a story in which sexual doings and solidarities assert themselves at the expense of often taken-for-granted assumptions about the pull experienced by British/Asian second generations towards what their parents might regard as their Indian/South Asian 'homeland'. The authors describe feelings held by some of their interlocutors about their homes being 'unhomely' in their heteronormativity. The 'gay Asian scene', on the other hand, formed partly within a cradle, or in the mirror, of white British gay youth culture, is reported to be a cultural space in which new senses of 'homely' home could flourish and develop, although these do not follow inevitably. This is an example of sexual imperatives and idioms asserting themselves within or alongside homes defined in national and/or ethnic terms.

Rapport and Overing (2007: 176) argue that, given a world shaped by migration and movement, Douglas' approach is 'anachronistic, providing little conceptual purchase on a world of contemporary movement'. Therefore, they suggest, we need to find ways of working with notions of home and identity 'that transcend traditional definitions in terms of locality, ethnicity, religiosity, and/or nationality and that are sensitive instead to allocations of identity which are multiple, situational, individual, and paradoxical'. They claim that anthropological notions of home need to be founded on 'the intrinsic migrancy of identity', suggesting that everyday movements of people across national and state borders render the making of simplistic associations between home, nation and the routinization of space and time redundant. They argue that in a world of layered identities, we should adopt the position of being reflexive hybrids. Weber-Feve (2010) also commends the use of the notion of hybridity, frequently linked as this is to the work of Bhabha (1994) and others.

However, the work of our authors suggests that rather than placing time/space regularities at one pole and hybridity at the other – and by so doing implying that we have to choose between them – we may advance the understanding of home by adopting and asserting the necessity of both.

In fact, as implied above, Starin Basi and Qureshi's work provides a powerful illustration. Their young British-Asian interlocutors seem competently to operate within a culturally 'hybrid' universe by adopting sexual ways of doing that are routine and regular amongst the wider gay community. This suggests that Rapport and Overing miss the point. Let us remind ourselves that we live at a time of the burning of Grenfell Tower, increasing homelessness in our cities and the multiple tribulations of refugees. Additionally, and for many reasons, including housing shortages and property price rises, there seems to be a weakening, in some places and in some senses, of more general social (including kinship) solidarities. Given all of this, the challenge is to find political and intellectual modes of thinking and proceeding in which the homeless can regain the power and capacity to convert 'unhomely' states of being in the world to 'homely' ones.

Family Histories and Materials of the Everyday

In their different ways, Anton Chekhov (2011 [1904]) and E.M. Forster (1973 [1910]) both wrote of the poetics of emotional and cognitive interpenetration of houses and families. Both the Cherry Orchard as an estate and Howards End as a house appear as intimates, almost kin, of the families and their guests who made them homes. Both narratives contain references to persons and families of varying wealth and poverty, and it seems indisputable that both Chekhov and Forster touch on universal processes having to do with relations between homes and family histories across classes, ethnic affiliations and incomes.

Colin Murray writes of his anthropological research in the early 1970s into the family histories of displaced people in the 'remote and desolate rural slum' of Pitse's Nek in Lesotho. Many such families are broken and fractured by the demands for migrant labour in the mines and elsewhere in apartheid South Africa. In his chapter in this volume, he weaves his African research into a search for his own senses of personal and professional belonging during his own life. He describes how, as an anthropologist fashioned by Cambridge anthropology of the late 1960s, his interest in the intricacies of 'kinship' transformed into a concern with 'family history', a shift that demanded a broadening of his theoretical boundaries from anthropology into history and political economy. In Lesotho he became kin to families in Pitse's Nek. In later years, well after his original field research, he came to be regarded by the children and grandchildren of his original interlocutors as a valued expert in their family histories and, as such, was able to help those who wished to know more about their ancestors. As to the thinking about his U.K. home and the sense of belonging that went with it, he describes how his life became associated with a remote and uninhabited Hebridean island that he had visited as a child with his parents and later as a parent with his own children. Late in his professional life, he embarked upon what he called the 'Island Project', which focused upon the relations his family had to other families who also made holiday visits to this Scottish island and who had, like his own family, developed strong emotional attachments to it. He further describes how his professional life had elements of homelessness about it, spending as he did only two years in an anthropology department and the remainder in departments that bordered on political economy, history and development.

In these and allied ways, Murray draws together a number of fine threads to illustrate how place, memory, kinship and scholarship intersect to create senses of home. Furthermore, his chapter shows how a geographically unsettled life may nevertheless be laced with serendipitous and resonant links that made it possible for families whose members are spread over extensive territorial and historical domains to retain and even develop senses of being together.

One aspect of Murray's writing that arguably forms the ground base of his chapter is found in the references he makes throughout to the material features of life, work and being in both southern Africa and in Galloway. One such material feature is the weather itself and the heat, cool, sun and rain with which it is composed. He talks of the 'hilly, open and undulating landscape' of his first experience in Uganda, the 'hot and arid summer months' in Lesotho and the thoughts of 'soft, driving rain' of the Scottish Hebrides. He draws our attention to other material features of his life, describing the physical bodies of Pitse's residents, his own hut in the township during his research and, further, of the cottage that his family and the others who stayed there in his Hebridean island.

Like Murray, Shuhua Chen also draws our attention in a rather particular sense to the ways in which 'materials of the everyday' play central roles in the construction of a sense of home in the mind of one of her informants. She focuses on the rubbish that builds up in the boarding house she shares with migrant workers in a provincial Chinese city. Her informant explains that in her 'real' home far away in the countryside, such piles of rubbish could not be imagined. Her chapter may be read as showing us an example of material (rubbish in this case) serving as a metaphor to distinguish between place of residence and home.

The Political Economy of Homemaking in the Contemporary World

Much of the literature on the topics of home and homemaking in a contemporary world characterized by the movement of individuals and families starts from the consideration of relationships between local and global political economies of migration, on the one hand, and personal and collective homemaking practices, on the other. Braziel's distilled summary is worth quoting at length. His description of migration and diasporas helps frame our effort to understand homemaking:

> Migrations and diasporas are part of global capitalism: the international divisions of labour; the trans-nationalizations of production and finance; the consolidation of

the 'international' monetary fund; the regulation of world trade in goods and services; and the interstitial relations of development and international (or 'world bank')
lending have all led to massive displacements in human capital – some voluntary,
some not – as people migrate to work, or flee violence and political repression, and
as developing countries strategically export labour and import multinational corporations, or ground national economic development polities within a three-pronged
strategy of exported labour, returned diasporic remittances, and imported multinational corporations. Migratory flows and diasporic communities are both produced
by the discordant flows of globalisation, even as they are productive of its disjunctures
and cultural cacophony ... global traffic is not one-way; nor is it simply two-laned;
its traffic moves through multiply striated vectors and cross-wired flows of myriad
exchanges ... international migrants without cultural capital, and especially those
lacking in monetary capital, continue to cross international borders illegally – often
smuggled across geopolitical borders in unheated semi trucks, huddled in the backs
of minivans, or sewn into the seats, perilously adrift in small boats tossed on waves
crossing the ocean. (2008: 2–3)

Throughout the period of writing this Introduction, stories appeared daily
in newspapers echoing Braziel's words. On 3 November 2016, for example,
it was reported that 15 people, including two children and a baby, had been
found in a refrigerated lorry at the Albert Bartlett potato factory in Norfolk.
Before their discovery, they were said to have pushed sweet potatoes out of
a hole in the lorry to attract the attention of workers in the potato fields in
the hope and expectation that help would be forthcoming. However, having
been identified by the police, they were taken into the care of the Home
Office Immigration and Enforcement Agency. From previous reading of stories of this kind, it is unlikely that their fate will be recorded further in the
national press. This is a small episode that is illustrative of a larger and more
significant theme, namely the relation between forces of law, order and authority, on the one hand, and the everyday practices of those in search of
home and homeliness, on the other.

In one way or another, a majority of our authors frame their chapters in
relation to politico-economic processes at the various territorial levels Braziel records. Following the bloody ethno-religious conflict in the Maluku
Islands between 1999 and 2002, Frost describes the views of asylum seekers from the islands in Sydney, Australia as they oscillate between regarding
their 'homeland' in Indonesia as both idyllic and hellish. As we have already
seen, Murray's chapter considers homemaking in southern Africa through
the prism of detailed studies of the histories of families living and working
within the economic and political conditions of migrant labour in the region.
Chen's study is set within a Chinese economy based on widespread internal
migration. Starin Basi and Qureshi, and Sapritsky too, describe homemaking driven by global politico-economic processes which have brought Asian
families to London and Jewish families to Israel and then back to Ukraine

containing multiple ingredients including sexual dispositions, nostalgic memories of homelands, everyday experiences of friendships, and conversations between the generations. Although Shioji's Cotswold migrants, with their fine attention to tea sets and elegant front gardens, seem worlds away from some of the other subjects in the volume, they too are subject to a dynamic national political economy giving rise to flights of urban dwellers to country towns and villages, some of whose inhabitants are themselves displaced in the process. Webster-Kogen's rap group's repertoire combines many of the features described above: displacement from homes by incomers, intergenerational negotiations about identity, innovation by youth in thinking and rethinking the nature of home and belonging, and extensive and intensive imagining of homes here and there.

Symbols and Connotations

In her analysis of the symbolic relation between windows and women in Dutch social history and seventeenth-century paintings, most notably Gabriel Metsu's (1663) well-known painting *Woman Reading a Letter* (in front of a window looking out on to a seascape of rough water with a boat heaving in the waves that Irene Cieraad interprets in terms of sexual turbulence, implying that the letter the woman is reading is a love letter), Cieraad (1999: 50) writes that 'the hymen as the historically vital physical borderline of the woman coincides with the windowpane as the vital physical borderline between public and private space'. As she acknowledges, her treatment of borders (of house, home and body in this case) leans heavily on the work of Mary Douglas. For the present purposes, Cieraad presents us with an example of the extent to which the spatial characteristics of houses and homes mirror and enter into the connotative structures of the human body. Sarah Pink's (2004) account of how a London family's home is constructed in relation to the objects that decorate its interior spaces and how such objects all carry connotations and associations that bear upon the social relations within the home (Pink is particularly interested in gender relations) is another fine example of how the material features of homes, together with the objects that they house, take part in the shaping of identities.

In their respective attention to the symbolic and connotative roles of rubbish in domestic settings in Shantou City and gardens, thatched roofs, saucepans and baskets in Chipping Campden, Chen and Shioji follow Cieraad's preoccupation with the relation between outer and inner landscapes. Like her, they are concerned to show symbolic associations between bodies, identities and those material objects that take part in the formation of houses and homes.

The more general point for us in this volume is that discussion about home and homemaking in all of our chapters is conducted with regard to material objects and places together with their symbolic connotations: countries, regions and their imagined landscapes (Frost), townships and a Hebridean island (Murray), sexual bodies (Starin Basi and Qureshi), a city (Sapritsky), and the hills and coasts of those living between the Jordan and the Mediterranean (Webster-Kogen).

Self as Mirror of Home

All of the above leads directly on to considerations of the extent to which ideas of self and of home are intertwined. Clare Cooper Marcus' (2006) *House as a Mirror of the Self* explores the emotional and cognitive processes involved in the shaping of self (from early childhood onwards) in relation to topography of homes. She documents with precision how child development proceeds in relation to the tangible and intangible contours of home, how coming and going, leaving and returning to and from home are part of the struggles of selves for independence, how the home (with its furnishings and decorations) is, inevitably, an active party to the making of such social partnerships as marriage, and how (as in *Howards End*) family homes take part in the construction and expression of individual and collective identity.

The lesson for us stems from Marcus' insistence on the links between senses of self and identity, on the one hand, and ideas of home, on the other. This link is expressed in various ways in our chapters. Frost's description of the ways that her informants find themselves 'between despair and desire' exemplifies how the identities of members of the Moluccan diaspora in Australia are fashioned in large part by deep (and deeply painful) images and imaginative conceptions of the nature of their homes in Indonesia. Webster-Kogen's rappers are caught in between conceptions of home within ethnically defined and delimited space and/or by space unencumbered by ethnic or religious affiliation. The question this begs, in turn, is of central importance to us. Perhaps it is the most important question of all: who controls and determines the natures of the borders and boundaries of our home?

Home, Language and Meanings

As Shelley Mallett (2004: 65) observes, many scholars have examined the etymology of the word 'home'. Her own reading starts from observing that 'the Germanic words for home, heim, ham, heem are derived from the Indo-European kei meaning lying down and something dear or beloved', whilst the Anglo-Saxon 'ham' refers to 'village, estate, or town'. These observations suggest a particular place where rest and safety may be achieved within a larger and familiar collective space.

Recent writings of scholarly work concerned with migration, including forced migration, movements of refugees and asylum seekers, go beyond these etymologically drawn linguistic meanings without displacing them. Mallett points to Brah's (1996) work, picking out her assertion that home refers to the 'lived experience of a self in a locality' as being especially illuminating.

Amongst the chapters presented here, there are several that are concerned with meaning. As noted above, Chen's chapter is revealing for its capacity to inform us of the historical progress of ideographs for home whilst placing these linguistic insights within a detailed ethnographic analysis of a contemporary dwelling. The chapter is a compelling argument for searching for meaning within the interplay between language, ethnography and historical context. Murray's text also stresses the centrality in our definitions of historical as well as geographical context and illustrates as persuasively as any that the meaning of home is to be found within the doing and feeling of it, whether in Pitse's Nek or Galloway. Shioji's chapter demonstrates the extent to which the meaning of 'home' in Chipping Campden is shaped by class and wealth (wealthy incomers have a monopoly on 'traditional'-looking homes in the town), whilst Sapritsky's Israeli returnees to the Ukraine find themselves poised between (Israeli) conceptions of home as homeland and feelings that Odessa is not only an elegant city, but is also one that lends itself to homely and familiar networking, reciprocal care and a strong sense amongst individual family members of comforting familiarity.

Thinking Ahead

How may we draw this Introduction to a close whilst maintaining the sense of movement implied by the volume's title? Bearing once more in mind that we are looking at the nature of home through the lens of people making journeys of various kinds, what can we contribute to the general and wide-ranging literature on the nature of home?

Our chapters, taken together, suggest to us that in order for the notions of 'home' and 'homemaking' to take their rightful place at the core of anthropological theory and practice, as well as a central place in discussions of the nature of home, we need to adopt an approach that by now has a number of recognizable features. These include the facts that home and homemaking are best approached as part of interlocking processes that are at once global and intimate, tangible and intangible, material and symbolic.

Marina Sapritsky's work places her informants' notions of home within a global and/or regional political arena in which material realities of territory and city are fashioned by ideologies of homeland and Jewish destiny, on the one hand, and elegance and familiarity, on the other. Her returnees find themselves in a mobile and changeable world in which home may be found here and there at almost the same time. In this way her ethnography destabilizes any sort of binary of home and away in the context of ongoing movement and simultaneity. Furthermore, attitudes towards home and feelings of 'being at home' can and do change. Many of those she spoke with did not see their return to Ukraine as final, but envisaged moving again, either back to Israel, or on to a third location.

The idea, expressed by our authors in a variety of ways, that individuals may have two (or more) homes is not unique in the existing literature. Charlotte Williams' (2000: 195) reflections on her own movements between the homes of her physical parents in the Caribbean and of her adoptive mother in Wales are a case in point. She describes her Welsh 'white mother', who has a 'language of care and protection', and her own granddaughter 'with her eyes shining like the blue of the Atlantic', and observes that she herself feels 'a sense of the 'presence' connecting us all'. From this she reflects on the role of women as communicators of culture and of their capacity to embrace hybridity, loss, change and transitions as creative forces, and to feel and interpret identity as a process of 'becoming' rather than as fixed and static.

Cases such as those described by Sapritsky and Williams thus encourage us to work with notions of 'home' and 'homecoming' in landscapes of movement, thinking, rethinking and reimagining. They demonstrate that the global and intimate, on the one hand, and politico-economic and symbolic, on the other, need understanding within a system of interlocking relationships that is far from being a direct translation. Shioji shows us how class, wealth and the property market influence attitudes towards 'heritage' properties and opinions of what constitutes appropriate local development, but they do not predetermine it. As her detailed longitudinal ethnography illustrates, attitudes to home also combine very personal questions of taste, memory and experiences. Nevertheless, it does underline the necessity to look not *just* at the symbolic or the politico-economic, but, much more interestingly, at the complex architecture of the relations between them. Frost's description of expatriates from Maluku watching from afar as their region was swept by brutal communal violence, changing voluntary migration into involuntary exile in the process, confirms the point. Not only did (and does) this experience polarize characterizations of Maluku into images of a (pre-conflict) peaceful paradise, contrasted with a dark and bloody present, but it also brings into relief the relationships between thoughts and feelings about identity that had previously been mostly private and a public discourse involving independence struggles and global political movements.

This collection thus aims to exemplify the theoretical value of thinking about home and homecoming from the perspective of individuals and communities on the move. 'Home' as a conceptual space is in this sense usefully poised between the material (land, buildings and human bodies), the politico-economic (interrelated processes at global, regional and local levels) and the symbolic (identity, memento and practice) realms as well as inner and outer landscapes, as explored above. At a time when a nuanced understanding of these elements (and the implications of their disruption) is increasingly important for effective and empathetic policy-making, we feel that greater prominence for these concepts, both within anthropology and beyond, is not only desirable, but also necessary.

Tom Selwyn is Professorial Research Associate in the department of anthropology at SOAS, University of London, and visiting professor at Breda University, the Netherlands, and Bethlehem University, Palestine. He was awarded an Emeritus Fellowship in 2014 by the Leverhulme Foundation. He is widely published (including six edited/coedited volumes) in the field of the Anthropology of Travel/Tourism/Pilgrimage (ATTP) and has directed/codirected five multinational research and development projects in the Mediterranean and Balkan regions for the European Commission, as well as projects for other international agencies elsewhere, including Ethiopia. He was Honorary Librarian and council member for the Royal Anthropological Institute for ten years and was awarded the RAI's Lucy Mair medal in 2009.

Nicola Frost has a Ph.D. in Social Anthropology from Goldsmiths, University of London. She has conducted fieldwork in Indonesia, Australia and the United Kingdom, working on community organization, multiculturalism, and the cultural politics of food and festivals. She has held postdoctoral fellowships at City University London and SOAS. She recently travelled home to Devon and now works for the Devon Community Foundation, doing research, data analysis and evaluation.

NOTE

1. A subtitle that is also inspired by Clara Marcus' *House as a Mirror of Self*.

REFERENCES

Bhabha, H. 1994. *The Location of Culture.* London: Routledge.

———. 2012 [1997]. 'The World and the Home', in C. Briganti and K. Mezei (eds), *The Domestic Space Reader.* Toronto: University of Toronto Press, pp. 358–62.

Bourdieu, P. 1979. *Algeria 1960.* Cambridge: Cambridge University Press.

Brah, A. 1996. *Cartographies of Diaspora: Contesting Identities.* London: Routledge.

Braziel, J.E. 2008. *Diaspora: An Introduction.* Oxford, Blackwell.

Chekhov, A. 2011 [1904]. *The Cherry Orchard.* London: Faber & Faber.

Cieraad, I., 1999. 'Dutch Windows: Female Virtue and Female Vice', in I. Cieraad (ed.), *At Home: The Anthropology of Domestic Space.* New York: Syracuse University Press, pp. 31–40.

Douglas, M. 1991. 'The Idea of Home: A Kind of Space', *Social Research* 58(1): 287–307.

Forster, E.M. 1973 [1910]. *Howards End.* London: Edward Morgan.

Lawless, J. 2016. 'For UK's Europeans, Post-Brexit Attacks Bring Shock and Fear'. *Associated Press,* 27 October.

Marcus, C.C. 2006 [1995]. *House as a Mirror of Self.* Fort Worth: Nicolas-Hays.

Mallett, S. 2004. 'Understanding Home: A Critical Review of the Literature', *The Sociological Review* 52(1): 62–89.

Pink, S. 2004. *Home Truths: Gender, domestic objects, and everyday life.* Oxford: Berg.

Prakash, G. 2015. 'Everyday Tactics of Survival in the Unhomely City', *Quaderni Storici* 2: 501–22.

Rapport, N., and J. Overing. 2007. *Social and Cultural Anthropology: The Key Concepts.* London: Routledge.

Sugars, C. (ed.). 2004. *Unhomely States: Theorizing English-Canadian Postcolonialism.* Plymouth: Broadview.

Travis, A. 2017. 'UK Asylum Seekers' Housing Branded "Disgraceful" by MPs', The *Guardian,* 30 January.

Weber-Feve, S. 2010. *Re-hybridizing Transnational Domesticity and Femininity: Women's Contemporary Filmmaking and Lifewriting in France, Algeria, and Tunisia.* New York: Rowman & Littlefield.

Williams, C. 2000. '"I Going Away, I Going Home": Mixed-"Race", Movement and Identity', in L. Pearce (ed.), *Devolving Identities: Feminist Readings in Home and Belonging.* Aldershot: Ashgate, pp. 179–195.

CHAPTER 1

HOMING DESIRES

Queer Young Asian Men in London

CHAND STARIN BASI AND KAVERI QURESHI

Introduction

During our fieldwork at a support group for young Asian gay men in London, a meeting took place on the topic of 'coming out: the parent's perspective'. Given that young gay men's parents could often seem to embody a 'traditional' culture that was unable or unwilling to articulate same-sex desire and confronts expressions of gay identity with plain incomprehension, we were intrigued to see what would happen at the session. When Amir, the group leader, announced his idea for the session, it sparked off worried discussions among the young men. Would anyone bring their parents? What would the atmosphere be like? And given that the meetings were held in a building in Soho, how would they get their parents there without parading them through the heart of 'gay London' – Old Compton Street? Amir reassured the others that 'we're not going to take them through "Batty Boy" street, I don't want my relationship with my mother to go back ten years'. He and another group member worked out a route to get the parents from the underground station to the support group venue without passing any porn shops or rowdy gay bars.

In the event, only Amir and one of the service users, Rohit, were able to bring their mothers along to the meeting. Amir's mum arrived dressed in traditional Pakistani *salwar kameez,* head covered in a *dupatta* scarf, while Rohit's mum presented herself with a middle-class British accent and a tightly tailored and fashionable Punjabi suit. As the group members piled into the room, the mood, normally raucous and convivial, turned formal and serious.

Some of the young men stood in a quiet and deferential gaggle around Amir's mother, whilst others maintained polite conversation with Rohit's mother. There was also a white English woman hovering awkwardly outside the two circles; she was representing another organization that provided support to the parents of gay children.

As the group got ready to start, the young men sat in a circle on cushions. The two mothers sat on chairs at the back. Once the group settled down, Rahul, the facilitator, struck a Buddhist singing bowl to indicate that the session was about to start. He said how important it was to understand parents' perspectives on coming out and thanked the two mothers profusely for coming. He suggested an ice-breaking game: each person was asked to introduce themselves and give the name of the first album or single they had ever bought. There were laughs at the tackiness of the first albums, with the exception of Amir's mother's first buy, which was the Pakistani national anthem.

The representative for the parents' support organization introduced herself. She started by acknowledging the difficulties of having gay children. Both of her children were gay; she said she knew this when they were in their early teens and encouraged them to be open with her about their sexuality. She told the group that she understood the difficulty of having to tell other members of the family – the most common response she heard was 'what – both of them?'. At this she laughed slightly, but there is no response from the rest of the group. The next exercise was to break off into pairs and discuss the topic of 'what coming out means to family'. Chand was paired with a service user, Narinder, and they weren't able to talk about the topic; Narinder was feeling too emotional. They talked about his experiences of other gay support groups, which he said were helpful but didn't really understand him and his culture, particularly around issues of marriage. After the second topic was announced, 'how we can help our parents', Narinder looked more and more distressed, and quietly got up and left the room. Finally, it was time for Amir's mother to address the group:

> When I found out I was very depressed – my religion . . . back home . . . but what can I do? He is my son; I want him to be happy. I cried, I cried, I feel guilty. It was like an atom bomb; dad still loves him but doesn't want to talk to him about this gay thing . . . [voice breaks] I did something wrong in bringing him up . . . Looking around it's OK – you are all gorgeous boys, but inside you are hurting.

Aseem, a service member who had benefited hugely from Amir's emotional support over his two years attending the group, said to her in a deferential voice: 'aunty, you have done nothing wrong because Amir is so good, he has changed my life'. This comment was translated into Hindi by Rahul, but when Amir's mum responded, Rahul fell silent. Later, Rahul explained to Chand that he had been unable to continue the translation because the sense of disappointment she conveyed about her son's sexual orientation had brought tears to his eyes. Then it was Rohit's mother's turn. 'Well, I always knew he had a feminine side 'cause he was looking at bangles more than I did', she laughed:

> After he finished school he left home and he sent an email to us saying that this is who I am and I pray to God that you can accept me. I was so hurt that he was sad – he's my son. I didn't have a problem with it at all, Rohit is Rohit and I will always love him. My problem though was with telling the family, I didn't know how to say it. You know parents have to come out as well, it's painful . . . it's painful for us too.

After each meeting, the members would usually go to a coffee shop across the road to socialize and often onwards for a light meal and a group trip to one of the many gay clubs in Soho. It was at these times when Amir would come into his stride, buzzing around the tables checking on people, joking and making exaggerated South Asian-style head nods. This time, however, after making sure that people had had time to say a respectful goodbye to his mother, he escorted her out of the door and slipped away. Rohit and his mother hung around outside the building before the remainder of the group went on to the coffee shop.

It was a deeply affecting meeting and, by the end, many were moved to tears. Narinder told Chand that he had to leave the room for half an hour because it was too overwhelming and he just needed some time alone. Weeks later, Narinder spoke to Kaveri about how Rohit's mother reminded him of his own. He could imagine his mum trying to engage with his 'gayness' in a similarly 'cool' and understanding way, but deeply hurting inside, and against Amir's hopes for the session, this experience made Narinder all the more certain that he would not tell his parents and inevitably upset and disappoint them.

This meeting struck a chord with us as it illustrated with particular salience the painful emotions provoked for the young men by the question of broaching their sexual preference with their parents. At the same time, the very organizing of the session illustrated the young men's desire to make their lives intelligible to their parents, secure their approval and to wrought into being a coherent sense of self that was free of the painful disjunctures between the constructions of same-sex desire and their families and contexts of origin.

This chapter explores ethnography and life histories with this group of gay-identified male Asian twentysomethings in London: we have retained the men's use of the category of 'Asian', which in the British context refers to people of South Asian heritage. Speaking about their childhood homes, the young men talked about homes that were somehow unhomely, in which the workings of heteronormativity and respectability alienated them from their families of origin and 'Asian culture', which they felt was less accepting of homosexuality than mainstream British society. Their attempts to negotiate a space where they could feel 'at home' raise questions about our theorizings of home and homeland.

By way of introduction, we will briefly outline how seminal work in gay and lesbian studies has approached questions of home and homeland, before turning to our ethnographic material and returning to these debates in the discussion.

Home and Homeland

Alan's Sinfield's (1996) engagement with diaspora theory is highly suggestive for this collection. Sinfield suggests that queer experience can be thought of as a kind of reverse diaspora. Whilst the archetypical Jewish and Black diasporas invoke the idea of an originary home, exile and forced migration, the identity of queer people is constituted almost in reverse. The diasporic sense of exile experienced by queer people may in fact attach itself to aspects of the heterosexual culture of their childhood homes:

> Most of us are born and/or socialized into (presumably) heterosexual families. We have to move away from them, at least to some degree; and into, if we are lucky, the culture of a minority community. 'Home is the place you get to, not the place where you come from' . . . Instead of dispersing, we assemble. (Sinfield 1996: 280)

In this model of dispersal-as-assembling, the estrangement from home is conceived in terms of moving into a gay or lesbian subculture that is invested with the qualities of a diasporic return. These subcultures are a 'cultural homeland' (Sinfield 1996: 285) for gay and lesbian people. The gay bar, Sinfield suggests, is 'a place where he [as a gay man] is in the majority, where some of his values and assumptions run'; 'a place of reassurance and sharing' (1996: 287). Importantly, and illuminatingly for us here, this is a complicated journey without a fixed point of arrival. For Sinfield, home is indeterminate and perennially deferred, as queer people are 'stuck at the moment of emergence . . . we never quite arrive' (1996: 280).

Sinfield's musings have been seminal in inspiring work on queer diaspora. Yet later work has been critical not only of his celebration of dispersal-as-assembling, but also, more searchingly, of the conceptualization of home that he assumes. In Anne-Marie Fortier's (2003) subtle exploration of gay and lesbian autobiographies and memoirs, she demonstrates that the movements effected by gays and lesbians are more complicated. She breaks away from a linear concept of migration and shows that, rather than simply leaving the childhood home behind, gays and lesbians are drawn to, remain attached to and may actually return to their childhood homes, attempting to find a different way of living there. For example, in Bob Cant's (1997) *Invented Identities? Lesbians and Gays Talk about Migration,* he reminisces about his childhood in a farming community in the east of Scotland:

> Eventually I was able to look at the culture of normality which affirmed that 'everyone' lived in families and 'everyone' subscribed to the values of the Church of Scotland. It was a culture which made me feel like an outsider; it was only after I left that area that I realized I was not the only outsider. (Cant 1997: 7)

Similarly, in Mary Cappello's (1998) *Night Bloom,* the author returns to her Italian-American upbringing and sees it as the source of her queerness, queer unshackled here from sexuality and expanding to all non-normative difference:

> What I could never fail to notice about the men and women in my Italian/American family ... was [how] the men failed miserably and with varying degrees of unhappiness in conforming to the mask of white, middle class masculinity, and the women wielded word, story, their own bodies, in ways that could never pass for demure. By Anglo-American standards, to put it crudely, the male members of my family were soft and the females were hard. Mightn't the fraternal demolition parties that Hollywood cinema has invented for Italian/American subjectivity [as epitomized by *The Godfather* sequels] be indicative of precisely the fear that those dark, curly-haired, music-loving, flower-tending Italian/Americans are queer? (Cappello 1998: 96)

Fortier is drawn to explore these returns and re-memberings of childhood homes. This complicates considerably a model of queer diaspora in terms of dispersal-as-assembling. But even more provocatively, Fortier offers a critique of the conceptualization of home as emblematic of comfort, care and belonging, and opens it up to queer belongings. For inspiration she draws from Avtar Brah (1996), who writes of 'homing desires' in the context of migration and diaspora. Brah suggests that home is not necessarily defined by feelings of being 'at home', but by the longing that results from the loss of leaving home. Fortier pushes this even further and asks whether it is possible to conceive of homing desires that are already 'engendered and lived *at* home' (1996: 124).

Fortier is equally critical of Sinfield's exposition of gay and lesbian 'cultural homelands' as a space of comfort, care and belonging. The concept of home is fetishized in this movement away from the familial home towards an imagined other space to be called home: 'while the fantasy of "home" and belonging is projected onto these "imaginary homelands", the material conditions that determine their existence are concealed' (Fortier 2003: 119).

Whilst the autobiographies and memoirs Fortier analyses consider returns to ethnicity, in the sense of Cappello's re-inhabitance of her Italianness, she does not explore Italy itself, as the homeland of Cappello's immigrant parents. Gayatri Gopinath's (2003; 2005) thoughts on nation and diaspora are useful here. Gopinath argues that the nation is inherently heternormative, depending on familial metaphors of belonging and on the family as the reproductive unit through which the stability of gender roles and hierarchies is preserved. She states that this makes the queer subject 'impossible', making a play here between the 'impossibility' of a queer subject in the sense of cultural constructions of the nation and the sense of irreconcilability felt by nonheterosexual Indians about their sexuality and national identity. She goes on to show that these formations persist in the cultural politics of the Indian diaspora. However, she also sees diaspora as generative of resistive, critical locations and positions. Examining the alternative queer sensibility that allows for the depiction of a marriage without a groom in Indian American Shyam Selvadurai's 1994 book *Funny Boy,* or two sisters-in-law in bed together in Deepa Mehta's 1996 film *Fire,* she writes that:

> A queer diasporic logic displaces heteronormativity from the realm of natural law and instead launches its critique of hegemonic constructions of both nation and diaspora from the vantage point of an 'impossible' subject. (Gopinath 2003: 152)

Gopinath's work underlines the necessity, for a queer diasporic subject, of returning to the concept of nation. The ethnographic material discussed in this chapter brings together these three bodies of work; Sinfield's 'reverse diaspora' from childhood homes to the cultural homelands of queer subcultures, Fortier's problematizing of home as a space of comfort, care and belonging, and Gopinath's queering of national homelands. The chapter proceeds through four ethnographic sections exploring young men's reflections on their childhood homes; queer cultural homelands; India, the homeland of their Indian immigrant parents; and finishing with a description of a queer *yajna* ritual aimed at bringing together a gay identity with the traditional religious domestic sphere. Finally, we will return to the theorization of home and homeland and will suggest how our ethnographic material speaks to these debates.

Childhood Homes

We start with Jaz, whose conversations with Chand offered windows onto his profound feelings of discomfort with his family and 'community', feelings that were echoed by other young men in the group. Jaz was twenty-four years old and studying for a Master's degree in London. He had grown up in a working-class Asian area of Birmingham, which he referred to as a 'ghetto'. He painted a very negative portrait that seemed to speak to many pathologized or stereotyped accounts of South Asian families, describing his parents as 'married off by seventeen' and stressing his parents' lack of choice and fulfilment in their marriage. Their unhappiness with each other, he said, gave them a vicarious desire for their children to study hard, go to university and make a more satisfying future for themselves. This game plan was laid out very clearly before Jaz, yet he knew from an early stage that he would not fit his parents' ideal. He recalled himself at the age of eight going through the free magazines at home and trying to amuse himself with the pictures of women advertising bras, but finding himself more aroused by the men's underwear instead. He tried to suppress these early feelings, but as he explained:

> From the age of eleven till about thirteen I remember going to bed every night and playing this sort of movie in my head about how it would be when I marry a woman, how the honeymoon would be, what I would do to her in bed, how I would be sexually, you know active with her. And I would, kind of try and wipe . . . to brainwash myself, kind of wipe the memories away, of my homosexuality. But then when I was thirteen I realized that you know, I can't live a lie.

Jaz was a good-looking guy, turning up to the support group meetings with a trim indie look, a monkey hat and army coat with shoulder lapels. He was clean-shaven, with fashionably messy hair, but he had begun life with the orthodox Sikh look of long uncut hair and a *patka* (topknot). He played the tabla at the local *gurdwara* (temple) on the weekends until he left home. The incommensurability of his homosexuality with Indian culture and the Sikh religion struck him from an early age, he said. He recalled how his own reflection in the mirror, as a turbaned Sikh youth, used to unsettle him and make him consider himself an anomaly:

> I had long hair until I was fifteen, that's a constant daily reminder of my religion and who I was. Every day I was reminded when I looked in the mirror, when I touched my head, whatever whatever – who am I, this very conservative Sikh Indian boy. I didn't know any Sikh gay guys I didn't even heard of what was gay or men who like men, you know that doesn't exist . . . After I found out I was gay I rejected all of that.

Growing up, Jaz felt that Indianness was incommensurable with gayness, which was substantially to do with the heterosexual life course expected of him – that after completing his education, he would get married, bring a daughter-in-law back to the family home and then have babies. He constructed a life history of progressively distancing himself from the Indian aspects of his upbringing. He said that he'd been trying to 'run away' from his Indian and Sikh background, 'trying to run away from it and try to find myself'. He reflected that his Asianness felt like a kind of 'baggage'; 'it affected my homosexuality and my homosexuality took precedence'. He cut out his Asian friends as much as he could: 'Completely shut off, didn't meet them, didn't want to meet them, didn't come across them.'

In Jaz's narratives we glimpse how the 'impossibility' of a queer Indian subject, as suggested by Gopinath (2005), is produced through the family as well as through a racialized visual field. For a queer Indian subject, there is a slippage between the family and wider co-ethnic circles, as we can see in Jaz's developed aversion to the Indian aspects of himself, his Asian friends and, by extension, the Punjabi Sikh community in which he grew up. In her work on gay and lesbian Italians in Montreal, Fortier (1999) has explored this tendency to separate out the ethnic and gay aspects of the self and maintain these two subject positions in disjunction with one another. Yet she observes that there is a difference between gay/lesbian and 'race-based ethnic identities', which revolves crucially around their in/visibility. The visual field takes precedence: 'one can choose to pass as heterosexual, but one cannot choose to pass as white if she is black or Asian' (Fortier 1999: 6). Jaz discovered this for himself during a university year abroad in Germany. Constantly quizzed about his ethnic heritage, he was forced to acknowledge the visual limits to his ability to craft his own identity and, he said, come to terms with his own Indianness. By the time he spoke to Chand, he described a kind of rapprochement with his Indianness during his new university life in London. He said he had become more open to making friends with Indian people. He had discovered some gay Indians as well as some gay-friendly nonjudgemental Indians, and he was able to revise his earlier understandings of Indian people as conservative, misogynist and homophobic:

> In Germany they would always say 'You're not British, you're Indian, or you're something else'; you're exotic y'know? 'Cause to them being British is being white. So therefore, now, they made me associate myself with my colour, so prior to that I wouldn't have done that. So to them I was some sort of exotic thing, or, y'know, I wasn't British, I wasn't British, I wasn't British. And that was new for me and it was really hard for me to swallow 'cause I was really trying to escape my Indian ethnicity, I was really trying to rid of it, really really really, I was really trying to not be Indian, I suppose, and it was just reaffirmed constantly, daily, and then I was like 'fuck it' I will . . . and then I was . . . I realized the importance of working with Asian gay people and the common things we have, but I have a lot of Black gay friends, but I've started to think about where I'm from now and I want to work in India and before I was like no I don't want to go to India. So I'm connecting back.

Jaz said he did not want to cut himself off from the Indianness of his childhood home and upbringing, and he continued to feel a strong attachment and loyalty to his family. He talked about having to live a 'double life', dividing his Indian social circles – family, neighbourhood and Asian peer group from school in Birmingham – from his gay circle. This impossible reconciliation, as Fortier puts it, is 'largely connected to the spatial metaphors which, much like languages of immigration, suggest that the meeting of the "two cultures" would entail moving from one to another' (1999: 2). However, Fortier suggests that the interaction is more complex than is conveyed by the spatial metaphors of a 'double life', recognizing the strength of queer attachments to home and origins at the same time as refusing to deny their sexual orientation. This complexity is captured by the bodily contortions Jaz described when he talked about going back to Birmingham, passing for straight in his childhood home:

> It did feel like living a double life yeah, for sure. It still does, my parents don't know I'm gay. But I think because I've lived away from home for so long I'm becoming more who I am, and therefore, it's harder for me to act in a different way when I'm home now. And I like that. I like that I act more like me. But at the beginning then it was definitely living a double life . . . I think at home maybe I tried to . . . maybe even still now, try to act, or try to be more masculine. My friend came from Germany, he was hanging out with me in my area, and he was like 'you walk more', sort of, I don't want to say 'straight' but more sort of, kind of, it's kind of a ghetto area, so more 'ghetto' I suppose. And so the body reactions and that kind of change. When I'm on the bus and stuff I definitely, I don't dress, you know, I wouldn't dress as extreme, I won't wear boots and things like that, I try to tone down a little bit. Mainly because of my parents, 'cause when we go to the temple they're like, 'why are you wearing what you're wearing' and stuff, so. It is kind of living differently.

Jaz said that the palpitations of fear he used to experience at the prospect of being publicly outed in the gurdwara dissipated after he clocked other gay Sikhs in there, even one who professed a Jat caste identity, he said – Jatness being associated with stereotypical dominant macho masculinity. He reflected that this was a major factor in his rapprochement with his 'Indian heritage'. He described a kind of reappraisal of his childhood home open to possibilities for queerness *within* it, rather than queerness being inimical to it:

> I [go to the gurdwara more now], 'cause I'm more comfortable with myself and also I recently met a guy who, when I worked at [retail job] when I was 18 he claimed to be straight, and he dates all the straight girls. He's Sikh Punjabi and he's a caste of Jat, which I don't believe in. Anyway, so I'm in a gay club, and he's like a model in Bollywood whatever. He's gay, and I always see him at the temple, and I was like, he's so hot, and now I'm realizing a lot of people are in the closet, a lot of people are bi, tri, confused, whatever. So now I feel a lot more comfortable.

This kind of rapprochement was described by the other young men too. It could be the discovery of a 'seedy' side to the respectable Asian community. One told Kaveri about a trip to West Bromwich High Street he'd undertaken with his father and his cousin, where the Asian boutiques and grocery stores were transformed by night into pole-dancing clubs styled in the fashion of *mujre* (a music and dance form from Punjab associated with seedy sexual-ized performances by women for a male audience). He described Eastern European women winding sexily around poles to the sounds of *bhangra* mu-sic to cater to the Asian clientele: 'My dad and my brother are dirty like that, but I don't mind.' Equally, it could be the suspicion of having a 'gay uncle' in the family tree or the possibility that apparently straight Indians might have secret other lives. Rather than Sinfield's (1996) straightforward model of dispersal-as-assembling, the young men were effecting highly complex 'different movements of the "queer" outside or inside the homespace' (Fort-ier 2003: 115), returning to their childhood homes and finding ways to make their queerness legible to those who might choose to read it as such, as well as reframing that childhood home *within* the possibility for queerness. The extent to which this was prompted by their realization of their Indianness as an un-erasable part of their racialized identity is explored further consider-ing their journeys through the queer subculture.

Queer Cultural Homelands

For Sinfield (1996), the queer subculture is the homeland of the gay 'reverse diaspora'. To an extent, the young men also talked about their initial steps onto the queer scene as liberating, coming into a true sense of themselves, providing space for an unfurling of their sexual difference or, as one put it, 'living out my sexuality'. Their first experience of going to gay bars and clubs was exhilarating. Melvir, a 27-year-old barrister, recalled:

> I remember feeling a bit lost and staying – well, definitely staying very close to [my friend] for the whole time I was there and noticing the other people who were sitting there, it was a Saturday afternoon so it was quite quiet so I noticed a lot of gay men there and they were, you know, some of them were sitting by themselves and not really yeah, talking to anyone but just the whole idea of being somewhere that you can relax and be happy with your sexuality was a fresh experience for me. And also walking along Old Compton Street which again was a new experience. Being in an environment where the majority of people were gay.

However, the queer subculture was not the idealized space of home as com-fort and seamless belonging that Sinfield depicts. Melvir described strong initial reactions at the highly sexualized nature of the gay subculture. When he first attended a support group for gay Asians, he was told in no uncertain terms what it was to be 'gay'. Rather than sexual orientation being part of a continuum, or same-sex desire being something that even straight people could experience, there was only one option: 'gay', an essential aspect of selfhood in which one's entire person is defined by sexual orientation. To be 'gay' was to be sexually voracious, aroused by hardcore sexual language and the spectacle of penises and men having sex:

> The first time that I met up with him [the group leader] was I think during the half term when I had a bit of time and went along . . . went to his offices spoke to him for a while and he spoke to me and then confronted- not confronted me but gave me a copy of Boyz magazine . . . I think in a bizarre way he almost objected to me reading so much and he just said, 'this isn't what you should be looking at' and he turned to a particular page which was, well, it was a photograph of someone completely nude. He just said 'you know you've never seen this so you know, have a look at it and there you are, this is what it means to be gay'. And that frightened me at the time. I felt a bit, not disturbed but, just slightly intimidated by this obvious sexuality. Yeah, it was like 'blimey, I've only just come, this is the first gay man I've met and now I'm being shown a bit of porn'.

Melvir identified the discomfort he felt with this highly sexualized take on the gay subculture as the product of his 'Indian upbringing' and 'family values'. Another area of dissonance was the normatively white and middle-class aesthetics of the gay scene. Melvir, who was still wearing a turban when he spoke to us in 2010, said:

> I would always think that when I was walking in to a gay bar, that people were looking at me and staring at me, cos I hadn't seen anyone that was Sikh going into a gay venue. I was very self-aware and quite intimidated by it. I was only about nineteen at the time, eighteen, nineteen. So it's understandable. I was stopped a number of times before I went into a gay venue as well, because people would say 'you do realize it's gay here'.

Melvir made sense of this sense of exteriority with reference to his turban and to his Asian-looking body. Similarly, others recounted experiences of being rejected or unable to 'pull' because the Asian look was regarded as unsexy or inadequate in light of the physical ideals touted on the gay scene. Some said that white men would expect them to perform sexual acts that white guys would not do because they were 'looser', because of their titillating exotic racial difference. Others felt 'fixed' as Indian by their white lovers: pressurized to eat out at Indian restaurants, do Indian things and perform up to their expectations of cultural otherness.

Many young men said that their first impulse to seeking out a queer South Asian scene was to escape the racism and orientalist discourse they felt within more mainstream queer spaces. They hoped that the queer *desi* scene would be a place to meet others who were struggling with similar issues with family and upbringing, a place where you could riff in Hindi/Urdu or teasingly call each other *penji* ('sister'), where language and culture lifted from their childhood homes could be given new meanings in new contexts.

The queer *desi* scene in London is not immense. Club Kali, a night held once a month in Tufnell Park in north London, is the most widely known. Various studies have celebrated the transgressive and carnivalesque culture in such venues. Manalasan writes of how gay New York Filipinos' nostalgic performances of drag incorporating the national flag, iconography from the Catholic Church and dominatrix garb effect 'a remapping of the mercurial notions of here and there', establishing 'a tension between the nation of birth and the nation of settlement, thereby unravelling the exigencies of home' (2000: 194). Similarly, in Club Kali cultural symbols metonymically iden-tified with South Asian nationhood – national treasures such as the play-back singer Lata Mangeshkar and statespersons such as Benazir Bhutto – are taken up to provide a space for diasporic readings that unsettle the heter-onormative narration of the nation, the cultural stuff of childhood homes taken up and reapplied in a queer context. In Club Kali the hyperbolic fem-ininity of the South Asian bride provides the stuff for drag acts riffing on the heterosexual culture of home. The young men expressed some relief and excitement at being in a place where parts of themselves that had previously felt painfully inimical were able to exist in playful connection. Melvir, who had spoken of feeling sidelined in mainstream gay spaces, recalled how he felt during his first visit to Club Kali:

> This is it, I was home. But not home that's . . . this was actually home; *home*. It's where I belong, honestly [cries]. Actually after all of those years of . . . it didn't have anything to do with just sex, cause then I would have been OK in GAY [a commercial gay club]; you know I think I just wanted to be able to dance to Lata Manjeshkar like a *penji* [sister]! It's like coming back to a home I never knew . . . kinda like a dream that you kinda half remembered, like you knew it but you didn't.

With infectious pleasure spreading over his face, Melvir described here the complexities of 'homing' that many young men expressed. Of interest here is that, as with the gay 'cultural homelands' more broadly, not everyone expe-rienced the queer *desi* scene as a place of emergence and belonging. For Jaz, for example, at that particular time in the movements he was effecting inside and outside the homespace, Club Kali was a bit *too* homely:

> All the Asian gays in that club were very cliquey and they were all standing at the side in their groups and looking at everyone and they were looking at me like crazy like eighteen, nineteen years old, skinny, boots – it was fashion that people didn't wear back then, they wear it now – with my army coat and whatever and my eyeliner on. They were like who is this? I had all my confidence and I was dancing like you know I was Beyonce and they don't like it and they didn't like my confidence. And I didn't like them, I didn't like them either. I thought 'if this is the Asian gay scene then I'm getting out of here', cos they seemed to be people who lived with their parents but on the weekend came out and let it all out and I wasn't living with my parents at that time

and I was looking at things in a different perspective, I wasn't giving anyone a chance I was prejudging them all. I thought they're living in their Asian suburbs in London and they've come out for a weekend, they're very insecure and they're really bitchy for no reason. To me they came across as those Asians I lived with when I was growing up; narrow minded, stupid, homophobic, unintellectual and just you know bitchy, and they were, they came across as really bitchy.

The 'queer cultural homelands' envisaged by Sinfield are perhaps no more sites where all gay men can enjoy comfort and seamless belonging, any more than all heterosexuals are able to enjoy the privileges and power of heteronormativity (see Cohen 2005 for a wider critique of White homonormativity). Melvir's experiences of being warned off by bouncers – 'sorry mate, this is a gay bar' – and Jaz's visceral response to the Asian clientele he encountered at Club Kali illustrate how Sinfield's homelands are troublesomely 'devoid of any individual bodies or, rather, he assumes that any (gay and lesbian) body will feel at home in its hub' (Fortier 2003: 119). And what of the homeland of their migrant parents – was that a place of belonging?

National Homelands

During the informal socializing that took place in coffee shops and gay venues in Soho following the support groups we attended, India was omnipresent in the conversations. Somebody's parents were going to India; somebody else was planning a trip; somebody else was travelling to India with work; speculations circulated about the different ways of reading sexuality in India and the emerging gay scene over there. The focus was on the big metropolitan cities of Delhi and Mumbai, but the homelands of Punjab also featured. 'Is Jalandhar really a cruising ground?' (Jalandhar is the provincial city nearest to the villages from which the majority of British Indian Punjabi families originated.) 'Is it just the elites who can be gay?' 'What are gay venues like?' 'What are gay people like?' 'Are they very camp?' 'But aren't all Indian men camp anyway?'

These light-hearted conversations did important work in exploring the possibility that same-sex desire existed 'indigenously' in India, although perhaps not in the form in which it was apprehended in the West. Stories were exchanged about the possible meanings of the practice of hand-holding among young men in India. Did this mean that the homoerotic possibilities of male friendships were recognized? India was said to be a place where male homosexuality was a prosaic reality, tacitly accepted if conducted 'under the radar', but not recognized by what they saw as a hypocritical public culture and morality.

Much of the men's relationship to family in India centred around themes of loss, family and belonging. The men felt that their same-sex desire was an intimate and important part of their sense of self, and also that it would not be possible to communicate this part of their self to their family in India. Many expressed a deep sense of loss about this; loss of the possibility of 'authentic connection' in familial ties, and through this loss there was often a sense of separation from a wider belonging to a 'homeland'. However, all the men we spoke to felt it important to continue deepening their sense of rootedness and belonging in India, despite sometimes having to bypass their families of origin. Many spoke of India as a place to embark on a 'journey of discovery', and including an exciting place to explore and develop their sense of a gay identity. Melvir, who had been to India in 2008, told us that:

> I was once told that if you want to find a cruising ground in India, just go to the alley behind the mosque and there'll be plenty waiting for you – I thought that was bizarre. It's all furtive liaisons, often unsafe liaisons in cruising grounds.

The young men wanted to experience the queer scene in India for themselves. Like other so-called 'second-generation' youth visiting the homeland, they had a strong desire for a touristic experience of India (cf. McLoughlin and Kalra 1999; Mand 2003; Bhimji 2008) and were bored with the parochialism of the sleepy out-migrant villages and small towns that they visited with their parents. They wanted to shrug off the relatives and get to the freedoms of Mumbai and Delhi, travel with friends and stay in hotels or backpack on the hippy trail instead of compulsory socializing within the family. A lot has been written about the neocolonial aspects of queer tourism involving travel from the 'first' to the 'third world' (Puar 2002). Yes, there was an undercurrent of exotic sexual intrigue, exploration and consumption. Melvir felt even sullied by the gay venue he had visited in Mumbai:

> You have to pay a lot of money at the door, cos the management have to pay off the police. Then whilst I was there, I felt like homosexuality was similar to prostitution. The club was on two levels. At the bar you had all these sugar daddies watching the gay men on the dance floor. Then on the upstairs dance floor it was all straight men, and the only women who were there were prostitutes. It was like they were linking one stigmatized identity to another. So I didn't feel very comfortable there.

For Bobby, a 29-year-old media professional, travel to Calcutta, Mumbai and Delhi had been eye-opening. These cities showed him a face of India that was socially elite, metropolitan, open about sexual orientation and politically engaged. He commented on how refreshing it was to encounter a queer Asian scene that was recognizable, but not 'Westernized':

It was very similar in bits, sort of, Indians, whereas, what I mean by that is, 'cause we're all . . . we were a lot more Western, just in the way we talk and the way we are with each other, the way we socialize the way we dress the way we look. I know they're not as Westernized as we are over here, it's slightly different, but that's us, it's not a bad thing, it was really nice, really good, really friendly.

He commented at length that the gay scene in India was more 'political' and less oriented around sexual encounter and 'pulling' than the queer Asian scene that he knew from the United Kingdom. Comparing Gay Mumbai favourably with London's Club Kali, he said that:

I found it to be a lot more politically 'out there' than what it is over here, there seems to be an agenda, a cause, people are kind-of attuned to and that was good. It was far more political than what it is over here. Whereas everyone here tends to be out to have a good time, over there it was like, well, ok, 'we'll have a good time but we're also activists as well' . . . I think just generally it isn't about sex.

For Bobby, like others, India was also a place of danger. Progressively he evaded his relatives in Punjab and neglected to let them know that he was even in the country. The last time he had visited India with his parents was in 2005, and he vowed never to return to India with them due to the mounting expectation that he should marry soon:

It was a mix of everything and the fact that I was like twenty-five, twenty-six, and the fact that I'd come out as well and there was that pressure that oh well, you know, I don't think I would have had that much pressure to get married if I hadn't come out, I think they would have eased up a bit. I think because I was in that environment they almost had me into a corner and they kind of took advantage of that a little bit.

Puar (2002) writes of queer diasporic tourism as more complicated than other 'second-generation' youth visiting the 'homeland'. These are journeys of self-discovery, of not just 'going back to their roots' but reconfiguring those roots to provide a space for same-sex desire. Yet India, too, was not a seamless place of belonging. These journeys could be laced with fear as the spectre of marriage began to loom in their interactions with their families.

These extracts from the young men's narratives point to the conclusion that our conceptualization of home and homeland needs to be prised away from ideas of comfort, care and belonging, as the young men worked against the unhomeliness of their childhood homes, in the queer cultural homelands *and* in the homelands of their immigrant parents. However, in all three cases we can see the young men responding to their estrangement not by simply dispersing, but by returning repeatedly and trying to negotiate a space where they can feel 'at home'. These movements are illustrated in the final vignette, which shows the young men trying to convince their parents of the possibility of reconciling gay identity with the domestic sphere, appealing to traditional authority to legitimate their life choices through ritual.

A Queer *Yajna*

Rahul, a civil servant in his late twenties, had been planning a religious ceremony called a *yajna* at his house for some time. He would for the first time in his life be making his own ritual offerings, sublimating herbs into a holy fire and reciting holy verses, as he had seen many generations doing before him in his Hindu Punjabi family. He had intended this event to be an 'open invite' so that people from different parts of his life would be present. However, several days before the *yajna,* his parents told him that they would be near London on that day and would like to attend. In fact, his father wanted to officiate at the ceremony. This presented Rahul with a problem. He had been 'out' to his parents for over thirteen years – when he was fifteen, he told them he was gay and would never marry. After some fairly rocky years, they had managed to rebuild their relationship wherein he and his parents painstakingly avoided making any references to marriage and sexuality. While his parents had been to his home in London before, these were always stage-managed events with any sign of his sexual orientation erased from their view. This would be the first time they would come into contact with any of his gay friends. Rahul's response was to narrow the invite list to only his gay South Asian friends. He realized that he had before him an opportunity to demonstrate the possibility of the cohabitation of a gay identity within the traditional and religious domestic sphere. He told his parents beforehand that some of those present would be gay and afterwards told them that the entire congregation was gay. However, he did not want those who would be 'outrageously camp' to be invited and encouraged those who were invited to wear traditional Indian dress. The following message was sent out to those he wanted to be present:

> *Just to say that my parents have decided at the last minute to attend the Yajna. My father will be officiating the ceremony.*
> *Can I please ask everyone to respect their comfort levels. No hugging or kissing. No wearing eye-liner, bangles or bhindis! LOL*
> *My parents are very friendly, although extremely conservative.*

Rahul wanted to use this as an opportunity to present his domestic space to his parents in the context of a religious ceremony where he would be singing a *bhajan,* a hymn in Sanskrit, the very picture of Hindu piety. The ceremony went ahead as planned; Rahul introduced his friends to his parents, Rahul's father officiated at the rituals, and small talk was exchanged on all sides. At the end of the ceremony, Rahul's mother stood up and warmly invited all the young men gathered to eat the food that she had prepared. The young men responded with similar warmth; a few went up to her to thank her for the food and the ceremony. After about ten minutes of this, she politely took her leave, and she and her husband got ready to go back to Birmingham. No words passed between Rahul and his father. After the parents left, there was the palpable sense of an easing of tension.

Discussion

This ethnographic material on young Asian gay men in London underlines the fact that important questions need to be asked about the mainstream theorizing of home and homeland. Our ethnography brought to the surface the subtle ways in which queerness can disturb, reimagine and re-create spaces of belonging. The men described complex dynamics of painful separations and exciting creations of home. Sinfield's notion of the queer diaspora as a 'reverse diaspora', of home as the place you get to, not the place where you come from, has strong resonances with the narratives of the young men with whom we worked, who talked similarly about how their journeys through youth culture and into the queer scene liberated them from certain pressures of their childhood homes. However, despite their difficulties in making their sexual orientation intelligible to their families, the young men felt emotionally unable to maintain the semi-estrangement from family practised by many (by implication white) lesbians and gay men, which is presumed in Sinfield's model of queer diaspora. Whilst Fortier's (2003) explorations of autobiographies and memoirs such as those of Cant (1997) and Cappello (1998) show that the notion of dispersal-as-assembling overlooks more complicated movements for white lesbians and gay men too, this was all the more important for the men in this research, as their sense of racial othering made them reconcile themselves with their Indianness – they could not 'pass' as otherwise. They returned to their families and attempted to make their sexual orientation legible to those who might read it as such, and they reframed their childhood homes as places within which queerness was possible.

The queer subculture offered them a place where they could 'fit in', to an extent, speaking to Sinfield's exposition of home as a place of comfort and familiarity. However, the young men experienced disconnections too within this queer subculture, unsettling the idea that the queer subculture provides home in the sense of comfort and familiarity. In this, there is a need to reconsider the queer subculture in its racial and class specificities. More searchingly, we echo Fortier's challenge to uproot the concept of home and homeland from the assumption that home is necessarily a space for comfort, care and belonging. We agree with Fortier (1999, 2003) that the notion of 'homing desires' is better able to capture the ways in which the young men remained so strongly connected to their families, attempting, through complicated moves, to deny neither their origins nor their sexuality.

The young men were obliged by virtue of their Indian identity to return to the concept of nation. However, whilst Gopinath argues that 'the consignment of queer male desire to diasporic space serves only to solidify the heteronormativity of the home space of the nation' (2005: 192), the young men's excavation of the possibilities of sexual difference entailed a return to India – both literally, through travel, and metaphorically, through the imaginary homelands they constructed – in pursuit of a differently constructed home. Here, they encountered another India where same-sex desire was a furtive secret or prosaic reality denied by public morality and where metropolitan elites had created queer publics that were more heavily politicized than those in which they engaged in Britain. These were journeys of self-discovery, but following a different trajectory from the standard 'second-generation visits homeland' trope as they were negotiating more complex terrain. Whilst Puar (2002) writes positively about the possibilities of encountering queerness in the homeland through queer tourism, the young men also spoke to us of the anxieties that India aroused in them as a symbol of everything that their parents had brought them up to want.

The queer *yajna* suggests the possibilities for eventual legitimation, in the eyes of family, for the alternative kinds of domestic lives that the young men could evolve. These were young men seeking and sometimes succeeding in creating ways of building a coherent sense of self without abandoning their 'Indian-ness' or their 'gayness' and rendering themselves a 'possible subject'. Yet the tensions are irresolvable, the wave of relief that the group of young men felt when Rahul's parents returned to Birmingham denying any easy celebration of 'homing desires', which are engendered by the longing that results from loss.

Chand Starin Basi is a therapist and mental health professional in London and specializes in developing mental health services for black and ethnic minority communities. He has also worked as an ethnographic researcher.

Kaveri Qureshi is Research Associate at the Institute of Social and Cultural Anthropology, University of Oxford. She has research interests in gender, life courses and their disruptions, and translocalism.

REFERENCES

Bhimji, F. 2008. 'Cosmopolitan Belonging and Diaspora: Second-Generation British Muslim Women Travelling to South Asia', *Citizenship Studies* 12(4): 413–27.

Brah, A. 1996. *Cartographies of Diaspora*. London: Routledge.

Cant, B. (ed.). 1997. *Invented Identities? Lesbians and Gays Talk about Migration*. London: Cassell.

Cappello, M. 1998. *Night Bloom: An Italian American life*. Boston: Beacon.

Cohen, C. 2005. 'Punks, Bulldaggers and Welfare Queens: The Radical Potential of Queer Politics', in P. Johnson and M. Henderson (eds), *Queer Black Studies*. Durham, NC: Duke University Press, pp. 21–51.

Fortier, A. 1999. 'Outside/in? Notes on Sexuality, Ethnicity and the Dialectics of Identification', Working Paper, University of Lancaster, Department of Sociology.

———. 2003. 'Making Home: Queer Migrations and Motions of Attachment' in S. Ahmed, C. Castañeda, A. Fortier and M. Sheller (eds), *Uprootings/Regroundings: Questions of Home and Migration*. Oxford: Berg, pp. 115–35.

Gopinath, G., 2003. 'Nostalgia, Desire, Diaspora: South Asian Sexualities in Motion', in S. Ahmed, C. Castañeda, A. Fortier and M. Sheller (eds), *Uprootings/Regroundings: Questions of Home and Migration*. Oxford: Berg, pp. 137–56.

———. 2005. *Impossible Desires: Queer Diasporas and South Asian Public Cultures*. Durham, NC: Duke University Press.

Manalasan, M. 2000. 'Diasporic Deviants/Divas: How Filipino Gay Transmigrants "Play with the World"', in C. Patton and B. Sanchez-Eppler (eds), *Queer Diasporas*. Durham, NC: Duke University Press, pp. 183–203.

Mand, K. 2003. 'Gendered Places, Transnational Lives: Sikh Women in Tanzania, Britain and Indian Punjab', unpublished Ph.D. thesis. Brighton: University of Sussex.

McLoughlin, S., and V.S. Kalra. 1999. 'Wish You were(n't) Here: Discrepant Representations of Mirpur in Narratives of Migration, Diaspora and Tourism', in J. Hutnyk and R. Kaur (eds), *Travel-Worlds: Journeys in Contemporary Cultural Politics*. London: Zed Books, pp. 120–36.

Puar, J. 2002. 'A Transnational Feminist Critique of Queer Tourism', *Antipode* 34(5): 935–46.

Sinfield, A., 1996. 'Diaspora and Hybridity: Queer Identities and the Ethnicity Model', *Textual Practice* 10(2): 271–93.

CHAPTER 2

HOMEAWAYNESS AND LIFE-PROJECT BUILDING

Homemaking among Rural-Urban Migrants in China

SHUHUA CHEN

Introduction

In contemporary China, most rural migrants working in cities return home only once a year, usually during the Chinese New Year (Chan 2010; Pun and Lu 2010; Huang 2011). According to the National Bureau of Statistics of China, by the end of the year 2011, the population of rural-urban migrants had reached 158.63 million.[1] This enormous army of migrants, constituting the main part of the travel rush population, has over the past two decades transformed the *chunyun* (Spring Festival travel rush) in China into an annual spectacle. The *chunyun,* which takes place in January or February each year, includes the movement of *fanxiang* (returning to rural areas) before Chinese New Year and that of *fancheng* (returning to cities) after Chinese New Year.

Thus, the migrants spend most of the year away from home. To some degree, their being *at-home* becomes an annual holiday, while being *away-from-home* comes to represent their everyday life. How does this affect their feelings concerning home and their ways of making home? Between *leaving* and *returning* home, how do the migrants possess (or how are they possessed by) their sense of being-in-the-world? Based on fourteen months of ethnographic fieldwork in Shantou city (in Guangdong, China), my research examines the interior experience of migration, attempting to present a fine-grained picture of rural migrants' everyday life in the urban space.

A Methodological Approach to (Rural-Urban) Migration

> It might be the core of an anthropological science, I would suggest, to give a comparative account of individuals' meaningful experiences: the experiences situationally accrued and the meanings ongoingly construed by particular individuals in one moment or milieu (and the consequences of these experiences and meanings for the course of individuals' lives) as against those accrued and construed in others. (Rapport 2002: 9)

The method I adopt in this chapter follows a similar model to that of Nigel Rapport. It pursues, through anthropological research, 'a comparative account of individuals' meaningful experiences'. While contextualizing them within specific social relations, my research into rural-urban migration in China focuses on individuals' experiences. I am less keen to identify possible new urban social structures than to explore how participants in the urban milieu construe their experiences as meaningful. I attempt to examine migration through the individual experience *within* the process of urbanization and the migrants' diverse perceptions *of* the social and spatial change as a result of this very process, in terms of their ideas of home and their ways of making home.

To be specific, I will scrutinize two moments in the migrants' daily lives – one when a migrant (Yang Cui) discards a plastic refuse bag in an old courtyard of a house and a second when another migrant (Xiao Bin) is packing to return home. As Rapport's statement also suggests, I explore 'individuals' various meaningful experiences . . . in one moment or milieu'. With regard to the act of littering in a courtyard-house, I question that how homeawayness was manifested at that particular moment by a migrant? What are the implications of this homeawayness and how does homeawayness relate to one's homemaking away from home? With regard to the sentiments expressed by another migrant while packing to return home, I ask whether these activities are best understood as a *re-turn* or a *new-turn* for the migrant. Are the movements between *leaving* home and *returning* home circular or linear?

In methodological terms, scrutinizing momentary experience involves the anthropologist in his or her own interpretive analysis construing the meaning-making – which may be fleeting, fluid or unsettled – of individual informants. Through the lens of migration, anthropologists are able to focus on and investigate individuals' ideas of home from a unique perspective, I further argue. One recognizes informants' *being at home in their imagination* and *making home away from home*. It is the movement of *leaving* and *returning* home that creates the space for a migrant to consider and reconsider the notion of home, and thus construct and reconstruct home through his or her everyday lived experience of the migratory journey.

Fieldwork in Bomaqiao (Shantou, China)

As an important port city throughout history, with strong links to Chinese overseas and great potential for foreign investment, Shantou[2] was established in the 1980s as one of the four original Special Economic Zone cities. The rise of manufacturing in Shantou has attracted a large population of migrant workers who have arrived there from all over the country. My fieldwork was carried out in Bomaqiao in Shantou, a neighbourhood that is undergoing fast urbanization. Bomaqiao was once a suburban village, but now has become part of Shantou city with hundreds of small factories. I witnessed first-hand what happened once this formerly agricultural area was designated for urban development. Bomaqiao is located close to my hometown and I have visited regularly since 2006, before living there for fourteen months while carrying out intensive fieldwork from November 2011 to January 2013 – working in a toy factory with migrant workers and living together with them.

Similar to many other villages around Shantou, Bomaqiao has in recent decades experienced a transformation from an agriculture-dominated economy to one primarily oriented towards manufacturing. In recent years, the profile of Bomaqiao has fundamentally changed: arable areas are no longer farmed; instead, the land now 'bears' an industrial park, lots of factories and new houses. New houses play new roles as multifunctional spaces: they serve as homes for the locals, workrooms for assembling manufactured goods, and warehouses for storing factory products. The migrant factory workers mainly live in the old courtyard-houses district, where the houses are in a state of near-collapse and are cheap to rent. Besides the migrants, some old villagers (for example, some parents of factory owners) also live in the courtyard-houses. They are reluctant to move to the new dwelling district and prefer to stay in their ramshackle courtyard-houses, which hold their lifelong memories. It was during my fieldwork in Bomaqiao that I stayed with a few migrant workers and a local elder in one of these old courtyard-houses.

The main interlocutors included in the chapter are Yang Cui, Xiao Bin and Grandma Chang. Yang Cui (in her mid thirties) and Xiao Bin (in her mid twenties) are migrant workers, both from Sichuan province. They have arrived in the coastal city of Shantou having left their homes approximately 2,500 kilometres away in rural inland Sichuan, currently doing assembly jobs at Shun Xin Toy Factory (named after the owner) in Bomaqiao. I met Yang Cui and Xiao Bin on the first day of my arrival in the field. Yang Cui and Xiao Bin soon became my key informants. Yang Cui then introduced me to the place where she lived: an old courtyard-house owned by the factory owner, Shun Xin. Grandma Chang is Shun Xin's mother, a Bomaqiao local. She also lives in the courtyard-house.

Littering in a Courtyard-House: Homeawayness

The Old Courtyard-House

It is early January 2012 and the first time I 'meet' the old courtyard-house. When I approach the house, stepping in and wandering around it, I find myself deeply attracted by its details and am filled with nostalgic feelings as well as confusion.

Right after turning from a narrow alleyway, Yang Cui points to an old gateway. 'Here it is. Come in.' It is a stone arched gateway with fine carvings on it, though very old. Together with the *duilian* (Chinese antithetical couplets usually including two phrases written as calligraphy on vertical red banners) placed on either side of the door, the gateway offers a special, almost festive, welcome, as though it is visually preparing for visitors to the house. The shiny couplets remind me that the Chinese New Year is coming. I wonder: what kind of migrants post couplets on houses they rent? To my knowledge, most migrant workers in Bomaqiao spend little money decorating the places in which they live. As soon as I step into the house and meet Grandma Chang, I find the answer: it is Grandma Chang, a Bomaqiao local, and not the migrants living here, who posted the *duilian.*

The architectural style of the house is a mixture of a traditional Chaoshan[3] *si dian jin*[4] (four points of gold) layout and lots of delicate Western-style decoration. Dressed with two tasteful classical columns, the veranda of the house delivers a strong foreign flavour within this traditional Chinese courtyard-house. In addition, the building materials also exude this foreign flavour: *ang mo hue* (a local name for Western cement) and green *xi yang zhuan* (Western ceramic tiles). The green tiles look bright against the crumbling old walls. Grandma Chang then tells me that every single one of these green tiles was imported, brought from Thailand by her father-in-law, who built this house in the 1920s, even though he himself spent most of his life in Thailand.

These delicate architectural details fill the space with an ambience that is an almost perfect mixture of the Oriental and the Occidental, local tradition and foreign fashion. Evoking a special human feeling, such an ambience flows; it is similar to what the geographer Yifu Tuan (1977: 118) calls 'frozen music', creating an architectural space that seems 'to mirror rhythms of human feeling'. However, the 'frozen music' is drowned by piles of rubbish in the courtyard and by half-finished plastic products piled up in the halls and rooms, assailing me as soon as I move my eyes away from these delicate details to take in the panoramic totality of the house.

Passing through the veranda, I see an entrance hall in the middle and two small chambers, all of which are filled to the brim with pieces of half-finished plastic toy products. During my tour, I find that much of the space in this house is now used for storing plastic products, including half of the back hall (the other part of the back hall is reserved for ancestor worship) and even the pigpen attached to the house. A pigpen filled with plastic products rather than pigs?

Many thoughts soon flash through my mind about the links between these households with pigpens and the Chinese ideogram for house, home, residence or family, 家 (*jiā*). The Chinese character '家' is a combination of the radical '宀' ('a roof of a house') and the radical '豕' ('a pig'), which is a pig under a roof. The following section shows a few milestones in the evolution of the Chinese symbol for the character 'home' (家):

Shang Dynasty (1600 BCE to 1046 BCE) in *Jia gu wen* (Oracle bone script)

West Zhou Dynasty (1046 BCE to 771 BCE) in *Jin wen* (Bronze script)

Qin Dynasty (221 BCE to 206 BCE) in *Zhuan wen* (Seal script)

The current character in *Kai shu* (Regular script)

So, the Chinese character 'home' shows a roof (of a house) with a pig beneath it. But how did 'a roof with a pig beneath it' come to signify home in China? The history of pig domestication in southern China can be traced back 10,000 years and represents an important transition from the fishing and hunting age to the agricultural period (Schneider 2011). Pigs, as an integral part of the home, provided the first metaphor for security of meat supply and the prosperity of a home. From this point of view, it was the pig that enabled a home to be anchored firmly in a place. According to Mindi Schneider, for millennia virtually every rural household in China raised at least one or two pigs each year. 'A roof with a pig beneath it' provided a neat metonym for the way of life of most Chinese households inasmuch as it represented the combination of shelter and animal husbandry.

Since the 1980s, this long tradition of domestic pig-raising has begun gradually to disappear, when industrial modes of production became predominant, especially in Special Economic Zones like Shantou. As the world changes, so too does the use of space and the relationship between human beings and livestock within the Chinese concept of home. This is clearly apparent in Grandma Chang's courtyard-house, which is filled with industrial products, including in its attached pigpen.

Wandering around the house, I become deeply fascinated with what the house is telling me, from its architecture, its delicate decorations and contents consisting of half-finished industrial products and piles of rubbish. As it is our (the house's and mine) first meeting, I try to show my respect for it by not asking too much, although I find that there are stories everywhere within the space, both visible and invisible. As on the face of a centenarian, age has left its traces on the walls of the house. Drowned in a flood of urbanization and industrialization, this courtyard-house is struggling to accommodate the rural-urban flow of migrant workers.

Besides plastic products, the industrialization in Bomaqiao also brings factory workers, who migrate thousands of miles from other provinces, to the old courtyard-houses. Grandma Chang has told me that in total there are six migrant workers now living in this house.

'Yang Cui and her man stay in this room; Xiao Bin stays in the next one and three other girls just moved into that room last week...', Grandma Chang shows me. 'This is my room, come in.'

It is a bedroom fully appointed with old-fashioned furniture. What catches my eye is the gallery wall next to a washstand.

'Look at this one. It is our whole family photo from when my husband returned home for the last time from Thailand, almost thirty years ago', Grandma Chang says.

'Oh, isn't it the courtyard of this house?' I ask.

Recognizing the distinct archway and pillars, I am surprised to realize that the family photo was taken in the courtyard of this house. A spring of nostalgic feeling wells up inside me suddenly while looking at a huge family gathering in such a blossoming and luxuriantly green courtyard – the courtyard as it was in the past. Although it is a black-and-white photograph, it still seems very colourful to me.

I move my eyes from the courtyard of the past (the one in the photo) to the courtyard of the present (the one outside Grandma Chang's room). I see a rather grey and gloomy image: the tidy and elegant garden courtyard has disappeared under piles of rubbish and filth, and it is starting to smell bad. The nostalgic feeling instantaneously shifts to a complex and ambivalent feeling, which then haunts me throughout the rest of the tour of the house. I become especially sensitive to words regarding the courtyard uttered by Grandma Chang:

> Yes, it was the yard outside. We used to have clan family gatherings in this yard, whenever our *xianluo fanke* [emigrants to Thailand] returned home, or on occasions such as Chinese New Year, *Qingming* Festival [Tomb-sweeping Day], or wedding banquets of any clan relatives. It [the yard] could hold more than ten dining tables ... Now the yard is empty. There are no family gatherings of those kinds anymore ... The young move to the outside world. Then after the young move out and these *ghua sen gian* [immigrants from other provinces] move in, here is not our family yard anymore but a public garbage dump ... It was our yard but now it is their dump...

I then turn to Grandma Chang while nodding my head slightly to show my understanding of her complex feelings. I fix my eyes on her when I am listening to her talking for a while, and her expressive face changes considerably. She is smiling and excited when she shares with me the memories of the big family gatherings in the past in this courtyard and falls into those beautiful (for her at least) reveries. Then her face becomes mournful and depressed when she starts telling me about the decline of the courtyard. Indeed, later on, after moving into the courtyard-house, I find that it is quite true that the yard now 'is *their* dump' – the rubbish dump of the floating migrant workers who stay in the house temporarily.

The Moment of Littering

One week after my first visit to the courtyard-house, I manage to move into the house, ready to listen to any stories it might tell: its silent storytelling echoed through every single piece of *xiyang zhuan* (Western brick), the shabby top of a wall or the rubbish piled up in the courtyard, but mainly through the people who had created and who are still creating stories within the space.

It is noontime. I am busy with my move into the courtyard-house while Yang Cui is preparing lunch for me. Yang Cui shares a room with her partner who works as a building constructor. She has a daughter (aged nine) who has been left behind in her rural Sichuan home.

Yang Cui: 'Xiao Chen, come and eat.'

Yang Cui always shouts loudly. She is calling me to have lunch in her room. Compared to Grandma Chang's room, Yang Cui's room is a rather empty one. A broken bed, a worn table with two stools, a small old television and a bamboo pole serving as a wardrobe; all of these old and gloomy pieces of furniture make the room look more dilapidated. However, within these ten square metres, the space is multifunctional: it is a bedroom, a living room and a dining room. I am asked to sit down on one stool, next to the shabby table with a dish (rib with bitter melon) and two bowls of rice on it.

Yang Cui: 'Oh! I almost forgot the braised goose meat I bought just now.'

Yang Cui walks towards the TV and gets the bag of braised goose meat, which she puts on top of the TV. She tears the plastic bag and empties the meat onto a plate. As my eyes have been following what Yang Cui is doing while waiting for her to start the lunch, I am searching for a rubbish bin in her room for the greasy bag. However, I am stunned by what I see at this very moment: the bag flashes through the doorframe and accurately lands on the top of a rubbish pile in the courtyard.

Yang Cui seems quite pleased with her successful long shot. But when she turns to the table, her self-satisfied smirk meets my bewildered stare of great astonishment and puzzlement.

Yang Cui: 'Ah, here, everyone does it like that . . . But we do not do it at home . . . And I never do it in front of my girl [Yang Cui's nine-year-old daughter] . . .'

Yang Cui explains herself immediately.

From her immediate verbal response, I read her interpretation of the surprised expression in my eyes as comprising at least two different layers:

1. How can you do that? – *Ah, here, everyone does it like that.*

2. Do you also do this at home? Don't you think it is not a good model for educating your child? – *We do not do it at home . . . I never do it in front of my girl.*

Let me be clear for what I mean by 'layers' here: one's flow of interior conversations. When Yang Cui threw the food bag into the courtyard rubbish pile, seeing my puzzled facial expression regarding her act of littering, she immediately became self-conscious. Trying to make sense of my momentary experience expressed through my puzzled face, she went through her flow of interior conversations within that fleeting moment and came out with her 'self-justification' at least with two aspects: 1) 'Ah, here, everyone does it like that'; and 2) 'But we do not do it at home . . . And I never do it in front of my girl'. She made sense of her act momentarily through the two aspects of the response to my momentary attempt to make sense of her act; in other words, our singular and personal experiences abutted – she read my mind (partially) at the moment when I tried to read her mind (partially as well, I think). In the following, I intend to contextualize the first layer of Yang Cui's response in order to 'return [her] elliptical behaviours to their true cognitive homes' (Rapport 1993: 129). Then, from the cognitive logic of this first layer, I will try to explore its social implications (within the very process of rural-urban migration) through an analysis of the second layer.

The Cognitive Logic of 'Here, Everyone Does it Like That'

How can you do that? [As indicated by the look of shock on my face]
Ah, here, everyone does it like that. . . [She answers.]

In the first layer, outwardly, Yang Cui gives a reason to explain her behaviour (her throwing the plastic bag into the courtyard) and claims that it is acceptable to do it 'here' – '*here, everyone does it like that*'. It is indeed a good reason for me, allowing me to make sense of the piles of rubbish in the courtyard and solve some of the puzzles that had been haunting me since my first house tour: who throws the rubbish here? Everyone. How can they do that? Because here everyone behaves in this way. The 'here' that Yang Cui refers to could be the courtyard-house or even the whole Bomaqiao. Serious littering makes the whole village look like a huge rubbish dump. It is every single long shot (or maybe a short one) performed by 'everyone' that has contributed to turning the courtyard into a rubbish dump.

However, if we questioned it further – 'why does everyone do it like that?' or, in other words, 'what is the point of littering?' – then we may need to explore a hidden psychological mechanism.

Let me list the possible meanings of 'Here, everyone does it like that' in this situation:

Here, everyone does it like that
1. So I think it is *right* to do it.
2. So I *should* do it as well.
3. So I just follow them.
4. So why not?

Obviously, we can easily rule out the first possibility from Yang Cui's two remarks: 'We do not do it at home' and 'I never do it in front of my daughter'. For the second one, it can also be readily discarded because it is not logical, in a very commonsensical way, to just litter more. For the third one, it agrees with popular psychology. It could be the one that reveals what Yang Cui claims as her right to do it 'here'. To her, the right to litter 'here' may come from her just following others and not from the very littering behaviour itself. Then, if the third one is what she uses to explain her behaviour, the fourth one may be the one through which I try to explore her inner world (her psyche) in order to explain her behaviour and the social phenomenon of littering, if possible.

'Here, everyone does it like that, so why not?' This logic implies that the very action of littering can bring some potential benefit for the actor. Or, if someone does not litter, he (or she) may be losing something. If this is the case, then how can one benefit from littering? What is the loss if one does not litter among a littering community? Temporary convenience? Even at the cost of a dirty living environment? But it is the only excuse I can imagine for them. It is similar to the very common phenomenon of drivers in Bomaqiao who are notorious for driving through red lights. I always wonder about the traffic violators who drive through a red light just for the sake of temporary convenience, even at the cost of their life.

'Here, everyone does it like that' is a very familiar statement to me. I heard it again and again during my fieldwork in Bomaqiao. It is not just an individual statement, but a common one, shared in the minds of people asserting their right to belong 'here'. It is a piece of formulaic exchange, which generates its own borders, by everyone involved and becoming involved, by whoever belongs to 'here'. 'Here' is not necessarily a fixed geographical concept, but an idea with fluidity. It differs according to the context in which it is employed. In the case of littering, Yang Cui may just be talking about the courtyard-house or she may also be referring to the whole Bomaqiao. But surely 'here' is somewhere that Yang Cui does not regard as home. I now turn to the second layer of the cognitive exploration of her response (to the shock in my sensitive face after her long shot): her concern about 'being not at home' and 'being at home'.

Analysis of 'We Do Not Do it at Home'

'Do you also do this at home? Don't you think that is not a good model for educating your child?' [What Yang Cui might read from my face.]
We do not do it at home . . . I never do it in front of my girl.

If the first layer serves to justify her right to litter 'here', then for the second layer, Yang Cui's deictic focus positions her somewhere else: not 'here' but there, i.e. home. On the one hand, she clarifies the conditions that led to her being drawn into a forceful littering habit: she only does this when she is participating within such a littering community, where everybody is involved in such a routine and formulaic practice. When she is at home, she does not do that, especially when she is with her daughter. On the other hand, she distinguishes herself from the local Bomaqiao people. In the first layer, the subject 'here everyone' may include both migrant workers and local people. In the second layer, she changes it into 'we', which excludes the locals. Quite often in our daily conversation (I usually sat next to her in the assembly workshop in the toy factory and worked while talking with her), Yang Cui uses the word 'we' to refer to herself and the migrant workers whom she knows well in Bomaqiao. In this case, 'we', used as a grammatical subject, immediately breaks 'everyone' up and separates the migrants from the locals. More than that, the 'we' behaves completely different in the two places – 'here' (away from home) and 'at home'.

No matter which 'here' Yang Cui refers to, the courtyard-house or the broader Bomaqiao area, neither is her true home. To her, home is somewhere else and other, far away in rural Sichuan; home is where she and her fellow villagers do not litter (at least as she claims). But why? Why is this activity associated with their being away from home? Following the logic of her first statement ('here, everyone does it like that'), one possible reason is that they (Yang Cui and some other rural-urban migrants) do not litter at home because there nobody litters. The other possible reason is that home is not a space for littering. If we adapt Mary Douglas' (1966) classic formulation of *dirt,* then on this occasion, to Yang Cui, litter at home (somewhere else and other, not *here*) is 'matter out of place'. However, for Yang Cui (and for other migrant workers who live in the house and also throw litter in the courtyard), the rubbish pile in the courtyard is not necessary 'matter out of place' because home is not here in the courtyard-house. In contrast, for Grandma Chang, because the courtyard-house is her home, the rubbish pile in the courtyard is 'matter out of place', as she believes that the courtyard is for family gatherings and clan activities; ideally, it is supposed to be tidy and clean, decorated with green plants and not used as a space for discarding waste. Here, I am less keen to further pursue people's perspectives of dirt (or litter) within home and nonhome spaces; I am more interested in people's (especially migrants') perspectives of space in their two ways of being-in-the-world – being-at-home and being-away-from-home – and the implications of these two ways, both socially and individually.

Homeawayness

In China, most rural-urban migrants return home once a year, usually during the Chinese New Year. Therefore, for most of the time in a year, they are not at home. However, they are not homeless. They are away from home. To some degree, being at home for them becomes their annual holiday, while being away from home comes to stand for their everyday life. Experiencing everyday life for most of the time somewhere that is not home, they possess (or are possessed by) an alternative sense of being-in-the-world, which I would like to term 'home*away*ness' (analogous to 'home*less*ness').

Deriving from either a sense of alienation or a lack of belonging, homeawayness is a state *in-between* being-at-home and homelessness. The term 'homeawayness' implies two crucial features: first, having a rooted home somewhere else, whether concrete or imagined; and, second, having one's everyday life being uprooted from that home, with spatial distance and/or temporal distance. It emphasizes the spatial dimension (somewhere else) of one's experience of home as well as the temporal dimension (either in the past or in the future; not at present). Since one anchors oneself to a home not here and now, one places oneself in a liminal position of being not at home, but also not homeless. The two features distinguish homeawayness from both of its extremes: being-at-home and homelessness. One can be *at home* when one 'inhabits a cognitive environment in which one can undertake the routines of daily life and through which one finds one's identity best mediated', while being *homeless* occurs 'when such a cognitive environment is eschewed' (Rapport and Overing 2000: 161). Since such a cognitive environment can be found or lost at any time and in any place, being at home is not necessarily bounded by a physical space within a certain time, while being homeless does not necessarily imply being expelled from it. So, neither being-at-home nor homelessness is like homeawayness.

For the Chinese rural-urban migrants, homeawayness represents a typical sense of being-in-the-world: a consciousness of being away from their rural home and floating in the urban space (before they have the mind to 'settle down' in the urban space). Their everyday life's absence of home defines the floating mindset of homeawayness. What attached to the rural-urban migratory process in China is a spreading sense of homeawayness that emerges within the urban space and is especially dense among the floating migrant population. As one sense of being-in-the-world, homeawayness expresses the migrants' perception of an urban or fast-urbanizing space. On a small scale, Bomaqiao represents precisely this kind of space, inasmuch as it accommodates a substantial population of rural-urban migrants. More specifically, in the case of littering, Yang Cui has never perceived the courtyard-house (a space that is used to accommodate migrants like her) as 'home'. Her sense of homeawayness thus manifests itself in the act of her long shot into the rubbish pile at that moment.

As I mentioned before, such a long shot is not peculiar to those living within the physical space of either the courtyard-house or in Bomaqiao more broadly. Littering has become a common behaviour; indeed, 'Here, everyone does it like that'. Mary Douglas (1991) argues that home is definable as a pattern of regular practices through which communitarian realities appear. Ironically, we find that littering, as one of these regular practices, contributes to the routinization of the space-time of the courtyard (or Bomaqiao) as a *nonhome* space. If we perceive home as the routinization of space-time, which, after Douglas, may 'provide a model for redistributive justice, sacrifice, and the common, collective good' (Rapport and Overing 2000: 157), then we can see the reflection of the *nonhome* image in such a courtyard by, on the one hand, the flood of rural-urban migration on the surface and, on the other, the flood of homeawayness underneath. It is the powerful flood of homeawayness that sweeps away the beauty of the courtyard garden and leaves the rubbish piles. Through the very act of littering in the courtyard-house, we can catch a glimpse of a moment when such a *nonhome* space-time is structured functionally, aesthetically and morally by a migrant worker.

Packing to Return Home: Life-Project Building

It is 20 January 2012. Chinese New Year is approaching. Throughout the nation, both the local media and the state news broadcast reports about *chunyun* (the Spring Festival travel rush) and *mingong fanxiang* (peasant-workers returning home). Bomaqiao is filled with advertisements from factories that seek to recruit migrant workers for the coming year, since many migrant workers move from one factory to another after their trip home over the Chinese New Year holiday. In her room in the courtyard-house, Xiao Bin is busily packing for her trip home for Chinese New Year.

Xiao Bin is also from rural Sichuan, where she left a six-year-old son when she came to Bomaqiao a year and a half ago. In that time she has worked in dozens of different toy factories and is currently employed at Shun Xin Toy Factory. As one of more than a hundred million rural-urban migrant workers, she is part of the army of people constituting the Spring Festival travel rush in China.

I attempt to help Xiao Bin pack. Not surprisingly, most of the things are for her son. The items she packs are mainly clothes, toys and sweets. What surprises me is a fancy brand-new mobile phone that she is about to pack into her suitcase. Seeming very pleased with herself, she informs me that it is a gift for her son. With her smiling face and shining eyes, she tells me that she will teach her mother-in-law how to use this smartphone to video-chat. She will then be able to see her son every day and see for herself how much he grows, and so on and so forth.

Xiao Bin talks and talks; as usual, whenever she mentions her son, she does not stop talking (about her son). She misses him very much. He is taken care of by his grandmother at her home in a small village in Sichuan province. Xiao Bin talks about her son almost every single day and thinks about returning home for a short while to see him (although she only returned home once last year). Holding the new phone that has the video-chat feature, it seems that she has found a solution to her homesickness. She knows that she will stay at home with her son for just a short while during the Chinese New Year holiday. Without that phone, she may again linger over the thoughts of her son when she comes back to work in Bomaqiao. So, to Xiao Bin, the phone will change things for the better. She is convinced that having the daily video-chat with him will help her adapt better to being away from her home and son. At first glance, it seems that the smartphone, with its video-chat feature – this new technology – has the power to overcome the problem of distance between a young migrant mother and her little son who is left behind. However, I soon find that beyond this, there is a more fundamental power that drives such a young migrant mother to be able to manage the difficult situation of distance.

Xiao Bin's Life-Project: Cosmopolitan Living

There is a bundle of recruitment ads from toy factories nearby, left on the floor while all the other things have been packed into the suitcase. With great surprise and curiosity, I hold them up to have a close look before I try to squeeze them into the suitcase. Right at that moment, Xiao Bin stops me. In serious tones, she explains that those recruitment ads are her *ming gen zi* (things as important as one's life), which should be kept in her backpack. She must not lose them.

This is the first time that Xiao Bin shares with me her future dream: to bring these recruitment ads back home and distribute them in her village, and bring fellow villagers to work in the factories in Bomaqiao. If success-ful, she will earn fees from the factories, which could become her 'first bucket of gold' to support her further plan of having her own business in Bomaqiao – a small clothes shop. She wishes to have her own business, no matter how small it may be. She does not want to be just a factory girl her whole life. I am reminded of Lao Jin, a migrant who runs a noodle shop in Bomaqiao; Xiao Bin's eyes fill with envy and admiration whenever she mentions Lao Jin.

Xiao Bin looks triumphant when she describes her plan. She holds up the recruitment ads carefully, as if holding a seed of hope that will grow up to be a flourishing tree. She then hugs the bundle of recruitment ads. At this very moment, I can feel that her imagination is filled with visions of future brightness. Her trip home for Chinese New Year will be a crucial step in that future – to plant the seed. She emphasizes that if she succeeds in bringing fellow villagers to work in Bomaqiao, these recruitment ads will not only bring her money (through recruitment fees), but, more importantly, *people.* 'The more *laoxiang* [fellow villagers] here, the easier it is to do something.' I show that I agree by nodding. She speaks with a smile: 'you know, last year when I returned home, the villagers treated me differently. I felt that I had become important because I had seen the outside world.'[5] Xiao Bin is one of several who have moved out to 'the outside world' from her home village in a remote mountain area in Sichuan.

'The outside world is my future. Maybe, for my home, I was born to be-long in the outside world.' Xiao Bin continues, and her voice is filled with more and more confidence. To her, the idea of home exists because there is an outside world, and the outside world exists because there is a home, but the two may become one.

Inasmuch as a migrant's idea of home may change from time to time, so may one's idea of the outside world varies depending on one's idea of home. In other words, the relationship between one's ideas of home and the outside world is not fixed; they are mutually constitutive from case to case, or from moment to moment. In what follows, I offer some examples of the relation-ship articulated by Xiao Bin between ideas of home and her correspond-ing understanding of the outside world. These emerged over the course of a year's worth of conversation in different situations.

TABLE 2.1. Xiao Bin's interpretations of home and the outside world

Ideas of home	The outside world
'My rural village in Sichuan'	'Like here, where I am now [Shantou]'
'Rural areas'	'Cities'
'Here [Shantou]'	'Somewhere I've never been'
'Here [China]'	'You are in the real outside world [United Kingdom]'
'There, very few things I can do'	'Where with opportunities. . .'
'It's more about my childhood'	'My future'

Although she was born in a remote mountain village, Xiao Bin believes that she does not just belong to the small village. At the specific moment when she packs for home, to her, the outside world is the Chinese urban environment, especially eastern coastal cities such as Shantou. Having left her home village in inland China, and now planning to establish herself in a coastal city and make a home in that outside world, she has been building her 'life-project' (Rapport 2003). Her first step is to set up a small clothes shop in the near future. Through building a life-project, her ideas of home and the outside world are almost overlapping – to be at home in the world.

In order to be at home in the world, for one thing, one needs to have a home in one's mind, a clear idea of home, no matter whether this is an imagined one or a concrete one, from one's past, present or future. Those clear ideas of home exist in particular moments of individual consciousness – they are especially obvious in moments when one consciously attempts to make sense of one's self and others, home and the world, and the relations among them. What parallels the corresponding relationship between home and the outside world is the relationship between the self and others. As the former changes, so does the latter. For migrants, home can be a centre for their sense of who they are, but also somewhere to which they can return. It can also define what they are not: from the first step a migrant makes out of the home, home village, home town or home country, he (or she) begins to distinguish himself (or herself) from those fellow villagers who are staying still in the home place. Although this sense of being different from other villagers may be traced to this very first step, it may not be as obvious to a migrant at that moment since it could be concealed by their excitement (or anxiety) about being in the outside world for the first time. In contrast, when a migrant returns home after having sojourned in 'the outside world' for a period of time, his (or her) sense of being different is too obvious to ignore.

When Xiao Bin returned to her home village last year, she gained a specific sense of self-worth.

From Xiao Bin's perspective, although she believes that she belongs to the outside world, it is home that gives her the power to move out to the outside world. As she said: 'maybe, *for my home,* I was born to belong in the outside world'. Her ideas of *home* and *the outside world* are mutually constitutive: without home, there will be no outside world, and vice versa.

In order to be at home in the world, again, one needs to include the outside world in one's home, though one's comprehension of 'the outside world' may vary from time to time (see Table 2.1). For Xiao Bin, the outside world has not yet become her home in such a way that she can feel that she is at home in the world. However, with her life-project taking shape, her idea of home and the outside world may be merging towards a point – a point that harmonizes and synthesizes home and the outside world: a kind of cosmopolitanism. Her life-project, from this perspective, can be understood as a kind of 'cosmopolitan living' (Rapport 2012: 75).

According to Rapport (2012: 75), 'cosmopolitanism is a kind of space for human expression and for individual emancipation'. Rapport gives us three key words to describe the kind of human life that cosmopolitanism envisages: 'movement, voluntarism and fulfilment' (2012: 75). Here, in a world of movement as experienced by Chinese rural-urban labour migrants, 'cosmopolitan living' is understood as a *process* of syncretizing the migrants' ideas of home and the outside world through the fulfilment of their life-projects. At the point where home and the outside world merge into one, *time* replaces *space* in one's imagination (of home and the outside world). It is at this very point that cosmopolitanism can be said to come into being, occupying an individual's sense of being at home in the world. As Rapport concludes, 'fundamental to cosmopolitan living is that ethos of global guesthood whose anchor is time not space: *Anyone* is recognized as belonging fundamentally to the time of his or her life' (2012: 124).

Returning to the example of Xiao Bin specifically, her statement that 'the outside world is my future' tells us vividly of the time-space replacement: the outside world (space) is where her future (time) or her life-project is. For her, being at home in her future or in her life-project will be like being at home in the outside world. Each time she thinks about her plan or her future, she may think about her home – not only her present home, but also her future home.

Xiao Bin places the backpack on her shoulders, stuffed with the bundle of recruitment ads, lifts up her fully packed suitcase and leaves her room. Seeing the back of her, leaving the courtyard and heading to Shantou train station to take a train home, I wonder: will it be a *re-turn* (home) or a *new-turn* (for her life-project)?

Conclusion

Can a migrant really return home? Will it be a *re-turn* or a *new-turn* for Xiao Bin? In his book *Migrancy, Culture, Identity,* Iain Chambers (1994a: 74) argues that, for migrants, to 'go home' again becomes impossible since '[t]his means to find oneself subject to ever wider and more complex web of cultural negotiation and interaction'. Or, as Sara Ahmed (1999: 343) puts it, 'the movement of selves between places that come to be inhabited as home involve the discontinuities of personal biographies and wrinkles in the skin'. Both authors tell us of the continuous change selves undergo throughout the migratory process. Furthermore, their arguments point up the intimate relationship between one's self and one's home. As Ahmed reminds us: 'Home is not exterior to a self, but implicated in it' (1999: 343). In other words: 'Home is not a phenomenon that lies outside of the individual . . . The individual is embedded in the home-making process' (Cubero 2015: 6). From this perspective, one can never leave home since home is always within one's mind, and one can never return home since either one's self or one's home is ever changing. Ahmed (1999: 343) reasons: 'The process of returning home is likewise about the failures of memory, of not being inhabited in the same way by that which appears as familiar.' In short, as John Berger sums up, 'every migrant knows in his heart of hearts, that it is impossible to return' (cited in Jackson 2012: 69).

When Xiao Bin went back to her rural home, she found that she could not stay anymore; she belonged to 'the outside world'. The moment one finds one cannot stay anymore, the boundaries of home are renegotiated. One is negotiating with oneself a broader understanding of home or, if not broader, then multiple. As a conceptual space, one's original home (usually where one was born and grew up) may serve well to accommodate one's nostalgia, providing a context for one to trace one's origins. However, the space may not be enough for one to accommodate one's struggles of identity formation and of internal divisions within one's migratory experience. The movement of migration implies a future, an exploration or a discovery, and home becomes a cognitive space for one's constant *self-(re)definition* or *self-(re)discovery*. In this sense, the movement in-between *leaving* home and *returning* home is not circular.

If we agree that it is not possible for migrants to return home, then, is the movement linear? The answer is partly yes and partly no. It is partly yes since migration is a one-way trip in the sense that there is no home to go back to, as has just been discussed. It is partly no due to the fact that on no account can we prevent a migrant (or any human being) from taking steps to return home. At least, there is no way to root out one's very intention or desire to return home – regardless of the geographical territory of one's origin or cognitive home, of one's past or future. Home could be in the form of a text that, as for the religiously observant Jew, 'each re-reading was a return home' (Rapport 2012: 105). Home could also be marked in a photographic postcard that transports one back home by sustaining one's nostalgia of a remembered landscape (Naguib 2010). Or, again, one might return home through inscribing a sentiment on a piece of *qiaopi* remittance family letter and mailing it home (Chen 2015). In short, it is these attempts to return home, these real actions such as *re*-reading a text, *re*-viewing a postcard, and writing family letters *again and again,* that make the movement nonlinear.

As in Xiao Bin's case, each attempt to return home is also a construction of one's idea of home and a way of homemaking. Each time Xiao Bin collects a piece of recruitment leaflet from a factory, she is compelled to revisit her life-project that culminates (for now) with her plan to open a clothes shop in the future. Each time she is reminded of her plan, she experiences a return home – a home that is shaped by her sentimental attachment to her imagined future. To some extent, this shows us the way that home comes to exist in moments of individual migrants' consciousness, and the processes through which home is constituted when one is away from home. Life is like a flow, but we make sense of it in moments. Within a moment of being, we step back to review or to look forward (Rapport and Overling 2000: 257–61). But the momentary stepping back is still part of the greater flow of life, as returning home for migrants is still part of one's life-project. For migrants, each attempt to return home (whether physically or cognitively) itself becomes a way of homemaking. This is a nonlinear movement: with each return, one does not get back to one's starting point to form a circle, but instead one follows a spiral curve that always leads further and further away from the origin, though whether it has an upward or downward trajectory is debatable. In a word, each return forms a movement that is neither circular nor linear, but spiralling onwards.

So, how does a migrant's sense of homeawayness relate to homemaking in light of this spiralling trajectory? In Yang Cui's case, at the very moment when she sensitively defines the courtyard as *nonhome* space through her self-justification ('We do not do it at home') for her act of littering, simultaneously, she is fashioning a conscious image of her (ideal) home (at least in one aspect). Throughout her migratory process, each time she consciously builds an intangible wall between *home* and nonhome space, she may imagine home, either sketching its profile or colouring a detail of it. Again and again, she constructs and reconstructs a sense of home. In other words, it is the sense of homeawayness that brings us to a migrant's understanding of home and his (or her) imagination of what an ideal home is supposed to be. Since '[t]o imagine is to begin the process that transforms reality' (Hooks, cited in Chambers 1994a: 9), the imagination may be reflected in reality as one's aspiration of making a home, a home that is either based on a past one or a future one, or may be manifested as one's desire to return to the original home or to reach a future home. With either spatial distance or temporal distance, home is elsewhere when one possesses (or is possessed by) the sense of homeawayness. Home becomes 'where the self is going' (Ahmed 1999: 331). In other words, to a migrant, home may not be only where he or she comes from, but also where he or she is heading. The floating mindset of homeawayness expresses the continuing self-negotiation when identities are performed; there is a continual oscillation between one's reality and one's imagination, one's past and one's future, and one's rootedness and one's cosmopolitan openness. If home is understood as 'where one best knows oneself' (Rapport and Dawson 1998: 4), then the floating mindset of homeawayness manifests itself as the constant process of self-reconstruction or reimagination when one moves away from home, and the movement might instead become a fundamentally important process of coming home (a coming that is *not yet* home) within oneself. In other words, accompanied by manifest expressions of homeawayness, there is cognitive construction that undergirds the migratory process, which is to say that the making of home is a continuous process (of the making of the self) shaping a spiralling trajectory, which is essential to crafting the life-course of the migrants.

Along one's spiralling-onwards trajectory of home, the boundaries between home and away, between home and the self, and between home and the world are permeable. Home and away cannot exist without each other. The relationship between home and the self is dynamic. In relation to home and the world, they are each one's own shadow. When the two overlap – at home in the world – the shadow disappears. Being absent from one's original home, the movement creates the space for a migrant to rethink home and to make a home beyond a fixed, spatial and material one. Such acts of making home enable one to be at home in the world. 'Home', in a world of movement, therefore becomes less like a noun and more like a verb – 'homing', a *doing* (e.g. making, feeling, returning, writing, remembering or imaging) (Ahmed 1999; Jackson 2005; Chen 2017). Home becomes those very practices from which space-time unfolds so that home can be sensed, experienced and expressed.

Shuhua Chen has recently completed her Ph.D. in Social Anthropology at the University of St Andrews. While interested in cosmopolitan studies, anthropology of migration and home, and archival research of overseas Chinese remittance letters (*qiaopi*), her research is currently devoted to the studies of rural-urban migration in China. In particular, she explores the interior experience of migration, concerning individuals' phenomenology of home away from home, as well as their imaginative and practical construction of home and homemaking.

Notes

This research is based on my fieldwork in China between 2011 and 2013, supported with funding from the Foundation for Urban and Regional Studies (FURS) and the Centre for Cosmopolitan Studies at the University of St Andrews. I am also very grateful to Nicola Frost, Tom Selwyn, Walter Hakala, Nigel Rapport, Stephanie Bunn and Karolina Kuberska, for their incisive and insightful comments for this chapter.

 1. Retrieved 9 April 2018 from http://www.stats.gov.cn/tjsj/zxfb/201305/t20130527 _12978.html.
 2. In 1861, Shantou was opened officially as a port under the Treaty of Tien-tsin signed between the Chinese Qing government and France, Britain and the United States (Wang, Wang and Qin 1988).
 3. The Chaoshan region consists of three cities in Guangdong province: Shantou, Chaozhou and Jieyang. The term 'Chaoshan' has been used for both a linguistic and cultural region.
 4. *Si dian jin* is representative of the Chaoshan architecture styles: four rooms take up the four corners of the courtyard. Besides the four rooms, there are usually two other chambers, one on either side of the entrance hall. As the centre of the house, a courtyard connects the entrance hall with the back hall.
 5. 'The outside world' is the English translation of Xiao Bin's original Chinese word '外面的世界' (*waimian de shijie*).

References

Ahmed, S. 1999. 'Home and Away: Narratives of Migration and Estrangement', *International Journal of Cultural Studies* 2(3): 329–47.

Chambers, I. 1994a. *Migrancy, Culture, Identity*. London: Routledge.

Chan, K. W. 2010. 'The Global Financial Crisis and Migrant Workers in China: "There is No Future as a Labourer; Returning to the Village Has No Meaning"', *International Journal of Urban and Regional Research* 34(3): 659–77.

Chen, S. 2015. 'Making Home, Making Sense of the World: Archival Research with *Qiaopi* Letters', in K. Koehler and K. McDonald-Miranda (eds), *Letters and Letter Writing: Negotiating the Private and the Public*. Oxford: Inter-Disciplinary Press, pp. 59–76.

———. 2017. 'Cosmopolitan Imagination: A Methodological Quest for *Qiaopi* Archival Research', *Yearbook of the Center for Cosmopolitan Studies* 3: 1–27.

Cubero, C.A. 2015. 'To Know the World is to Advocate for it', *Yearbook of the Center for Cosmopolitan Studies* 1: 1–20.

Douglas, M. 1966. *Purity and Danger: An Analysis of Concepts of Pollution and Taboo*. New York: Praeger.

———. 1991. 'The Idea of Home: A Kind of Space', *Social Research* 58(1): 287–307.

Huang, P.C. 2011. 'The Modern Chinese Family: In Light of Economic and Legal History', *Modern China* 37(5): 459–97.

Jackson, M. 2005. *Existential Anthropology: Events, Exigencies, and Effects.* New York: Berghahn Books.

———. 2012. *Between One and Another.* Berkeley: University of California Press.

Naguib, S. 2010. 'Egypt in View: Postcards of Nostalgia', in S. Williksen and N. Rapport (eds), *Reveries of Home: Nostalgia, Authenticity and the Performance of Place.* Newcastle upon Tyne: Cambridge Scholars Publishing, pp. 109–24.

National Bureau of Statistics of China. 2013. 'National Monitoring Survey Report for Rural Migrant Workers 2012'. Retrieved 9 April 2018 from http://www.stats.gov.cn/tjsj/zxfb/201305/t20130527_12978.html.

Pun, N., and H. Lu. 2010. 'Unfinished Proletarianization: Self, Anger, and Class Action among the Second Generation of Peasant-Workers in Present-Day China', *Modern China* 36(5): 493–519.

Rapport, N. 1993. *Diverse World-Views in an English Village.* Edinburgh: Edinburgh University Press.

———. (ed.), 2002. *British Subjects: An Anthropology of Britain.* Oxford: Berg.

———. 2003. *I am Dynamite: An Alternative Anthropology of Power.* London: Routledge.

———. 2012. 'Part II Cosmopolitanism: Actions, Relations and Institutions beyond the Communitarian', in V. Amit and N. Rapport (eds), *Community, Cosmopolitanism and the Problem of Human Commonality.* London: Pluto, pp. 75–187.

Rapport, N., and A. Dawson (eds). 1998. *Migrants of Identity: Perceptions of Home in a World of Movement.* New York: Berg.

Rapport, N., and J. Overing. 2000. *Social and Cultural Anthropology: The Key Concepts.* London: Routledge.

Schneider, M. 2011. 'Feeding China's Pigs Implications for the Environment: China's Smallholder Farmers and Food Security'. Retrieved 9 April 2018 from https://www.iatp.org/documents/feeding-china's-pigs-implications-for-the-environment-china's-smallholder-farmers-and-food.

Tuan, Y. 1977. *Space and Place: The Perspective of Experience.* Minneapolis: University of Minnesota Press.

Wang, L., X. Wang and Z. Qin. 1988. *Shantou Da Shiji.* Shantou: Shantou Chorography Compilation Committee.

CHAPTER 3

Between a Home and a Homeland

Experiences of Jewish Return Migrants in Ukraine

Marina Sapritsky

Introduction

Despite the increase in migration and transnational patterns of life we observe across the globe today, the idea of home, or homes and belonging, remains extremely important in the way people define themselves and relate to others. This is especially apparent in the context of return migration and diaspora literature, where questions of what is a home or a homeland, where one feels at home and how one engages in homemaking practices are paramount and stand at the centre of academic discourse. In her latest book, *Diasporic Homecomings,* Takeyuki Tsuda describes 'the millions of Jews in the Diaspora who have migrated to Israel since World War II' as the 'most prominent example' of the world's major ethnic return migration, out of which 'the largest group of Jewish ethnic return migrants has been from the former Soviet Union; more than 770,000 Russian [speaking] Jews entered Israel between 1990 and 1999' (2009: 1). Although Jewish migration to Israel is often described as a return migration (including its problematic elements), Larissa Remennick, writing in the same volume, reminds us that 'the 'return' in the Israeli case is purely symbolic, as one cannot return to the land that one's ancestors left 2,000 years ago; yet the myth of *aliyah* (Hebrew, literally meaning 'ascent' or 'pilgrimage') as homecoming remains one of the chief pillars of Zionism (Remennick 2009: 209).

In this chapter, I attempt to grapple with return migration and transnational patterns among ex-Soviet Jewish emigrants and their family members

who have recently returned from Israel either to take advantage of new entrepreneurial, professional, educational and personal opportunities unat-
tainable abroad or just to feel 'at home'. Going beyond the debated statistics
and the stereotypes promoted by the media, I aim to present material about
the everyday reality of returnees,[1] including the motives for their return and
the various ways they adjust to their home environment following a prolonged period of absence. I analyse the ways in which returnees create and
undo ties within their social environments in order to construct and negotiate their sense of belonging. I argue that most ex-Soviet Jewish returnees
do not envision their returns as permanent. They entertain the option of an
eventual return to their original emigration destination or relocation to yet
another place. The freedom of choice guaranteed by a foreign passport allows returning Jews to approach 'home' as both a place of familiarity and a
place of discovery.[2]

Placing my research within the larger context of diaspora studies and literature on the subject of home and return, I end this chapter with an analysis
of the homeland–diaspora dichotomy, which I argue should be broadened
to include the multiplicity of belonging we see among Russian-speaking Israelis and others who are defined simultaneously by a number of diasporic
groups and homes. The notion of home vivid in this ethnography of Jewish
return migration from Israel is located within a complex, multilayered and
multidimensional space in which economic, religious and other personal
factors are framed by the larger context of state agendas. I want to suggest
that if we look outside of diaspora literature, where home is often embedded in ideological sentiments, it is easier to see the trajectory of Russian-
speaking Israelis in a similar light to many other migrant groups for whom
home refers, among other things, to the possibilities of creating a better livelihood and exploring new opportunities.

Debates on Ex-Soviet Jewish Return Migration

Jewish citizens of the USSR and its successor independent states were able to
emigrate with great difficulty during some periods of Soviet rule, and more
freely following its fragmentation. The breakup of the USSR saw massive efforts by Israeli officials, American Jews and others, including local activists,
that paved the way for one of the largest waves of Jewish emigration that
still flows today. Suddenly the possibility of leaving – to a myriad of destinations – became a reality for ex-Soviet Jews. However, far from everyone took
up the opportunity to emigrate and, when they did, Israel was by no means
always seen as the obvious place to go. The choice of the Jewish 'stay back'
population to remain in the Former Soviet Union (FSU) baffled many of

the human rights crusaders who, ever since the tiny crack in Soviet borders opened in the 1970s, had seen themselves as freeing Jews from communist repression and anti-Semitism: 'Emigration from the "land of state-sponsored anti-Semitism" has been the dominant lens through which everyone has seen Jewish life in Russia' (Aviv and Shneer 2005: 29, 49). The fact that most emigrating Jews were choosing destinations other than Israel was also highly disappointing for Zionists. Emigration from the former Soviet states has slowed down greatly and we can now analyse a new dimension of the ex-Soviet Jewish migration pattern: their return.

The emigration of Israeli citizens from Israel to the United States and Europe has been described previously in academic literature.[3] Yet the out-migration of FSU-born Jews from Israel has only recently captured the attention of politicians, scholars of Russian-speaking Jewry and journalists across the globe. The fact that, for the first time in the history of Russian Jewish migration, 'more Jews are migrating *to* Russia from Israel than the other way around'[4] elicited concern in Israel.

Statistics related to Jewish migration from Israel back to the FSU vary greatly. According to research conducted in Israel in 2004, between 2001 and 2003 alone, nearly 50,000 ex-Soviet Jews returned from Israel to Russia and other independent countries (Ash 2004). According to a report released by the Federation of Jewish Communities of Russia, while about 50,000 Jewish former emigrants to Israel have returned to Russia since 2001, only about 30,000 Russian Jews have left for Israel.[5] Meanwhile, Yevgeny Satanovsky, President of the Russian Jewish Congress, noted that over the same period, 100,000 Russian Jews returned to their countries of origin or other industrial centres and capital cities in the FSU (Satanovsky 2009). The figure for Israeli returnees in Moscow alone is estimated at 50,000 (Friedgut 2007). As Mark Tolts (2009) notes: 'There are a lot of ungrounded statements concerning huge numbers of FSU out-migrants from Israel.' Relying on the official statistics of the Russian and Ukrainian governments, Tolts reports that there were 17,438 registered returnees to the Russian Federation and 14,955 returnees to Ukraine in 1997–2009. Because many returnees do not register with the local passport office and hold on to their Israeli passports, the number of registered returnees (and hence the number who show up in official statistics) is much smaller than the mass of returnees who typically opt to hold on to their foreign passports. Many of the returnees also frequently travel back and forth from Israel, and are therefore automatically excluded from the statistics of out-migrants calculated by the Israeli state.[6] Nonetheless, Israeli officials have expressed concern about a possible Russian 'brain drain' and the general increase in Russian out-migration from the country. In a 2007 survey of 4,214 Russian-speaking Jewish respondents, most of whom (90 per cent) reside in Israel, 81 per cent said they had thought about leaving Israel.[7] Some Israeli sociologists including Elizar Feldman insist that many of the returnees are not 'failed cases of *aliyah*' (individuals who were unable to adapt to an Israeli way of life), but, rather, young, well-educated and capable individuals whose skills could not be accommodated in Israel's limited employment market and had reached a 'glass ceiling'.[8] Other specialists in Russian Jewish migration insist that, due to the nearly identical characteristics of emigrants *from* Russia to Israel and immigrants *to* Russia from Israel, the recent developments 'do not cause a "brain drain" in either place'.[9] Together with other groups of Israelis who choose to live outside Israel, the outflow of Russian-speaking Jews can be perceived as undermining the 'Zionist assertion that Israel is the best place for Jews to live'.[10] Evidently, the old narratives of Soviet repression still linger on. In response, Satanovsky has warned Western audiences not to read too much into this trend and to look beyond the Soviet days of repression: 'There is no Iron Curtain anymore, and that's what the phenomenon is . . . nobody is surprised when an American Jew goes to Nepal for a work contract and then returns to visit his aunt in New Jersey . . . All these are simply signs that Russia is a normal country now' (cited in Osipovich 2009: 1). While the old narratives of Soviet repression and anti-Semitism are still very much in force in the media,[11] new stereotypes are also being propagated in which 'returnees galvanize Jewish community life'[12] and 'revive Jewish culture'.[13] Those who have experienced life in the Jewish 'homeland' are thus perceived as becoming active and knowledgeable Jews who have something to teach local 'stay back' Jews about Judaism and Jewish community.[14]

Why Leave the Land of Milk and Honey?

Israeli returnees had different reasons for leaving Israel and for choosing to return to Odessa, whether on a permanent, undefined or temporary basis. These included family obligations, career development, the danger of living in the Middle East, and the improving economic and social prospects in the Ukraine. For the most part, the returnees I met were from Israel, with a smaller percentage from Germany and a few from Australia and the United States. This pattern may be explained by the fact that 'migration to the USA and Germany usually entails inter-generational families, rather than individual Jewish youth and young couples, as is frequently the case with Israel' (Golbert 2001: 347). Another explanation for the low frequency of returns from the United States and Australia is the distance and cost of travel. While visits from Germany were very common,[15] permanent returns are less frequent. European citizenship and highly praised social benefits were some of the main reasons presented by 'Germans' visiting Odessa to explain this pattern.

Among the returnees I met were people who had simply never managed to find their way in Israel and, facing economic, social or personal constraints, decided to return. Among such so-called 'failed cases of *aliyah*' were young Jews who had set off on their own and found it difficult to survive without the support of their family.[16] In other instances, elderly Odessans had found themselves too dependent on others for communication and everyday tasks, or middle-aged migrants struggled to make a living. There were also cases of well-to-do migrants lured back to Odessa by business opportunities. To this particular group of 'opportunity seekers', life in Israel presented no obstacles of acclimatization; the choice to leave was made because of better prospects elsewhere. These returns were often nonpermanent, with individuals frequently traveling back and forth. This group, whom I call 'transmigrants', divided their time between multiple destinations with split business and family commitments.

Odessa as a Place of Return

Some Israelis in Odessa moved to the city to study or work for one of the local Jewish organizations.[17] The returnees, transmigrants and long-term visitors I met were not all originally from Odessa. In some circumstances, returnees were natives of other cities of the FSU, drawn to Odessa by a personal or professional connection. Although the majority of ex-Soviet Jewish returnees chose to move to major cities in Russia and Ukraine due to their level of economic growth, the Russian-speaking Israelis I met chose Odessa for a number of reasons. For some, it was the place they had left and longed to return to, while others were reliant on the support of their local families and friends, and in many cases ownership of property played a major role. In one instance, an elderly couple who sold their apartment with heavy hearts upon their departure bought it back upon their return because it was the place where they wanted to spend the rest of their days. Non-native returnees were often spouses of Odessan locals or on work or academic postings. Yulik, a young entrepreneur I will describe later, was attracted by the city's small-scale yet urban life and the opportunities he saw in the city's tourist and market potential. Even non-natives spoke of Odessa as a place where they felt 'at home' and were touched by the intimacy of the place. 'Zdes' yutno' ('It's cosy here'), one returnee explained. At times, they shared some of the sentiments of native Odessan returnees who spoke of the place as 'radnoye', which roughly translates as 'native', 'homely' and 'dear'. In some cases, returnees said Odessa reminded them of Tel Aviv and other Israeli cities kissed by the sea and sun. The port atmosphere of the place also gave some returnees a sense of being part of the world and connected to their experience of travel. It was the small, cosy feel of the city as well as its airy openness and grandeur that returnees identified as unique. 'I love the fact that I am able to go see a different opera or theatre performance here, and at the same time I love the market where people talk to me like they know me', one returnee shared. Although pragmatic reasons such as property, kin, social networks and job opportunities most often dictated decisions to return, the decision to move to Odessa, rather than Kiev or Moscow for instance, was also infused with strong sentiments of 'home' and the city's 'homely' traits.

Natives and others described Odessa as a small, family-like place where you felt like you knew everyone and everything was within your reach. This is not to say that these sentiments were strong enough to keep returnees in Odessa or that they were not met with more negative feelings towards the place by some in the process of their prolonged stay, as I later point out. Many did move from Odessa to other locales and some ended up returning to Israel; yet others continuously engage in ongoing travel back and forth. Nonetheless, those 'rooted' returnees, like Nina described below, described their return as a reunion with their beloved city: changed, but nevertheless theirs.

Narratives of Returnees

Nina and her son Kostya were among the first returnees from Israel I met in the city. They were not acquainted with others who had returned.[18] Leaving Odessa in 1989, Nina had returned in 2000 and her son followed a year later. In our initial conversations, it had already become obvious that Nina's decision to emigrate to Israel had not been driven by any Zionist ideology of living in the Jewish homeland. She did not see her move to Israel as 'going home'. On the contrary, she described leaving Odessa as 'a difficult decision of leaving her native home'. At the same time, she told me, she was comforted by the idea that she was going to a place where no one would call her *zhidovka* ('yid') and, in that sense, to a place where she would be made to feel at home.

Nina reflected on her time in Israel with mixed emotions. She had struggled economically for all the eleven years she spent in Israel as she and her son changed jobs, apartments and cities in order to make ends meet. She also faced other social problems associated with an immigrant's life, including nostalgia and the unfamiliar local climate. At the same time, she spoke of Israel as a 'holy place' where she could feel history, see breathtaking landscape and take in the presence of God. In Israel, she started attending religious services, not at a synagogue but in a Russian Orthodox Church, which she described as being 'culturally close' to her. She recalled meeting a number of other Jews during services who were *vykresty* (baptized Jews).[19] It was during her years in Israel that she claims to have become closer to Jesus Christ, a relationship she still maintained through regular prayer and conversations with evangelical missionaries who visited her home. Other than occasional visits to the Jewish Club for the Elderly, *Gmilus Hesed,* she did not take part in Jewish activities in the city or identify herself as Jewish through any of the new avenues available to Jews in Odessa. Another returnee, Oleg, had had a similar religious experience in Israel, where he realized the importance of having God in his life through his interaction with the Russian Orthodox Church. When he returned to Odessa, both he and, more recently, his children were baptized.

Though Nina had formed some attachment to Israel, in the end it was not enough to make her stay. She was one of the few returnees I met who, on coming home, opted to change her Israeli passport for a Ukrainian one, which she needed in order to receive a pension and acquire a *propiska* (certificate of residency). Most returnees held on tight to their Israeli passports for travel purposes, and also for the advantages of having an alternative country of residence.[20] 'I came back to a lot that was new', she explained, 'but I still came back home.' When I asked Nina how others in the city responded to her return, she had little to say. 'I don't tell many people about it', she explained, adding, 'I don't want to brag about living abroad'. Referring to a painful incident after her return when one of her neighbours called her a *zhidovka,* she said that ordinary Ukrainians (especially newly arrived migrants to the city) were envious of the opportunities available to Jews. Her son Kostya had never experienced any such negative reactions as a returnee. Rather, he said, 'the people I told about Israel were always curious to know more'.

Kostya was nearly eighteen when he followed his mother to Israel. This was the first time he and his mother had left the Soviet Union. Soon after his arrival, he was admitted to one of Tel Aviv's leading art institutes, which he attended for several months, but eventually left because he needed a job. Despite his efforts, he had never managed to gain a degree or master the Hebrew language fluently enough to use it at a professional level, which had greatly limited his employment opportunities. Nonetheless, he saw his time in Israel in a positive light as being extremely meaningful. His return to Odessa was dictated primarily by his inability to support himself financially in Israel after his mother's departure.

Four years after returning, Kostya still defined Israel as his *rodina* (homeland) and held on to his Israeli passport. The idea of eventually going 'home' (to Israel) was a recurrent theme in his conversation – to the great irritation of his mother each time he voiced such thoughts aloud. His long absence from Odessa meant that he felt little if any connection to the city, the place where he was born and partially raised.

During the year before I met him, Kostya had become more observant of Jewish religious laws, had started wearing a *kippah* and regularly attended the synagogue – none of which had been part of his life in Israel. Once back in Odessa, however, he found that he wanted to live an active Jewish life. While in some cases returnees had become religiously observant during their time in Israel, for Kostya and some others it took returning to Odessa, rather than moving to Israel, to develop a desire and a need to be in an organized Jewish community. Kostya felt a sense of connection within Odessa's religious organizations where he could practise his Hebrew and discuss Israeli life. He also hoped that participation in local Jewish organizations could provide for an opportunity to return to Israel. I was told that Kostya did return to Israel a couple of months after I left Odessa, although without any settled prospects there.

Other young returnees behaved similarly, although with a less religious pattern of affiliation. Marat, a young entrepreneur in his mid thirties, explained that in Israel he did not follow any religious traditions: 'You don't need to do anything in Israel to feel Jewish.' However, when he came back to Odessa, he started visiting the Chabad congregation where his friends go for the major holidays and occasional Shabbats. He illustrated his participation with the religious congregation with an old joke: 'Rabinovich goes to the synagogue to talk to God and I go to talk to Rabinovich.' He had initially immigrated to Israel in the early 1990s when he could not get a visa for the United States. Thus, Israel was not his primary choice for emigration; rather, he explained, it was a way to leave Odessa and its stagnant economic and political situation. He had first returned to the city in 2002 for an experimental year and, having then returned to Israel, he made the decision to move back to Odessa permanently in 2004. He still considered Israel his historical homeland, but felt that the life of an immigrant was difficult to cope with. Back in his native city, he has started a construction company with another Israeli returnee who moved back after fifteen years in Israel. He enjoyed working as a manager and using a pencil and paper rather than the manual labour he had done in Israel. Although he did not imagine himself returning to Israel, other destinations such as Canada or potentially the United States, where his father lived, were not out of the question if Odessa's economic situation became difficult in the future.

Homemaking and Organized Jewish Life

In relation to Odessa, the media image of returnees actively reviving local Jewish life or even participating in its affairs is a considerable oversimplification. The generational differences in affiliation to Jewish Odessa we saw between Nina and her son Kostia and Marat were not atypical. Older returnees tried to ease back into their old lives almost unnoticed and usually avoided official affiliation (except for the sake of social benefits such as pensions). Most younger returnees strove to practise Hebrew, took part in Jewish holiday celebrations and often found employment in Jewish organizations, although others chose to remain on the periphery of Jewish activities. The behaviour of middle-aged returnees was largely determined by the nature of their employment and family circumstances. Some, seeking career benefits, used Jewish organizations to network, especially for possible clients; others, seeing no advantages, did not include Jewish gatherings in their busy routines. For families whose children were enrolled in Jewish schools, occasional Jewish activity was the norm, which sometimes led to more extended involvement, while others felt too constrained by lack of time or simply lack of interest.

One of my informants, Dina, who had returned after nine years living in Tel Aviv, said that she could not relate to Jewish life in Odessa as it was 'too religious'.[21] A young woman in her late twenties, she had moved back in late 2006 mainly to live closer to her family who had decided against moving to Israel. Her first encounter with Israel had been on a study abroad programme and, there and then, she had decided to emigrate. At the age of fifteen, she had made *aliyah,* leaving her sister and parents behind in Odessa. Prior to her move, she was an active participant in numerous Jewish programmes in the city. However, during her years in Israel, she drifted away from Jewish practices and her passion for being an active Jew slowly faded. As she saw it: 'When you actually live in Zion you don't need to do anything else to feel Jewish.' Returning to Odessa, she had chosen not to revive her old relations with Odessa's Jewish circles. She looked down on the policy of the Jewish Agency (known in the former Soviet Union as Sokhnut) of, as she put it, 'feeding Jews fairytales' about their 'home'. Equally, nothing about the religious observance of her friends struck a chord with her present Jewish identification. The new outlook she had adopted abroad now made them seem 'narrow and old-fashioned in their understanding of Jewish identity'. As other examples indicate, some returnees feel superior towards those who stayed behind because of their experience abroad (Stefansson 2004: 179).

Even outside the city's Jewish circles, Dina struggled to find her way among old friends. Most of her peers who had stayed in Odessa had graduated from college and found employment. Many of her old girlfriends were also married and starting their own families. By contrast, Dina was single, had 'lost two years to the army' and, despite her sustained efforts to work and study at the same time, had not managed to complete her college education in Israel. In Odessa, where most education is still free of charge, continuing higher education appeared more feasible. Within a month of her return, she had managed to register for several classes at the Engineering Institute of Odessa, which she attended with great interest. Despite her plans to remain in Odessa, after six years she returned to Israel, where she lives today. In our most recent correspondence, she explained that living in Ukraine, a place she described as a 'foolish country', proved more difficult than she imagined. In the end, she felt that she was, after all, more Israeli than Russian Jewish and therefore she belonged in Israel.

While some returnees intended their remigration to be permanent or at least long term, others did not. This group of transnational migrants, or 'transmigrants' as I call them, define their relationship with Odessa as one of partial belonging and residency. Genady, his wife Luba and their two children came to Odessa in the last two months of my fieldwork, having previously lived in Israel for ten years. They had decided to move to Odessa in order to grow their business of selling *Herbalife* health products, Israeli-made food supplements and skincare goods. They travelled regularly to and from Israel, as well as across Ukraine, in order to satisfy work and family obligations. They missed Israel for its food, music and natural beauty. Genady and Luba retained their Israeli citizenship, with Ukrainian resident visas securing permission to work. Although their primary identification was Israeli – a title they gave themselves and others used to describe them – Odessa, Genady's native city, served as a convenient business base in Ukraine. The fact that Genady's mother lived in Odessa and was available to mind their children made it easier for them to manage. As Genady put it:

> It is easy for me to come back to the Ukraine as opposed to moving to Canada, which is where my wife and I originally wanted to go once we decided to expand our business. In Odessa I know everyone that I need for any given situation and I feel free. In Israel, starting your own business is difficult, especially as an immigrant.

Other entrepreneurs I met had had similar experiences of conducting business overseas. Vova, a returnee from Haifa, told me of the difficulties he had faced setting up a business in Israel. 'You can't trust anyone in Israel', he told me. 'I had a business with a Moroccan guy but he tried to cheat me out of all my money.' Describing his motivation in coming to Odessa and his plans for the future, he was clear: 'I am here to make money.' Two months into his stay, he was still following his passion for Israeli food, working hard to open a hummus restaurant in the city. For that reason, he had attended a number of Jewish functions in the city and openly approached the Chabad rabbi to ask him for help in his entrepreneurial efforts. According to Vova, the rabbi knew a good many local businessmen to whom he could possibly turn for funding. Similarly, he approached other Jewish organizations in the city where he hoped to meet other Israelis and potential sponsors for his business idea. Although there are no specific returnee organizations in Odessa, returnees from

Israel take part in Jewish organizations in the city where they are regarded first and foremost as Israelis. In Vova's case, accessing social networks served as a key element of trying to secure his livelihood (Stefansson 2004: 178) and the success of his business. In his particular case, he relied on the larger 'kin group', the local Jewish population, rather than his own family or friends.

Vova was originally from Saint Petersburg, while his wife, Nadya, was a native of Odessa. The deciding factor between the two cities was that in Odessa there was an apartment available for their use. I also sensed from our conversation that Vova's determination not to return to Saint Petersburg sprang from the fact that he had missed out on opportunities that his friends there had made use of during his absence. 'Those people [in Saint Petersburg] were really able to grow and make something of themselves. I have been watching clouds and picking my nose for the last ten years living in Israel.' Furthermore, Nadya, having visited Odessa many times during the time they had lived in Israel, had assured Vova that she would be able to get a job in one of the city's Jewish organizations, where her Hebrew language skills would be in demand, and that he too would find interesting entrepreneurial opportunities in the city. Like the returnees to Sarajevo described by Stefansson, Vova, his wife and other business-oriented returnees were more concerned with solving their livelihood situations than with the questions of their own identity that seemed to preoccupy Kostya and his mother.

Like Nadya, Nina and Marat, many people who consider returning from Israel first make a number of preliminary visits to their potential destination. Yulik, originally from the Ukrainian town of Dnipropetrovs'k and currently living in Israel, was making such an exploratory visit to Odessa when I met him. Like Genady, Vova and Nadya, he was attracted to Ukraine for its business potential, in his case in the field of IT. Originally planning to relocate to Kiev, Yulik was now leaning towards a smaller city such as Dnipropetrovs'k or Odessa, where the IT industry was not nearly as saturated as it was in Ukraine's capital. His family in Ukraine had offered to help him get started if he was able to provide the finance. Unfortunately, when visiting his 'home town', he had found that Dnipropetrovs'k did not feel anything like home. Having spent most of his life in Israel, he felt like a foreigner. He spoke Russian with a Hebrew accent and knew no Ukrainian. His diet, dress and mannerisms were all marked by his experience abroad. Nonetheless, he felt a sense of curiosity in seeing a life that he was both close to and distant from.

Homecomings and Other Projects of Return

The same tone inflected the stories of many other returnees. Those coming back to Odessa described it as a place simultaneously known and unknown.

'In the course of [their] protracted absence', their home had almost inevitably undergone significant change, while they too had formed new habits and ways of thinking in the context of different resources and realities. For some, this made living in Odessa interesting, while for others, it was difficult to cope with. '[H]omecoming often contains elements of rupture, surprise, and perhaps disillusionment, besides the variety of practical problems that returnees usually confront' (Stefansson 2004: 4). In *Coming Home*, Long and Oxfeld similarly point out that 'as the act of returning unfolds, the specific experiences often contrast with the returnee's original dreams' (2004: 10). In the same book, George Gmelch describes how Barbadian returnees 'feel that their own interests are more cosmopolitan and transcend [those of] the local community . . . the place now appears as "narrow"' (Gmelch 2004: 213).

Returnees approached organized Jewish life in the city from different points of view. Some, like Nadya, looked to Jewish organizations for employment, others, like Vova approached Jewish gatherings as a way to facilitate their entrepreneurial efforts, and others, like Kostya and Marat, had become active participants in Jewish life (albeit for different reasons). The stories of Dina and Nina, even though they were from different generations, exemplify how some chose to remain on the periphery.

The experiences of those returnees active in the Jewish life of the city differed. Neither Genady nor his wife placed any importance on their own or their family's religious observance, but their children attended one of the city's Jewish Orthodox schools. Genady explained that Odessa has changed greatly since his departure and that most of the ordinary city schools were now taught in Ukrainian, a language that neither he nor his children ever learned. Deciding on schools upon arrival, they decided on a Jewish school where their children could learn in Russian and still practise their Hebrew. Even so, Genady saw little overlap between the ways he and his wife opted to raise their children as Jewish, and the other, more religious approaches that he found in Odessa on his return. As he explained:

> One of the teachers complained to me that my children were not paying attention to her lectures on Jewish traditions. I explained to her that, for Israelis, this is natural. In Israel, most of the Russians are not religious and we don't mix with them [religious Jews]. It is not a world I want them to be in.

Although his children had grown up in Israel knowing the Jewish calendar as a state-initiated agenda, he did not accept that Judaism had to be a crucial part of their identity, even if he did opt to enrol them in a religious Jewish school.[22]

This research demonstrates that returning to Odessa was complex and entailed much ambivalence. On the one hand, returning from Israel to Odessa often signalled that Odessa ultimately counted as home. On the other hand, some Ukrainian and other FSU returnees, both Odessans and non-Odessans, moved in order to follow their families or enhance their chances of prosperity without necessarily thinking of themselves as coming home. In general, when I would ask someone when they came back from Israel, many would respond by stating that they had not necessarily 'come back'; in other words, much was yet to be decided. In fact, many returning Jews continued to define themselves as Israelis, both legally and socially.[23] Still other ex-FSU Israelis considered other destinations, such as Canada or the United States.[24] The actual experiences of returnees displayed a mosaic of different orientations, attachments and associations constructed by returnees about their past and present locations and homes.

For older returnees, the decision to move back was typically a response to obstacles in Israel that were not encountered by younger or middle-aged immigrants. Their return was usually envisaged as permanent and experienced as more rooted; it felt like homecoming. Younger returnees still felt strong ties to Israel, where (despite being born in Odessa or the FSU) many had been raised, educated and/or served in the army, and thus felt acculturated to their Israeli way of life. For these returnees, Israel remained a place that partially defined them, even in Odessa. The orientations of middle-aged returnees were also mixed and largely depended on their familial and professional needs. However, in nearly all cases, returnees approached Odessa primarily geared towards 'creating better, more satisfying future lives' and were thus more likely to be engaged in 'feasible projects of homecoming' than those who were 'aiming at resurrecting a golden, but lost past' (Stefansson 2004: 4).

Now back in Odessa, many of my informants expressed their sense of connection with their multiple places of belonging through different modes of 'being Jewish'. For example, Kostya saw religious observance of Jewish laws as a way of maintaining a link between his Israeli past and his present, despite his entirely secular life in Israel. Others, similarly but in less extreme measure, simply opted to take part in Jewish holidays or educate their children in Jewish schools so as to maintain their Hebrew language and Israeli secular culture or simply to connect with friends. For a few disoriented or disenchanted returnees, it was difficult to tell how, if at all, they would bridge their multiple experiences locally.

Conclusion

The experiences of Israeli Russian-speaking Jewish returnees in Odessa are important to consider in the theoretical analysis of home and diaspora. Their patterns of migration and practices of homebuilding reorient the traditional model of Jews as a diaspora population connected to Israel as their 'home-land' and a cradle of Jewish identity, and offer more nuanced ways of approaching the question of belonging. Diaspora, a term defined by the *Oxford English Dictionary* as 'dispersion of the Jews beyond Israel' and in its more contemporary context the 'dispersion of any people from their traditional homeland', ultimately assumes a link between people and their *'proper* place' (Voutira 2006: 380, emphasis in original). Within diaspora studies, Jews have been identified as an 'ideal type' (Safran 1991: 84), a 'classic "old diaspora"' (Levy and Weingrod 2005: 4) whose dispersal from Babylon exemplifies them as a prototypical case of a diaspora population. Recent scholarship has challenged the negative connotation of diaspora as exile by offering a way to view diaspora in a 'positive light' (Tye 2001: 3; Gruen 2002; Wettstein 2002: 2). Some, including Boyarin and Boyarin, have even proposed 'a privileging of Diaspora', a structure of 'dissociation of ethnicities and political hegemonies', which they regard as the 'most important contribution that Judaism has to make to the world' (Boyarin and Boyarin 1993: 723). In the midst of its popularity, the term 'diaspora' has nonetheless been questioned and interrogated for becoming a 'catch-all phrase' that 'presumes that there is a single center of a given community' (Aviv and Shneer 2005: 22) defined by a 'natural bond' that people are said to have with their native home (Voutira 2006: 380). As a critique, many works on diaspora populations have highlighted the notion of multiple homelands that exist for and ultimately define any one group of people (Clifford 1994, 1997; Markowitz and Stefansson 2004; Levy and Weingrod 2005), while other scholarly work has pointed to the fact that people were no longer defined by places and 'identities have become deterritorialised' (Cohen 2008: 2; see also Lavie and Swedenburg 1996). Within Jewish studies, this shift in analysis has challenged the perception of Jews as a 'classic' diaspora model.[25] In many accounts of Jewish life outside of Israel, we can see how the supposed diaspora countries and various cities within those countries are perceived and experienced as homelands, and how Israel is regarded as a place of spiritual, religious and communal importance, but not necessarily a 'home' or a 'homeland'. The importance of the State of Israel and its claim to be *the* Jewish homeland has been questioned by a number of scholars and in some cases politically criticized.[26]

Research on 'Russian' Jews and other minority populations who have faced difficulty adapting within Israeli society or have been reluctant to let go of their cultural capital brought from overseas has also been instrumental in transforming the idea of Israel as a Jewish home.[27] The experiences of Israelis who choose to live outside of Israel exhibits another level of ambivalence between Jews and Israel apparent in the literature on *yerida* (emigration from Israel).[28]

The material in this chapter allows us to move further beyond the traditional assumptions of Jewish loyalties, attachments and orientations, and offers a more nuanced and multifaceted way of understanding the concepts of 'home' and 'diaspora' in today's global environment. On the one hand, returnees who choose to leave Israel and come back to Odessa might be seen as challenging the supposedly fundamental connection between Jews and their ancient homeland, returning to the supposed place of diaspora both as an old place of familiarity and roots and as a new centre of professional activity and personal growth. On the other hand, many of the returnees express strong ties to Israeli culture and define themselves as being Israeli through self-identification as well as citizenship, language, dress, music, food, worldview and even the idea of an eventual return. Many transmigrants continue to travel back to Israel and build their businesses, some utilizing Israeli products and services. Israel is undoubtedly regarded as an important place on the Russian-speaking Jewish map, even for those who choose to leave it behind. It now has the largest Russian-speaking population outside of the FSU and a growing network of economic, social and political links with the global Russian-speaking population.

For many of the returnees, the question of belonging remains tied to the economic and social situation at both home and abroad. The future for most returnees will be dictated to a large extent by the type of personal and professional opportunities that arise, and the economic and sociopolitical situation in the countries where they may settle. Now part of the global post-Soviet Jewish population spread over many continents and countries, the returnees described in this chapter are as much part of the Russian-speaking diaspora as they are part of the Israeli and Jewish diasporas whose 'cultural, [we can even add religious] geographic, and national boundaries are blurred and in flux' (Gershenson and Shneer 2011: 141). The overlapping worlds which define ex-Soviet Jewish returnees and transmigrants through the process of migration and remigration account for multiple understandings of homes, and ultimately transcend the common distinction of 'old' and 'new' diasporas in traditional diaspora discourse. Returnees, in effect, take up a role of being both transnational and Jewish, albeit in different ways.

It is understood that multilocal life and work patterns in the context of globalized and neoliberal economies challenge the empirical reality of home as a single location. This chapter illustrates that attitudes of Odessa's returning Jewish population towards 'homeland' and 'diaspora' were far from fixed. Like the other groups of migrant populations, their identity as a 'diasporic imagined community' is 'constituted within the crucible of the materiality of everyday life' (Brah 1996: 183). Contingent, negotiated and reflecting the socioeconomic and political circumstances of home and abroad, where one feels 'at home' or 'away from home', was a function of individual experiences. 'After all', as Stefansson points out, 'feelings of belonging do not rest on objective factors but are situated in the subjective realm' (2004: 186). Some emigrants had initially approached Israel as a place of belonging and their 'historical homeland',[29] but, suffering hardships in their new life, began to experience Israel differently, and themselves as living in the Russian-speaking diaspora. On the other hand, returnees coming back to a supposedly familiar place could also gradually come to see their city as more foreign, whether due to being treated as foreigners or through unmet dreams of the place once left behind. Ruth Mandel, writing about Turkish migrants in Germany who return to Turkey on a permanent or temporary basis, highlights that many 'returnees suffer from disorientation', unable to 'merge back into the Turkish mainstream' because they are judged by others, and by themselves, as 'Alamancilar' (i.e. German-like) (Mandel 1990: 160).[30] Moreover, in some instances the notion of 'home' or 'homeland' may be applied to more than one destination or, in the process of disorientation, may even cease to exist. This is particularly true for returnees who, having shared the experience of living as a Russian-speaking diaspora in Israel, on their return possibly viewed themselves, or were viewed by others, as 'Israelis' and in effect part of an Israeli diaspora in Odessa. As Clifford notes, 'at different times in their history, societies may wax and wane in diasporism, depending on changing possibilities – obstacles, openings, antagonisms and connections – in their host countries and transnationally' (Clifford 1997: 249). Thus, 'home' and 'diaspora' were not ideologically driven constants associated with centre (life in Israel) and periphery (life outside of Israel). Rather, they should be conceptualized as variable locations infused with memories and attachments that social actors inhabit and relate to through everyday experiences and life circumstances, which in turn shape their imagined reality and senses of attachment. If home, as Stephan Feuchtwang defined it, is 'a reference to a territory of belonging' (2004: 7), then ex-Soviet Jewish returnees have multiple and interconnecting homes that encompass their 'cultural norms and individual fantasies' (Rapport and Overing 1998: 8) and bring together their diverse experiences as locals, migrants, repatriates and returnees.

It is impossible to write about Ukraine today without acknowledging the political upheaval that took place in the region and its implications for Odessa specifically. I have been to Odessa on a number of short visits since my initial fieldwork, most recently in March 2014, on the brink of the tragic Odessa fire, when I saw some of the returnees and many of my local friends. A few of the people described in this chapter had already left Odessa before the outbreak of the conflict. Vova for instance, moved to China to pursue a new business idea; Genady returned to Israel, as did Dina and Kostya. Those who still remained in Odessa felt deeply affected by the tragic events in their city. 'I can't believe this is happening in my home town', one woman shared with me. 'The city is already crumbling and these hooligans, without any thought, vandalized and broke everything.' In her view, there were no 'real' Odessans involved in the fighting because no 'real' Odessans would vandalize their city in the way that the protesters and the police did. However, real Odessans (returnees included) were undoubtedly part of the pro- and anti-Russian camps involved in the chaotic attacks (see Richardson (2014) and Dima Khavin's film *Quiet in Odessa* for the accounts of local people). David, a young man in his thirties raised in a Russian-speaking Jewish intelligentsia family, returned to Odessa on a few shorter trips and finally settled in the city. He was a religiously observant man when we first met on one of his initial visits and I was surprised to learn that he had since enrolled in the self-defence league and was heavily involved in local operations. 'I am not a patriot', he told me when we met, 'but if some filth wants to enter my city, I will fight till the end.' He had previously served in the Israeli armed forces and he said he never thought that this training would be used in his everyday life in Odessa. According to him, there were over one hundred ex-Israeli soldiers volunteering with Odessa's self-defence league. In David's case, Odessa was now a home that needed to be 'protected' and 'defended' from an intruder – the Russian army, or 'the little green men' as he called them. Although David was among the minority of the people I knew who took an active part in physically defending his city, some locals and returnees volunteered to help the wounded, the refugees (who arrived in Odessa in great numbers from other affected areas of the country) and families of those who suffered. For some, the battle took place on Facebook and other social media networks, where people voiced their ideas, unfriended friends and formed new alliances. Neutrality was difficult to observe. Among the people I knew, most identified themselves, to one degree or another, as pro-Ukrainian (even if they were still critical of the corruption and politics of their nation) or anti-Putin. As a Russian national and a Russian speaker, I was worried that these tensions could, potentially, create a chasm in my friendships. However, I am happy to report that I did not witness any sort of negativity or aggression towards me, presumably because I supported their political views (although not the violence behind it). We continued to speak to one another in Russian, which was still the language on the streets and in most homes.

The upheaval in Odessa undoubtedly played a role in the way in which my friends now saw their city as part of Ukraine. While David found meaning in staying in Odessa and protecting his native home, other returnees took the opportunity to leave and were able to do so with their foreign passports. Ukraine's declining economy and political unrest have also stirred a new wave of emigration to Israel and a number of my Jewish friends have since applied for Israeli citizenship as a way to secure another option, another home. However, in their case, no one actually moved to Israel or spent a significant amount of time outside of the necessary length of stay required for receiving the Israeli 'papers'.

It is obvious that the local political and economic situation will continue to influence the way in which returnees and Odessan locals make decisions about their future. The recent appointment of Mikheil Saakashvili, some locals believe, may aid Odessa's economic and political recovery in a major way. While others await changes, returnees have the privilege of having an alternate passport, a status other local Jews (especially the younger generation) are drifting towards without diving straight into migration. Today, when ex-Soviet Jews in Odessa and elsewhere can judge the outcome of their migration or return based on the stories, pictures and anecdotes of others, knowing that Israel is always an option, they feel less pressure to make a choice between their home and their 'homeland'.

Marina Sapritsky is a visiting fellow in the Anthropology Department of the London School of Economics and Political Science affiliated with the Programme for the Study of Religion and Non-Religion. Her research interests include post-Soviet religious revival and community building, religious philanthropy and heritage travel, urbanity and Jewish studies. She is currently working on publishing her manuscript *Negotiating Traditions in Jewish Odessa* and conducting research for her new project, New Directions in Global Judaism: Russian-Speaking Jewry in London.

Notes

1. I use the word 'returnee' or 'returnees' as a descriptor rather than a literal category of people as some of the returns I describe are not permanent, as the label 'returnee' suggests.
2. Data for this chapter were collected during fieldwork in Odessa, Ukraine in 2005–7 and include in-depth interviews and participant observation with short-term and long-term returnees engaged in both provisional and permanent returns, as well as 'transmigrants' who regularly move between Odessa and Israel and other destinations. Thirty-two returnees were interviewed for this research. For the most part, I met returnees through other Jewish locals in the city who knew of my interest in return migration. I also met returnees in more organized settings of the local Jewish cultural centre Migdal, the two Orthodox Synagogues, the Jewish Agency (Sokhnut), Beitar Camp, the Medical Institute, the Israeli Cultural Center and communal Shabbats organized by religious families in the city. While I draw mainly on the experiences of returning migrants in Odessa in my analysis, I have also included interviews with returnees I met in Kiev. The overall goal of my research was to analyse change and continuity in the Jewish ways of life in contemporary Odessa where continuous residents ('stay back') and return migrants engage in many different pro-

cesses of identity formation and community building, negotiating Jewish traditions, values, practices and orientations from a number of competing cultural models of Jewish life.

3. See, among others, Rosenthal and Auerbach 1992; Goldscheider 1996; Cohen and Haberfeld 1997; Cohen 1999; Gold 2004.

4. Osipovich 2004; see also Finkel 2004: 329.

5. Osipovich 2004. I am not aware of a similar report produced in Ukraine.

6. According to Israeli authorities, the term 'out-migrants refers to Israelis who have left Israel and who have stayed abroad for a year or more (Tolts 2009: 9).

7. Retrieved 8 April 2018 from http://www.newsru.co.il/info/bigpoll/yerida2007 .html. A smaller survey of over 100 Russian Israelis (currently residing in Israel as well as abroad) conducted by Evgenyi Finkel on *LiveJournal* indicated that 20 per cent of his respondents have left Israel – 27 per cent returned to their countries of origin; 24 per cent left for the United States; 14 per cent for Canada; 23 per cent for Europe and 7 per cent for Australia. Another 25 per cent of Finkel's respondents who have not left Israel have entertained the idea of leaving Israel (Finkel 2004: 327).

8. Personal notes from the conference 'Russian-Speaking Jewry in the Global Perspective: Power, Politics and Community' Bar Ilan University, Israel, 17–19 October. See also Finkel 2004: 324–28.

9. Tolts 2009: 15.

10. Gold 2004: 445.

11. See, for example, article titles such as 'Return of the Jews: For Decades the Story of Russia's Jews Has Been One of Fear and Flight to Israel. Now Many are Coming Home' (*Newsweek International,* 9 August 2004) and 'Once Desperate to Leave, Now Jews are Returning to Russia, Land of Opportunity' (*The Times,* 28 April 2005).

12. *Jewish Telegraph Agency,* 26 August 2004.

13. *Los Angeles Times,* 3 February 2005.

14. Perhaps this stereotype is linked to the diaspora discourse discussed by Aviv and Shneer, which 'envisions the Jewish world hierarchically with Israel on top: "the diaspora" on the bottom' (2005: 19–20).

15. Belensky and Skolnik document that 92 per cent of ex-Soviet Jews in Germany have travelled back to their home towns, compared with 9 per cent in the United States and 19 per cent in Israel. They provide no data on permanent returns from Germany to the FSU. See Belensky and Skolnik 1998: 37.

16. A number of younger returnees I met had initially moved to Israel on their own initiative, often following their involvement with the Jewish Agency (Sokhnut), Betar or other Zionist organizations in the city. In many cases they had taken part in a three-year study abroad program, Na'ale, which invited Jewish youth to experience life in Israel with the ultimate goal of *aliyah* (see Fran Markowitz, 'Cultural Change, Border Crossings and Identity Shopping: Jewish Teenagers from the CIS Access their Future in Israel', in Noah Lewin-Epstein, Paul Ritterband and Yaacov Ro'i, eds., *Russian Jews on Three Continents: Migration and Resettlement* (London: Frank Cass Publishers, 1997), pp. 344–363.)

17. Odessa was home to a number of Russian-speaking Israelis who had come to the city to study medicine and other professions. A small number of returnees are affiliated with one of the two Orthodox movements in the city and the local branch of Sokhnut (the Jewish Agency, an Israeli organization that operates in the FSU to educate Jews about Israel and assist them in making *aliyah*). These individuals and families

usually stay in the city for a limited duration defined by their contract or the length of their course.

18. Returning Israeli Odessans did not form any sort of an organized network or community as they did in Moscow or in Kiev. However, Israeli students in Odessa's Medical Institute (including some former FSU residents) did organize events with each other on a regular basis.

19. For more on Russian-speaking Jews who have converted to Christianity or are attracted to Christian faith, see Deutch Kornblatt (2003); Gitelman, Glants and Marshall (2003: 201–2); Nosenko-Stein (2010).

20. Citizens of Ukraine need a visa for most destinations outside the FSU, which can be time-consuming and costly. Israeli citizenship facilitates less-restricted travel and an easier visa application process.

21. Chabad and a group affiliated with Ohr Sameach, organizations that encourage Jews to be more religious, are highly visible in the city.

22. When I recently enquired about Genady's and Vova's families, I was told by our friends in common that Genady has recently gone back to Israel and that Vova and his family now live in China, where they are following a new business idea.

23. All of the returnees I met, except Nina, who had reverted to a Ukrainian passport, could easily have opted to go back to Israel on their retained citizenship and legal documents.

24. In the survey published by http://www.newsru.co.il (http://www.newsru.co.il/info/bigpoll/yerida2007.html), 43.9 per cent of the respondents said that if they left Israel, they would like to live in Canada; 39.7 per cent said the United States; 25.1 per cent said Australia; 13.3 per cent said the United Kingdom; 12.2 per cent said Russia; 10.4 per cent said Germany; and only 5.8 per cent said Ukraine.

25. See, among others, Silberstein 2000; Tye 2001; Wettstein 2002; Aviv and Shneer 2005; Levy and Weingrod 2005.

26. See, among others, Boyarin and Boyarin 1993; Aviv and Shneer 2005.

27. Specifically for the Russian case, see Siegel 1998; Fialkova and Yelenevskaya 2007.

28. *Yerida* is translated from Hebrew as descent and is a term referring to the 'stigmatized path of Israelis who descend from the promise land into the Diaspora' (Gold 2004: 445). Emigrants from Israel are thus referred to as *yordim*.

29. For a number of returnees, the notion of Israel as a homeland was absorbed into settings of Jewish and Zionist education and through the teachings of Sokhnut.

30. Referring to the same material in a later book, Mandel describes 'a subtle reversal in the reference' of 'homeland' and 'host land', where, in the case of her informants, 'homeland [Turkey] assumes the status of a foreign, vacation destination', whereas Germany is considered their natal land (Mandel 2008: 18).

References

Ash, L. 2004. 'Israel Faces Russian Brain Drain', *BBC News,* 24 November. Retrieved 8 April 2018 from http://news.bbc.co.uk/1/hi/programmes/crossing_continents/4038859.stm.

Aviv, C., and Shneer, D. 2005. *New Jews: The End of the Jewish Diaspora.* New York: New York University Press.

Belensky, M and Skolnik, J. 1998. 'Russian Jews in Today's Germany: End of the Journey?' *European Judaism* 31(2): 30–44.

Boyarin, D., and Boyarin, J. 1993. 'Diaspora: Generation and the Ground of Jewish Identity', *Critical Inquiry* 19(4): 693–725.

Brah, A. 1996. *Cartographies of Diaspora: Contesting Identities.* London: Routledge.

Clifford, J. 1994. 'Diasporas', *Cultural Anthropology* 9(3): 302–38.

———. 1997. *Routes: Travel and Translation in the Late Twentieth Century.* Cambridge, MA: Harvard University Press.

Cohen, R. 1999. 'From Ethnonational Enclave to Diasporic Community: The Mainstreaming of Israeli Jewish Migrants in Toronto', *Diaspora* 8(2): 121–137.

———. 2008. *Global Diasporas: An Introduction*, 2nd edn. London: Routledge.

Cohen, Y., and Haberfeld, Y. 1997. 'The Number of Israeli Immigrants in the United States in 1990', *Demography* 34(2): 199–212.

Deutsch Kornblatt, J. 2003. 'Jewish Converts to Orthodoxy in Russia in Recent Decades', in Z. Gitelman, M. Glants and M.I. Goldman (eds), *Jewish Life after the USSR.* Bloomington: Indiana University Press, pp. 209–33.

Feuchtwang, S, 2004. 'Theorising Place', in *Making Place: State Projects, Globalisation and Local Responses in China.* London: UCL Press, pp. 3–33.

Fialkova, L., and Yelenevskaya, N.N. 2007. *Ex-Soviets in Israel: From Personal Narratives to a Group Portrait.* Detroit: Wayne State University Press.

Finkel, E. 2004. 'Na dvukh stulyakh', *Otechestvenye Zapiski: Migratsia: ugroza ili blago* 4(19): 324–356.

Friedgut, T.H. 2007, 'The Problematics of Jewish Community Development in Contemporary Russia', in Z. Gitelman and Y. Ro'i (eds), *Revolution, Repression, and Revival: The Soviet Jewish Experience.* Lanham, MD: Rowman & Littlefield, pp. 239–72.

Gershenson, O., and Shneer, D. 2011. 'Soviet Jewishness and Cultural Studies', *Journal of Jewish Identities* 4(1): 129–46.

Gitelman, Z., Glants, M. and Goldman M.I. (eds). 2003. *Jewish Life after the USSR.* Bloomington: Indiana University Press.

Gmelch, G. 2004. 'West Indian Migrants and Their Rediscovery of Barbados', in L.D. Long and E. Oxfeld (eds), *Coming Home? Refugees, Migrants and Those Who Stayed Behind.* Philadelphia: University of Pennsylvania Press, pp. 206–233.

Golbert, R. 2001. 'Constructing Self: Ukrainian Jewish Youth in the Making', Ph.D dissertation. Oxford: Oxford University.

Gold, S. 2004. 'The Emigration of Jewish Israelis', in U. Rebhun and C. Waxman (eds), *Jews in Israel: Contemporary Social and Cultural Patterns.* Lebanon, NH: Brandeis University Press, pp. 445–64.

Goldscheider, C. 1996. *Israel's Changing Society: Population, Ethnicity and Development.* Boulder: Westview Press.

Gruen, E.S. 2002. 'Diaspora and Homeland', in H. Wettstein (ed.), *Diasporas and Exiles.* Berkeley: University of California Press, pp. 18–46.

Lavie, S., and Swedenburg, T. 1996. *Displacement, Diaspora, and Geographies of Identity.* Durham, NC: Duke University Press.

Levy, A., and Weingrod, A. 2005. 'On Homelands and Diasporas: An Introduction', in A. Levy and A. Weingrod (eds), *Homelands and Diasporas: Holy Lands and Other Places.* Stanford: Stanford University Press, pp. 3–26.

Long, L.D., and Ellen Oxfeld, E. 2004. 'Introduction: An Ethnography of Return', in L.D. Long and E. Oxfeld (eds), *Coming Home? Refugees, Migrants and Those Who Stayed Behind.* Philadelphia: University of Pennsylvania Press, pp. 1–16.

Mandel, R. 1990. 'Shifting Centers, Emergent Identities: Turkey and Germany in the Lives of Turkish Gastarbeiter', in D. Eickelman and J. Piscatori (eds), *Muslim Trav-*

ellers: Pilgrimage, Migration and the Religious Imagination. London: Routledge, pp. 153–171.

———. 2008. *Cosmopolitan Anxieties: Turkish Challenges to Citizenship and Belonging in Germany.* Durham, NC: Duke University Press, 2008.

Markowitz, F. 1997. 'Cultural Change, Border Crossings and Identity Shopping: Jewish Teenagers from the CIS Access Their Future in Israel', in N. Lewin-Epstein, P. Ritterband and Y. Ro'I (eds), *Russian Jews on Three Continents: Migration and Resettlement.* London: Frank Cass, pp. 344–63.

Markowitz, F., and Stefansson, A. 2004. *Homecomings: Unsettled Paths of Return.* Lanham, MD: Lexington Books.

Nosenko-Stein, E. 2010. 'Aliens in an Alien World: Paradoxes of Jewish-Christian Identity in Contemporary Russia', *East European Jewish Affairs* 40(1): 19–41.

Osipovich, A. 2004. 'Reverse Exodus'. Russian Profile. http://russiaprofile.org/culture _living/a2473.html.

Rapport, N., and J. Overing, J. 1998. *Migrants of Identity: Perceptions of Home in a World of Movement.* Oxford: Berg.

Remennick, L. 2009. 'Former Soviet Jews in Their New/Old Homeland: Between Integration and Separatism', in T. Tsuda (ed.), *Diasporic Homecomings: Ethnic Return Migration in Comparative Perspective.* Stanford: Stanford University Press, pp. 208–24.

Richardson, T. 2014. 'Odessa's Two Big Differences (and a Few Small Ones): Life after the Maidan and 2 May', *Eurozine,* 1 September. Retrieved 8 April 2018 from http:// www.eurozine.com/odessas-two-big-differences-and-a-few-small-ones.

Rosenthal, M., and Auerbach, C. 1992, 'Cultural and Social Assimilation of Israeli Immigrants in the United States', *International Migration Review* 99(26): 982–91.

Safran, W. 1991. 'Diasporas in Modern Societies: Myths of Homeland and Return', *Diaspora* 1(1): 83–99.

Satanovsky, Y. 2009, 'Russian Jews: The Variant of the Future'. *Euro-Asian Jewish Congress,* 19 November. http://eajc.org/page34/news14038.html.

Siegel, D. 1998. *The Great Immigration: Russian Jews in Israel.* New York: Berghahn Books.

Silberstein, L.J. 2000. *Mapping Jewish Identities.* New York: New York University Press.

Stefansson, A.H. 2004. 'Homecomings to the Future: From Diasporic Mythographies to Social Projects of Return', in F. Markowitz and A. Stefansson (eds), *Homecomings: Unsettled Paths of Return.* Lanham, MD: Lexington Books, pp. 2–20.

Tolts, M. 2009. 'Post-Soviet Aliyah and Jewish Demography Transformation'. Paper presented at the 15th World Congress of Jewish Studies, Jerusalem, 2–6 August, pp. 1–36.

Tsuda, T. 2009. 'Introduction: Diasporic Return and Migration Studies', in T. Tsuda (ed.), *Diasporic Homecomings: Ethnic Return Migration in Comparative Perspective.* Stanford: Stanford University Press, pp. 1–17.

Tye, L. 2001. *Home Lands: Portraits of the New Jewish Diaspora.* New York: Henry Holt and Company.

Voutira, E. 2006. 'Post-Soviet Diaspora Politics: The Case of Soviet Greeks', *Journal of Modern Greek Studies* 24(2): 379–414.

Wettstein, H. 2002. 'Introduction', in H. Wettstein (ed.), *Diasporas and Exiles.* Berkeley: University of California Press.

CHAPTER 4

WHO MAKES
'OLD ENGLAND' HOME?
Tourism and Migration in the English Countryside

YUKO SHIOJI

Introduction

Images of the English countryside, featuring historic buildings, quiet villages and picturesque landscapes, have been reproduced since the end of the nineteenth century in guidebooks, tourist brochures and the mass media. Such images have also informed local and national tourism policies (Shioji 1997). It should be noted that people visit the countryside because its landscape and customs are established symbols of Old England (Urry 1990: 96–99). The image of 'Old England', evoking a green and pleasant land, traditional customs and a quiet rural life, has attracted British people as an ideal home to live in and retire to. In this chapter, I use the idea of Old England as a means for analysis of people's reasons for living in the countryside, and of the impacts of the idea on the resident community and on their lifestyles. The Cotswolds in southern England is an area redolent with such images and attracts not only tourists but also incoming migrants from other parts of the United Kingdom. This chapter is based on anthropological participatory fieldwork carried out between 1996 and 2016[1] in Chipping Campden, a country town in the Cotswolds.

Anthropological studies of tourism have noted that ethnic, political, economic or cultural minorities in host societies often experience negative effects from tourists and tourism development, such as having to sell their traditions and lands as touristic commodities (Smith 1989; Boissevain 1996). Concurrently, it has been claimed that new traditions are formed or that disappearing traditions are reconstructed as a result of tourism (McDonald 1987; Boissevain 1992; Yamashita 1999). Throughout these debates there has been a presupposition that hosts and guests live in exaggeratedly different worlds, often characterized as the wealthy north and poor south.[2] However, in parts of the English countryside, we find former guests who have become part of host communities, bringing with them their images and expectations of English rural life.[3] As reported by Fees (1996), a 'place myth' brought in by incomers – who tend to be retired, wealthy, middle-class people – can influence the politics and social relationships in a country town. In Chipping Campden, incomers resemble tourists, but they can have substantial influence on the local community when they become permanent residents.

In this chapter, local reactions to tourism, migration and the development of housing lands are discussed in an effort to consider who and what makes Old England home. The chapter also describes differences in lifestyles for local people and incomers in a town with many legal restrictions, such as listed buildings, a conservation area, the designated Area of Outstanding Natural Beauty (AONB) and even public footpaths. These restrictions not only affect people's lives, but they are also used in negotiations about the landscapes of homes and the development of housing lands in the process of making Old England home.

The English Countryside and Tourism

The English Countryside as an Ideal 'Home'

Beginning with the Industrial Revolution, Britain as a 'World Factory' experienced rapid urbanization; population density in cities rose, and historic buildings and natural environments were lost to development. A total of 200,000 hectares of farmlands and forestlands in Britain disappeared in just fifteen years between the late nineteenth and the early twentieth centuries. In parallel with this rapid social change within the country, the nineteenth century saw the dramatic expansion of the British Empire overseas.

During this period, the English countryside came to constitute an 'ideal type', representing stability and morality in an unfamiliar world. Many of the descriptions of countryside in literary works of this period tend to emphasize (and conflate) rural virtue and rural landscape. Rural landscape was drawn symbolically in landscape paintings so that countryside came to be focused on as a motif in works of art (Pevsner 1956: 167). As Raymond Williams points out, for the British who went to work in colonies in the era of British Empire, the idea of England as 'home' endured (Williams 1973: 281). Many of the images of this 'home' are of an idea of rural England. The reward for hard service in British colonies was 'a return to a rural place within this urban and industrial England' (Williams 1973: 282). Feeding this demand, the well-known nationwide magazine *The Country Life,* launched in the 1890s, carried regular articles and advertisements for houses in rural towns and villages. Thus, the rapid changes both inside and outside the country in the nineteenth century precipitated the idea of the English countryside as an imaginary 'home' to belong to. This idea maintained and developed throughout the twentieth century, constructing the countryside as an ideal residential area.

Tourism in the English Countryside

In the early twentieth century, countryside had become a kind of quintessential representation of Englishness. In the Great Depression of the 1930s, BBC radio lecture programmes emphasized traditional English rural life, and Longman's *English Heritage* series and Batsford's *English Life* series were published one after another (Wiener 1981: 73). At that time, guidebooks and travel writings described the English countryside in aesthetic terms for urban middle-class residents (Potts 1989: 172–73). Later, improvements in transportation and an expansion of leisure time made the countryside an attractive, easy-to-access tourist destination. With the spread of motorcars after World War II, travel to the countryside for new aims, such as sports and country walks, became possible. From the 1980s, this was accompanied by an interest in limiting the impact of tourism on the environment (Countryside Commission 1987, 1991a, 1991b, 1992).

Nowadays, consciousness of the importance of preserving the natural and cultural heritage of the English countryside is high. Indeed, tourism based on these natural and cultural resources is the basis for plans to revitalize many rural areas. The British Tourist Authority promoted 'countryside', 'heritage' and 'culture' as the most important characteristics of Britain. Two-thirds of foreign visitors gave these as a reason to visit Britain (Shioji 1997; 2003: 96–98). The English countryside is now an attractive tourist destination not only for artists and aristocrats as in the eighteenth century, but for everyone who wants to explore the Old England.

A Community in the English Countryside

Chipping Campden in the Cotswolds

The Cotswolds is a hilly area in the southwest of England, primarily located in the county of Gloucestershire, but with parts in four other counties. The population is around 80,000, in 145 small towns and villages. The Cotswolds has been designated by the government an AONB, considered to have significant landscape value, and many of its historic buildings have been preserved. These natural and cultural resources attract about three million visitors a year.

Chipping Campden is a town in the north of the Cotswolds, with a population of 2,000. It was a market town in the Middle Ages and from the fifth to the tenth centuries was a regional political centre. It flourished as a result of the wool trade and wealthy wool merchants built St James' Church, almshouses and the market hall. With the Industrial Revolution, the town became more peripheral as many people moved to the cities to work after the agricultural depression of the 1870s, leaving their houses and cottages in disrepair. However, in 1902, C.R. Ashbee, an architect of the Arts and Crafts Movement, relocated his Guild of Handicraft from London, and the town began to revive culturally, socially and economically. Since Ashbee's time, Chipping Campden has seen a steady stream of wealthy incomers; not only middle-class artists, but also colonial civil servants and successful urban businessmen retired to the town (Figure 4.1).

Chipping Campden has now the second-densest incidence of listed buildings in the country and is a conservation area. The High Street, curving for a mile through the centre of the town, has the highest concentration of listed buildings lining both sides of the street. Chipping Campden's local cultural heritage, such as morris dancing (a form of English folk dance), the Scuttle-

FIGURE 4.1 Chipping Campden surrounded by rolling hills (photo by the author)

brook Wake (a local May Day festivity) and the Cotswold Olimpick Games (locally known as the Dover's Games, a sports festival originating in the seventeenth century), also attracts people from outside the town as well as shaping the local community spirit (Shioji 2003).

Local Responses to Tourism

Situated twenty minutes' drive from Shakespeare's birthplace, Stratford-up-on-Avon, and not far from Oxford and Bath, unsurprisingly, tourism is the major industry in Chipping Campden. In high season, from June to September, over 250 visitors a day come into the Tourist Information Centre (TIC) in the town centre (Figures 4.2 and 4.3).

However, Chipping Campden is a living community as well as a popular tourist destination. There are plentiful facilities for tourism, such as hotels, bed and breakfasts, restaurants, tearooms and antiques shops along the High Street, which also has the necessary shops for community life, such as a post office, banks, a bakery, a butcher, a greengrocer, a chemist and a supermarket. Nevertheless, more than 40 per cent of the buildings in High Street are residential (Shioji 2003: 69). There can be tension not only between local residents and tourists, but also between long-term inhabitants and incomers, something that is explored in the following sections.

FIGURE 4.2 An open-top touring bus in summer (photo by the author)

FIGURE 4.3 Tourists looking at shops and tearooms in the High Street (photo by the author)

Few of the residents who do not directly depend on tourism are willing to promote tourism in the town. Several local clubs and the Women's Institute opposed the establishment of the TIC inside the town hall in 1997, claiming that this use conflicted with the purpose of the town hall as a community resource. Although the town council, recognizing the benefit of tourism to the town, funded the first two years of the TIC, in this instance they prioritized residents' interests. Most residents understand that tourism is essential to maintain the vitality of the town, but those who do not benefit from tourism directly can see it as an inconvenience. There are very few people who do not mind strangers with cameras gazing at their gardens and houses.

The group promoting tourism in the town has consisted of local accommodation providers and members of the Chamber of Trade, such as shopkeepers on the High Street. Those running bed and breakfasts in the area set up and have managed the TIC since 1995. However, since the internet became popular for booking accommodation, this role has gradually been taken over by local volunteers. One of the main organizers of the TIC in 2014 was a retired local bank manager. He is eager to attract tourists to the town and inform them about the town and its heritage through the TIC and the town's website.

Incomers: Social and Cultural Change

Most incomers to Chipping Campden previously visited as tourists. They can therefore bring with them a tourist's sensibility, and move to the town intent on making the English ideal of retiring to the country a reality (Figure 4.4). However, their arrival has brought about several social and cultural changes. The sharp increase in the number of older and retired incomers since the late 1980s, together with a reduction in the numbers of young people employed locally in agriculture and their subsequent exodus to the city, has resulted in a gradual ageing of the population. A total of 37 per cent of the population is over the retirement age and pensioners make up 23 per cent of all households. Most Campdonians, born and brought up in the town, are working-class people reliant on local industry. Incomers, in many cases, are retired middle-class people who were successful in cities (both 'incomer' and 'Campdonian' are locally used terms). The inflow of new residents has pushed up house prices out of reach of local young people. Incomers tend to inhabit the historic centre of the town, while Campdonians live in twentieth-century developments in back lanes and on the outskirts (Shioji 2003).

FIGURE 4.4 A thatched cottage in Westington – incomers' and tourists' favourite (photo by the author)

With their professional and business skills and experience, incomers have come to dominate local organizational and political life, establishing conservation societies and trusts that help to maintain the Old England landscape that originally attracted them to the area. For example, the biggest nonprofit organization in the town is the Campden Society (CS). Originally formed in 1924 when incomers began to arrive in the town in search of a narrative of Old England, it was revived in 1970 by incomers and aims to protect Campden's beauty and history. It has about 350 members, most of them retired incomers, and runs activities such as lectures and study tours. Very few native Campdonians are members of the CS, seeing it as an 'outsiders'' organization and preferring to join social groups and to support charities helping the elderly. The CS also examines planning applications and submits its opinions of plans for the rebuilding, extension, construction and restoration of buildings in the town. In this sense, the CS has the role of an advisory body for local government and its opinions are referred to as the voices of 'Campden residents'. As a high proportion of town councillors are also incomers and tend to share the opinions of the CS on planning matters, such judgements carry some weight, provoking the reaction from Campdonians that 'outsiders' have gained control over the town. Paradoxically, therefore, although Chipping Campden is situated in a political and economic periphery, ideas of traditional rural life, developed since the time of Ashbee and the Guild of Handicraft, have attracted incomers from the centre who come to control the town's organizational landscape (Fees 1996: 129–38).

Conflicts between Campdonians and Incomers

As was hinted at above, conflicts and tensions between Campdonians and incomers have become increasingly prominent. Many of these are based on differences in socioeconomic status, lifestyles and values. One example of this is the complaint from incomers in 1988 that large lorries driving through the centre of the town spoiled the landscape. In response, the county council, at the town council's suggestion, proposed a weight restriction for lorries running through the town. After consulting local businesses, the town council received the following angry comments from a representative of a local company supplying dairy products:

> This proposal is typical of the wrinkly yuppies who are destroying this town. The reason they all move to Campden is because people whose families have been here for hundreds of years have made it so pretty. But because of the newcomers, trade suddenly is not a concern. They are turning Campden into a wrinkly paradise. What are they trying to do to this town? Townies are coming into Campden in their droves and we are expected to convert to their lifestyles. We are just trying to earn a living.
> (*Evesham Journal*, 2 June 1988: 1)

Such sharp conflict between incomers and Campdonians did not come to the surface in the late 1990s when I was carrying out my fieldwork, but a few residents explained to me their different ways of thinking and attitudes.

Life in 'Old England'
The Life of Campdonians

In this section, I take up four examples of longstanding residents (Campdonians) whose ancestors have maintained the landscape of Old England for centuries, with a focus on their experience of the bureaucratic and financial implications of owning and developing property in the town.[4] It is mainly based on my research from 1996 to 1997 and also reflects some changes in their lives over the past twenty years.

Three Generations of a Campdonian Family

Mary (in her eighties in 2015) lives with her Campdonian husband in a modern bungalow in Calf Lane, just south of the High Street. Mary said that her husband's construction company built the bungalow in the 1960s when there were not so many houses in Calf Lane. They like their house; it is built of Cotswold stone and is large and bright.

Her late father, Tom, was related to the local farming family, Izod, who had been established in this area for over 400 years. He was a typical working-class Campdonian, engaged in construction work in the town. He lived in a small thatched seventeenth-century cottage next to St James' Church, where development is highly restricted now, but at that time he could put in a new staircase, and added a kitchen behind the house for convenience without any planning permission. Tom once said to me in the 1990s: 'I don't want to live in a modern red brick house.' He loved the historical but comfortably rebuilt cottage. He was an honorary member of the local Historical Society as he remembered the town's people and places from the past very clearly. The Society published a book of his memories of old days in the town in the 1990s.

The eldest and youngest of Mary and her husband's three daughters live nearby. Mary hopes that all of her daughters can live in Campden, but she thinks that it will be quite difficult for her second daughter and her husband to buy a house there even if they sell their house in Birmingham. Mary's eldest daughter, Lucy – in her late fifties – lives with her engineer husband in a house in Catbrook (on the southern outskirts of the town). Their house was built by C.R. Ashbee in the early twentieth century and it is a white-walled, semi-detached house, totally different from the traditional Cotswold stone buildings in the area. Catbrook is outside the conservation area and is therefore free of many of the planning restrictions. There is a lot of social housing in the area and property is relatively inexpensive. The couple said to me in 1996 that they chose the area because it was a conducive and affordable setting for them as a young couple with small children. Their grown-up children are now living in London. Mary's youngest daughter, who is in her forties, lives in a council house in Littleworth, a residential area on the northern outskirts of the town developed in the 1960s. Mary told me that they could live there because of the reasonable rent (Figure 4.5). In Campden, there is a waiting list for these council houses and it is difficult even for the children of Campdonians, who have a high priority, to live in them.

Thus, the younger generations of Campdonians tend to prefer living in a modern, convenient way over living in historical houses. Tom, respected by the local Historical Society, had, like others of the older generation of Campdonians, lived in historical houses by rebuilding them quite freely to adjust to changing lifestyles, as in previous centuries, before planning restrictions came into force. However, nowadays, as in the next example, even if working-aged Campdonians can buy historical houses, they have to apply for planning permission and may receive criticisms for the alterations made to their houses from local conservation societies such as the CS.

FIGURE 4.5 Houses on the outskirts built by local council in the 1990s (photo by the author)

A Campdonian Living in a Historic House

John Brave lived in a seventeenth-century cottage in Park Road next to the High Street. His grandfather used to perform as a Christmas mummer, a tradition passed down in Campden. The Brave family are longstanding representatives of the Campdonian working class. John worked as a fireman in the town for over twenty years and he ran an antiques shop on the High Street for ten years. He was interested in old stone buildings, antiques, and the natural and also historical environment of the area he has known since he was a child and where he walks every day. As a member of local Historical Society, he was keen on collecting old photographs and interviews of Campdonians. When he bought his cottage, it was very outdated; not surprisingly, it was quite expensive to renovate. Fortunately, the local government gave him a grant. He consulted his brother William, who ran a construction business, and proceeded to rebuild the house. However, he had an antipathy towards the CS and the Cotswold District Council, both of which he said demonstrated their preference for preserving the landscape over the needs of the town's residents. In the 1980s, John added an extension to the back of his house, which drew considerable criticism from the town council and the CS on the grounds of aesthetics. It took him a year and several revisions to correct the application for listed consent and obtain planning permission.

John died several years ago and his house was sold to a Londoner who owns the house next door to John as a weekend cottage. The new owner is now renovating John's former house as a luxurious holiday cottage. Some long-term residents who knew John are puzzled that the house needs renovation, saying that John lived there perfectly happily. Recently, it is not unusual to see wealthy city people buying houses from Campdonians and making them into weekend cottages or holiday cottages as investments.

A Campdonian who is the descendant of an incomer also lives in a historical building, but has a more traditional lifestyle. He has a different approach to living with historical architecture.

Third Generation of Incomer

Graham White, who is in his late seventies, is a grandson of the silversmith whom C.R. Ashbee brought from London in 1902. His grandfather married a woman from a local farming family, the largest landowner in the town; thus, the Whites have a strong tie to the town. Graham works with his son and nephew, shaping silver with his hands according to the same technique used by his grandfather on the first floor of the workshop in Sheep Street. His two daughters live and work in the nearby city.

Graham and his wife had lived in a three-storey seventeenth-century house on the High Street for forty-two years (Figure 4.6). They moved to a

FIGURE 4.6 Graham's house on the High Street taken
from the back garden (photo by the author)

smaller house built in the 1930s in Station Road, slightly away from the town
centre, in 2013. Graham's three brothers also live in the town; their various
occupations include farming, gardening, and running a car maintenance
and repair business. Graham helps his farmer brother with harvesting and
haymaking. He was a leader of the Campden Morris Men and is a committee member for the Scuttlebrook Wake. He is also a bellringer for St. James'
Church every Sunday. He has a strong affinity for the community as it was in
the past, lamenting in the late 1990s: 'I don't know at all [those] who are in
my neighbourhood – even on High Street.'

    With its long and narrow garden, Graham's former property retains the
shape of the medieval burgage plot (Shioji 1999: 66–69) (Figure 4.7). The
family grew vegetables and fruit, and they raised chickens and kept bees for
a self-sufficient lifestyle. The first floor is leaning, but because of its historical
importance as a listed building, renovations or repairs are quite expensive,

FIGURE 4.7 Graham's medieval burgage plot back garden (photo by the author)

so the family lived in it as it is. He and his wife had considered looking for a smaller house before all their children leave to become independent for a long time. They said that the former house and its garden were too big for just the two of them, and that it was cold and dark inside with not enough views from its windows. They finally bought the present house when their former house was sold in 2013. The new owners are from London, but they are interested in historic buildings and are trying to preserve the house, as the only one on the High Street retaining its burgage plot.

On the other hand, a returned Campdonian with an intellectual background was an active member of the conservation society and keen on preserving landscape, which is similar to the incomers' lifestyles explained in the next section. He lived in a thatched house, one of many in Westington, which is the most popular spot for tourists and incomers, but he tried to live in a traditional local way.

A 'U-Turn' Campdonian Living in Westington

George Knight used to live with his wife in a thatched house in Westington, to the south of the town centre. His two sons have left home and now live with their own families in cities. George was born and raised in Campden. He taught sociology at Manchester University, then after his retirement, he came back to the house in Westington, which his parents left him. He guided visitors through the exhibition at the Old Silk Mill as a trustee of the Guild of Handicraft Trust, and he also researched historical documents and archives about the town as an honorary member of the local Historical Society in the late 1990s. He edited and published a book about the history of the town in the 2000s.

George's father was a Campdonian as well as a craftsman for Ashbee's Guild. He was engaged in building architecture, and designed and constructed the house in Westington. After George and his wife moved in, they rebuilt the entrance hall and kitchen; the roof that covered these innovations was tiled. George's wife once explained that the original floorplan was characteristic of early twentieth-century buildings, with a bathroom near the entrance and a small ground floor. The family made use of a small field behind the garden by growing vegetables and fruit. George said: 'The thatched roof has moss on [it], which damages the roof so that it ought to be re-thatched, but it costs a lot. Furthermore, in 20 years' time, my sons will have to re-thatch the roof. We are thinking it may be easier to re-roof the whole roof with tiles.' However, it was difficult to obtain permission for architectural changes to houses in Westington, as it is a conservation area. George also explained that a thatched roof adds comfort and looks more beautiful; since his father designed the house with a thatched roof in mind, they were wondering if they should reroof it. George died in 2007 and the house was sold to an incomer who rethatched the roof.

The above four examples show that Campdonians are not monolithic; their lifestyles and engagement with historic buildings and landscape differ according to age, background and social class. The first two cases show the typical attitude of working-class Campdonians towards their life in the town. Younger working-class Campdonians choose to raise their children in areas not constrained by building restrictions; therefore, they can renovate and rebuild to accommodate their families' needs. If they live in historical buildings, they favour not just preserving old things such as restoring old buildings and collecting old records of the town, but also transforming them when necessary for ease of living. They criticize the CS as the group privileging preserving landscape over local people's convenience.

However, Graham White, the third-generation silversmith, and George Knight, the academic returning Campdonian, both tend to live traditionally and modestly in historic or thatched houses of the type usually preferred by incomers. Graham shows that a Campdonian caught between the working class and middle class sets a high value on a connection with the community. George, perhaps because of his experience of living in cities, has an interest in the history of the town and its buildings more commonly seen in incomers. Both Graham and George inherited houses from their families; because they are not as wealthy as incomers to the area, they live thriftily, choosing not to rebuild a seventeenth-century house or rethatch a roof.

The Life of Incomers

Over the last twenty years, several Campdonians whom I have known have moved to peripheries from the historic centre of the town or have passed away, and their houses were sold to incomers or city people seeking second homes. It is still difficult for younger Campdonians under forty to live in the town, and even then it tends to be in council houses. How does this experience compare with that of incomers moving to and living in the town? Next, I consider three examples of incomers in order to examine how their lifestyles differ from those of Campdonians and also how their life has changed in these twenty years.

An Incomer Couple Living on the High Street for Twenty Years

Mike, who is in his eighties, retired from his work as an executive in a leading department store in London to live in Campden with his wife in 1994. Their adult son and daughters are now living in cities. Mike has a good memory of Campden from when his parents lived there; thus, he regards it as his hometown, where he has many friends. He inherited his house on the High Street in 1989 from a friend who had no family or relatives. After obtaining planning permission from Cotswold District Council for renovations on the house, it took eight months from 1992 to complete the restoration.

Mike has sympathetically restored the house, installing a stone floor and rebuilding the fireplace. He expanded the living room by taking off the wall in front of a bathroom on the ground floor. He applied for a grant to rebuild the house from English Heritage, which judged the house as a Grade II listed building, but his application was denied. Therefore, he personally paid to renovate the house. However, the medieval fireplace was found behind a wall during renovations, indicating that the house was not built of stone, but of earthen walls older than stone. He had the stones removed from the external wall at the back of the house so that the earthen wall could be restored under the guidance of a conservation architect associated with the District Council.

Mike and his wife said that they were very proud of and pleased to live in the restored historic building. They showcase a small part of the earthen wall's interior to enlighten friends and relatives who visit them about the house's antiquity (Shioji 1999: 70, 74). His wife also tries to express the history of the house as a farmhouse by putting up saucepans and baskets from the hooks of the ceiling (Figure 4.8). The hooks were used to hang hams and sausages in farmhouse kitchens. Apart from that, she likes her comfortable modern fitted kitchen with a microwave, a dishwasher and an Aga oven.

FIGURE 4.8 The kitchen in Mike's house (photo by the author)

The couple are also very interested in protecting the town from development. They support the CS, which bought farmland on the outskirts of the town to build a car park fifteen years ago. A line of cars parked on the High Street and traffic congestion had been a problem in the town and it was necessary to build a big car park to improve life for residents. The CS bought the land, which was thought to be the only suitable location, and obtained planning permission from the District Council. As there were several objections to the plan, the CS ended up lending out the land to the local school, which uses it as an environmental and agricultural study area for children to plant fruit trees. Mike and his wife think that the CS protects the town from housing development by acquiring the land.

An Incomer Couple Living on the High Street for Thirty Years

Pat, who is in her seventies, moved from a city to a seventeenth-century house on the High Street with her husband in 1988. She worked in the business world for a long time and her husband is a painter. She has a thorough knowledge of local history and has been President of the Campden Historical Society for many years. She is proud of their house, which was used as a part of the Arts and Crafts School opened by C.R. Ashbee. They maintain the historic house very well and the only change they made in thirty years was installing a shower in the bathroom (with planning permission). She is also a member of the Cotswold Warden, which is the voluntary conservation group maintaining the Cotswold AONB, and often leads a guided walk for tourists as a volunteer guide and explains them the history of the town.

The previous owner of Pat's house obtained it by auction very cheaply and, after keeping it for only six months, sold it for a profit to her and her husband. This owner replaced the window frames with plastic ones without planning permission, which was reported by neighbours after Pat and her husband moved into the house. In recent years, she said, it has been common for people from outside the town to buy historic properties and, after rebuilding and renovating inside, sell them for a profit. It is difficult for the authorities to find out about these unauthorized alterations unless they are reported by neighbours or subsequent owners. Through such transactions, the price of houses in the town rose and it became more difficult for local people to afford such houses. Pat pays attentions to rebuilding and changes of use in neighbouring buildings in order to prevent such destruction of the town's landscape by investors of this kind.

Incomer Brothers Living in Westington

The Collins brothers – both were in their sixties and single – moved to Campden from London upon retirement in the 1990s. The older brother was a schoolteacher and the younger worked for a company. They decided to look for an appropriate house in the countryside that they could share as they grew older. They came across an old farmhouse in Chipping Campden advertised in *Country Life* in 1994. They initiated a contract to purchase the house ten days after seeing the ad. The farmhouse had been owned by the Izod family, who have been in the area over 400 years, and it featured the traditional combination of a main house, barn, stable, and dovecote. When the Collins brothers purchased their home, the inside of the main house and the barn had been modernized, so they purchased only the main house (Figure 4.9). The brothers had 'a busy retirement life', looking after flowers in their front garden and participating as members of the Camera Club and Campden Historical Society. They obtained photographs of the house from

FIGURE 4.9 The Collins' house (photo by the author)

its restoration in the 1950s and were interested in the original building structures. The older brother, who taught history to foreign students, once said
to me: 'We can feel a history of England in the countryside.' He planned to
relate the history of the house by decorating the old fireplace with the old
meat-roasting machine and trunk, which were left in the house when he and
his brother purchased it. They used a sofa covered in fabric featuring the
willow pattern designed by William Morris, and bought antique furniture
to complement the local countryside and antiquity of the building (Figure
4.10). Apart from being attracted by the elements of Old England, such as
the history of England and the farmhouse itself, they cited as the reason for
moving to Chipping Campden the convenience of life there, especially for
the elderly; the reasonable size of the town is conducive to walking to the
shops on the High Street. The brothers have since died and the house was
sold to another incomer.

The above three examples of incomers highlight their various backgrounds, reasons for migration and periods of residency, but also some
common, if not universal elements. Taken together with the examples of
the Campdonians, it is possible to trace some patterns with regard to their
approach to the local landscape and historic buildings. There is a tendency
for working-class Campdonians to seek modern and comfortable lifestyles,
whereas middle-class incomers are interested in history and tend to prefer

FIGURE 4.10 The living room of the Collins' house (photo by the author)

the preservation of old things and support the activities of the CS in relation to this. However, these categories are not always applicable: the respective groups of residents are far from monolithic and represent a range of life-styles, values and opinions.

Negotiated Landscape by People in the Town

The development of housing land in Chipping Campden, which can have a huge impact on the cultural landscape of the town, usually involves compli-cated negotiations between the differing interests of groups and individuals. An example is the controversy over the planned construction of a nursing home in 1998.[5] When the development was proposed, Campdonians and in-comers approached the plans in different ways, yet both opposed it. After exchanging their opinions in a public meeting and in the local newspaper, they gradually reached a consensus as 'Campden residents' and were able to influence the usually all-powerful external interests.

In March 1998, S company submitted a planning application to build a residential nursing home in Badgers Field. The area around Badgers Field is an old area of Campden that includes St James' Church, almshouses and the ruins of a manor house. Badgers Field is part of a green belt enclosing the old area; it is a pastureland still used by farmers as a water source. The company specializes in constructing large, respected medical facilities, and the planned construction site was recommended as an ideal location by an inspector for the District Council's planning committee. Consequently, the Campden Voluntary Help Group (CVHG), which had been questioning the necessity of building such a facility in Campden, agreed to support the plan. Two Campdonian representatives from this group assumed leading roles in examining the planned site over a five-year period, and S company accepted the commission to initiate the project. The CVHG announced publicly that S company's planning application had been submitted to the council. The development plan presented by the company included the following:

> The building is measuring sixty-one by forty-eight metres and eleven metres high, and the roof is steeply pitched because that is the style of the Cotswold vernacular. It has fifty-two single bedrooms, [each] with its own bathroom, and also has specialist equipment and a hairdressing salon. It needs about fifty-five to sixty people working in it and there will be twenty-one parking spaces which are regard[ed] as adequate [for the] site. At times other than those at which the junior school opens and closes: there will be no clash of traffic. The admissions policy will be decided upon after consultations with the social services because [the] home is not a facility for privately paying residents only. A certain number of beds could be reserved for Chipping Campden residents, but this should not be necessary as people from outside are not expected to live in it. (*Chipping Campden Bulletin*, April 1998: 4)

In the same month, a public meeting was held, and all residents who attended the meeting and made statements opposed the plan. Therefore, the town council unanimously rejected the application; the Campden Society also rejected the plan. Below I cite excerpts from ten of thirteen such statements that were reported in the town's newspaper in April 1998. Further, I include a brief profile of each person in parentheses to clarify their positions and local roles.[6]

A Vicar of St. James' Church (graduated from the Department of Theology at Cambridge University; an incomer arriving with his wife and two children in 1996):

> This building is much more than just a local facility, and residents of Badgers Field will lose a lot of light. There is a green belt around the ancient part of Campden, from this field to the Conyegree with Baptist Hicks' ruined house, the church, and alms houses facing the open spaces. To build on this area would be a tragedy . . . Calf Lane and Pear Tree and Cherry Orchard Closes are utterly unsuitable for many more cars in the morning and evening, particularly during the term times of the junior school. Why must such a home be in a central site? Will the elderly and infirm be popping regularly to Londis [supermarket]?

Mr B (chairman of the Campden Society, ex-major general, an incomer):

This is in the area of outstanding natural beauty; the access is abominable and it will overpower the town. In the recently completed town plan, the inspector placed particular emphasis on this field and the need to keep it open: to smash the town boundary at such a sensitive position is unacceptable. Is a home of this size wanted? Put it on the Wolds End Orchard as we do not need a car park.[7]

Mr S (ex-district councillor, an incomer):

The district council, when I was a member, negotiated with the Badgers Trust to maintain this field as it was in order to protect the view of the residents of Badgers Field and the overall feeling of openness in Calf Lane. The sooner this is officially declared a protected open space, the better.

Mrs W (an executive committee member of the Campden Historical Society, in charge of a column in the town's newspaper, an ex-schoolteacher in her seventies and an incomer):

How much of the Badgers Field dwellings will be in shadow at midday in mid-winter after this building is erected? Many might not see much sun at all. Since the twelfth century, this has been a town field – when the High Street was laid out in the 1170s. Campden is studied around the world as a fine example of an existing, medieval, urban pattern with the hills visible on three sides of the bowl in which it rests. There could be a lot of history in this field and if any building takes place, a geophysical study and an archaeological dig should be done. Baptist Hicks laid a lead pipe from Conduit House on Westington Hill to bring spring water to his mansion, the alms houses, and the vicarage, and that pipe runs straight through this field; farmers still use water from it.

Mr C (vice-chairman of the Campden Historical Society, an incomer in 1991):

The pipe had a branch to Badgers Farm as well. This proposed building is far too big and will generate a lot of traffic. We do not need a car park, so put it on the Wolds End Orchard instead.

Mrs L (owner of a shop in High Street, an incomer in her sixties who has lived in the town over thirty years):

This is totally inappropriate, particularly as we have Campden Home Nursing working very successfully here. Do we need a building of this size, as very few people have left town for homes in the past 10 years? . . . Twenty-one parking spaces are utterly inadequate. The registration authorities oppose large ghettoes like this and Fred Badger wanted no other building on this site after he had given his farmyard to create Badgers Field sheltered housing. It is unethical to do this.

Mrs M (in her forties, associated with Campden Home Nursing, wife of Campdonian whose family has owned an Old Silk Mill, which C.R. Ashbee and his Guild of Handicrafts used as an workshop, and surrounding land for three generations):

> Smaller homes than this can and do thrive and there are other sites available in town; one in particular (the land in back of the Old Silk Mill in Sheep Street) could take a home of 30 beds plus a day centre. There are alternatives to this.

Mrs G (second-generation incomer; her mother ran Woolstaplers Hall Museum, which had attracted tourists until its closure in 1996):

> This building will employ up to 50 people, but there are only 21 parking spaces. Where will visitors park? There are plans being discussed to attach a nursery to St. James' School. More cars mean more danger in the narrow streets around.

Mr P (ex-colonel, incomer, President of the Campden Historical Society, member of Campden Trust and the Campden Guild of Handicraft Trust):

> Agreed with everything said and was appalled at the sympathy shown to this proposal by the planning officers. Mrs. M's site was perfect, so please look at the alternatives and 'scrub this nonsense'!

Mr F (husband of Lady X (who is in her eighties), who is a descendant of the lord of the manor family in the town; they live in Court House near the ruin of a seventeenth-century manor house and next to St James' Church):

> [I am] staggered at the degree of opposition. After all, it is a medical requirement. If this site is unsuitable, let us find another.

Of these residents who spoke during the public meeting, eight were incomers: three ex-servicemen, two present members of the Campden Historical Society (CHS), an ex-district councillor, a woman living in Campden for over thirty years and the pastor of the Anglican Church living in Campden for two years. Three were Campdonians: two spouses of Campdonians and the second generation of incomers.

Speakers were members of certain local organizations, including the CS, the CHS, Campden Home Nursing, the Campden Trust, and the Guild of Handicrafts Trust, and their comments give an indication of organizational attitudes. The CS has often been mentioned in this chapter and it grew as it incorporated the declining Campden Trust that had preserved the historic buildings in the town by purchasing them. The CS consists largely of incomers and it is one of the organizations that represent incomers' opinions on the local landscape very well. Incomers generally accept the CS as an organization preserving the town's landscape and protecting the town from housing development. However, few Campdonians are members of the group and they even have an antipathy towards it because it has been demonstrating the preference for preserving the landscape over the needs of the town's residents. CHS members are interested in local history and are keen on preserving old documents, items, lands and landscape related to the local history. It is also organized by incomers, but there are several Campdonians who try to record the old days and people in the town such as typical working-class Campdonian John Brave and intellectual Campdonian returner George Knight mentioned above. Campden Home Nursing is managed by the group of Campdonians who have been looking after the old people in the town by visiting and taking them to hospital, which is appreciated by Campdonians. The Guild of Handicraft Trust preserves old documents and designs of C.R. Ashbee and his Guild of Handicraft. Its members are mainly incomers; the few Campdonians who are members of this group are artists themselves or have some connection with artists of the Arts and Crafts Movement in this town like George Knight, as his father worked for Ashbee, or Mr M, the Silk Mill owner whose wife suggested it as an alternative site for the development.

The contents of people's statements in the public meeting show that questions about the proposed development primarily addressed two points: the necessity of a residential nursing home and the impact on the environment from construction of the facility. It is clear that the approaches to this issue were different for old and new residents. Most of the incomers initially presented their concerns about the impact on the environment of the proposed medical facility. They pointed out that the scale of the facility was too large and would spoil the landscape and sense of the pastureland as an open space; they also claimed that the facility would increase traffic on the narrow roads around the site and would decrease light for existing houses. Incomers' perceptions of the landscape are reflected in the opinions of the pastor and members of the Historical Society. Incomers criticized the potential environmental impact and suggested looking for another site. They opposed construction of car parks in the town, mentioning Wolds End as the site proposed for car parks and as another possible site for the medical facility.

Although Campdonians understand the necessity for a residential nursing home in the town, they have, like the incomers, expressed their concerns about the impact on the local surroundings. Campdonians do not oppose preserving the cultural landscape of Badgers Field; when incomers supported a move to protect it, Campdonians suggested looking for another site. According to the presentation by the town's doctor, the population of the town is ageing and more than thirty elderly Campdonians have left the town to enter medical facilities in other areas in the last five years – a serious problem for Campdonians.

The number of letters to the editor of the town's newspaper increased in June after the public meeting. Correspondence appeared as a circular notice to all residents of the town in the June issue of the paper from 'a concerned group of Campden residents' under four people's names, including a Campdonian. The letter addressed the development plan and points regarding the proposed construction in Badgers Field and Sheep Street. It encouraged 'Campden residents' to consider the plan from the perspective of all town residents. This group recommended that residents observe the joint meeting of town and district councils in June and added the following three points:

1. It will be a purely commercial venture. The developers have stated that no priority will be given to Campden residents. The fees are expected to be about £600 a week and it will be open to anyone, whether from Gloucestershire, London, or elsewhere in the country. It is unlikely that social services would be able to fund beds at this high cost.
2. The site of Badgers Field is outside the recently confirmed development boundary of Campden. The reason given for favouring a breach in the district's plan is the 'overriding need' for the development. We consider this to be spurious.
3. The development would involve re-routing or blocking several rights of way (public footpaths) over the field. (*Chipping Campden Bulletin*, June 1998: 14)

The Chairman of the CVHG wrote a letter that appeared the same month in the town's newspaper:

The majority of people in Campden seem to recognise that there is a definite need for a nursing home in the town. What the CVHG is anxious to see is a high-quality home of good design, well-staffed, efficiently run, and financially viable . . . We would wish the home to feel part of the community, not pushed into isolation as so many have been in the past and many still are. Apart from these general objectives, the group is open-minded and would hope to be able to support any venture that met these standards, whatever the choice of site. We are looking only to secure for Campden the best possible facilities for its older people. (*Chipping Campden Bulletin*, July 1998: 9)

Mrs L, who opposed the development in the public meeting, wrote to the town's newspaper saying that she understood the efforts of CVHG members and the necessity of the facility; she also acknowledged that people's criticism of the construction plan during the public meeting was overheated. However, she explained the need to re-examine the scale and the construction site without accepting the opinion of S company without question since it is an enterprise pursuing profits. The September issue of the town's newspaper published two sketches of the site labelled 'Badgers Field before and after the development', drawn by a local painter in Campden. The sketches provided an overview of a public footpath and clearly showed the difference in the landscape before and after the proposed development.

Subsequently, the highest number of letters ever received about the planning application for this facility was sent to the Cotswold District Council.

More than 200 letters of opposition from residents of Chipping Campden, letters of protest from representatives of six conservation groups in Campden and other areas, and eighteen unregistered letters of approval were received (*Chipping Campden Bulletin,* November 1998).

In December, S company withdrew its application, citing as its reasons the discovery of a public footpath through Badgers Field and unsuccessful negotiations with the landowner. According to the local newspaper, it became clear that the company's potential profit would decrease because the owner of the farmland boosted the price of the land on the strength of the public footpath, which probably led to the withdrawal of the application. The substituted application for a Sheep Street facility will continue to be examined, but residents of Campden presume that it will be as difficult as the former one because the land houses the Old Silk Mill, a Grade II* listed building with connections to C.R. Ashbee.

Developments of housing land in Chipping Campden have been influenced by the conflicting interests of landowners, developers, administrations and conservation groups. However, the right to make decisions about the appropriateness and contents of developments is in the hands of developers and administrators from outside the community. Depending on the scale and nature of a development, some complicated relations in the town, including social relations among the residents, are inadvertently exposed in public opinions. After residents in various positions discussed the issue in a public meeting and via the local newspaper, incomers showed their understanding regarding the necessity of the facility, advocated by Campdonians who had originally agreed that the cultural landscape should be protected. As a result, a common attitude that an 'outside' trader could proceed with such a development (for profit) emerged, but residents specified that they would have to consent to the contents of the facility and examine the construction site to ensure that the cultural landscape of the town and surrounding area were not harmed.

Conclusion

The imaginary world of Old England has had social, cultural, political and economic influences on a country town by attracting tourists and incomers. Tourists indirectly maintain the vitality of the town by visiting and consuming all that represents Old England. Tourism can also be effective in causing people to move and become residents of their former tourist destinations. In fact, incomers are the most influential people in terms of transforming an imaginary world into reality. They preserve historic buildings by actually living in them, with all the attendant planning restrictions. They enjoy showcasing the antiquity of their historical houses, but they also improve the insides of the houses in a modern comfortable way (while Campdonians tend to value modern convenience and to accommodate their family's needs over historical interest). These houses characterize the landscape of the town, and the local conservation societies and the town council support such a landscape, which incomers claim and preserve. The ongoing arrival of incomers ensures that the local community is constantly changing, and potential tensions arise, given the frequent gaps between incomers and Campdonians in terms of class, economic power, lifestyle and values. However, neither group of residents is monolithic; there are several examples in the chapter of reasonably wealthy Campdonians, locals and incomers alike, who inhabit old properties without needing to improve or restore them. Some Campdonians are busy contributing to the local Historical Society, which incomers are mainly keen on organizing.

In the face of a potential threat to the landscape of Old England by huge external powers for housing development, incomers and Campdonians reached a consensus as 'Campden residents' after exchanging their opinions in a public meeting and in the local newspaper. Campdonians accepted incomers' perceptions of the cultural landscape and incomers also understood Campdonians' need for a medical facility.

In contrast with the tendency within anthropological tourism studies to describe host communities as relatively powerless in comparison with visitors, the Chipping Campden example paints a rather different picture. Incomers within the community had similar viewpoints to tourists, thereby forming a strong conservative force aiming to preserve the landscape of Old England. Furthermore, native Campdonians were not always 'the weak', as they expressed their viewpoints and claims as articulately as incomers, ultimately coming to the same conclusions. It was not just a simple relationship of the weak 'versus' the strong, but it could be regarded as the strong 'within' the weak. Tourism and migration not only bring a gaze from outside the community, but also create strength within the community towards outside powers that could destroy the commonness of Old England as home.

Yuko Shioji has an MA in sociology and anthropology of travel and tourism. Focusing on English culture from the Japanese point of view, she has a Ph.D. in literature (anthropology) based on ethnographic research on the preservation of cultural heritage and promoting tourism in the Cotswolds. She has carried out fieldwork in the English countryside for over twenty years. She is now a professor at the Faculty of International Tourism, Hannan University, Osaka, Japan, where she teaches anthropology of tourism and European culture. She is currently conducting research on the social and cultural construction of footpaths in Britain and Japan.

NOTES

1. Fieldwork in Chipping Campden was conducted in several stages from 1996 to 2016. I carried out the participatory long-term fieldwork from April 1996 to October 1997 and from April 2009 to March 2010. Between and after the two long-term fieldwork periods, from 1997 to 2009 and after 2010, I have carried out short-term research in the same town almost every year. I wish to thank all the people in Chipping Campden who supported my research over these twenty years.
2. Some recent works relativize this point of view by discussing the possibilities of community-based tourism or community development as well as tourism, which requires a partnership with a local community (Hall and Richards 2003; Singh, Timothy and Dowling 2003; Moscardo 2008; World Tourism Organization 2009).
3. Some factors presented in incomers' motivation and background link with several issues discussed in 'lifestyle migration' (relatively affluent individuals relocating to places that have meanings of identity and location to them), in a quest for a better quality of life (Benson and O'Reilly 2009).
4. Both examples of Campdonians and incomers are based on the author's research by gathering information through daily conversations and visits to or stays at their houses from 1996 to 1997. For the sake of their privacy, I use pseudonyms.
5. Here I use interview data from fieldwork in 1996 and 1997, letters to and from several residents in the town, and contents from the town newspaper after 1997.
6. For reasons of privacy, I use arbitrary capital letters for their names.
7. At the same time as the development of Badgers Field, a planning application for a car park in the town was submitted, and unoccupied ground (Wolds End Orchard) at the north end of the High Street was mentioned as its site. The CS strongly objected to the application, claiming that building a car park would bring more cars and tour buses to the town.

REFERENCES

Benson, Michaela and Karen O'Reilly (eds). 2009. *Lifestyle Migration: Expectations, Aspirations and Experiences.* Farnham: Ashgate.

Boissevain, Jeremy. ed. 1992. *Revitalizing European Rituals.* London: Routledge.

———. 1996. *Coping with Tourists: European Reactions to Mass Tourism.* Oxford: Berghahn Books.

British Tourist Authority and English Tourist Board (BTA/ETB). 1996. *English Heritage Monitor.* London.

Countryside Commission. 1987. *Policies for Enjoying the Countryside.*

———. 1991a. *Visitors to the Countryside.*

———. 1991b. *Area of Outstanding Natural Beauty: Policy Statement 1991.*

————. 1992. *Enjoying the Countryside: Policies for People.*

Fees, Craig. 1996. 'Tourism and the Politics of Authenticity in a North Cotswold Town', in T. Selwyn (ed.), *The Tourist Image: Myths and Myth Making in Tourism.* Chichester: John Wiley & Sons, pp. 121–46.

Hall, Derek, and Greg Richards (eds). 2003. *Tourism and Sustainable Community Development.* London: Routledge.

McDonald, Maryon. 1987. 'Tourism: Chasing Culture and Tradition in Brittany', in M. Bouquet and M. Winter (eds), *Who from Their Labours Rest?: Conflict and Practice in Rural Tourism.* Aldershot: Avebury, pp. 120–34.

Moscardo, Gianna. (ed.). 2008. *Building Community Capacity for Tourism Development.* Wallingford: CABI.

Pevsner, Nikolaus. 1956. *The Englishness of English Art.* London: Architectural Press.

Potts, Alex. 1989. '"Constable Country" between the Wars', in R. Samuel (ed.), *Patriotism: The Making and Unmaking of British National Identity. Vol. III. National Fictions.* London: Routledge, pp. 160–88.

————. 1997. 'Myths of the English Countryside: An Interpretation of the Language and Images of Tourist Brochures', *Language and Culture* 8: 183–200.

————. 1999. 'Living with Heritage', in K. Sato (ed.), *Houses are Telling.* Kyoto: Gakugei Shuppansha, pp. 63–80.

————. 2003. *The Creating Englishness: Sensing Boundaries and the Preservation of Cultural Heritage in the Cotswolds of England.* Tokyo: Akashi Shoten.

Singh, Shalini, Dallen J. Timothy and Ross K. Dowling (eds). 2003. *Tourism in Destination Communities.* Wallingford: CABI.

Smith, Valene (ed.). 1989. *Hosts and Guests: The Anthropology of Tourism.* Philadelphia: University of Pennsylvania Press.

Urry, John. 1990. *The Tourist Gaze.* London: Routledge.

Wiener, Martin. 1981. *English Culture and the Decline of the Industrial Spirit 1850–1980.* Harmondsworth: Penguin.

Williams, Raymond. 1973. *The Country and the City.* London: Chatto & Windus.

World Tourism Organization. 2009. *Tourism and Community Development: Asian Practices.* Madrid: World Tourism Organization.

Yamashita, Shinji. 1999. *Bali: What Can We Learn from the Anthropology of Tourism?* Tokyo: University of Tokyo Press.

CHAPTER 5

Modalities of Space, Time and Voice in Palestinian Hip-Hop Narratives

Ilana Webster-Kogen

Introduction

Among the Arab world's musical genres, Palestinian hip-hop enjoys an especially prominent and favourable media platform. Among Palestinian rappers, one group dominates scholarly study and media fascination. For those reasons, DAM's long-awaited second album, *Dabke on the Moon,* was released to a flurry of scrutiny and debate in November 2012. However, perhaps to the musicians' surprise, the album attracted attention not only for its groundbreaking material or its record-breaking sales, but for a political firestorm over its lead single, which was accused initially by critics online of overlooking the key element of Palestinian lives: the occupation. The debate calmed down within a few months, but that moment of eruption was fascinating for scholars invested in the mobilizing power of hip-hop, because it enacted a negotiation of boundaries and taboos for politically active musicians, raising substantial questions about the convergence of gender relations and political violence in an intractable conflict.

The song 'If I Could Go Back in Time'[1] tells a provocative story of an 'honour killing', a term queried by some feminist and legal scholars of the Middle East. Nadera Shalhoub-Kevorkian (2011), for one, argues that this constructed category of gender violence evokes disgust from Western audiences and justification on the part of Western leaders for taking control of populations (see also Abu-Lughod 2002). The song explores subjectivities of violence and agency, and after its release, a debate ensued online in *Al-*

Jadaliyya between DAM and anthropologist Lila Abu-Lughod with activist Maya Mikdashi, who criticized DAM for presenting gender violence through a skewed, Israeli lens, decontextualizing family life from the wider problem of occupation.[2] Some audiences found 'If I Could Go Back in Time' provocative because it paints a negative portrait of the status of young women within the Arab family and decouples it from the wider political reality of power relations.[3]

At the same time, the rather extraordinary song presents musical, lyrical and gestural cues that undercut the accusations of depoliticization, and, indeed, I will demonstrate that what audiences were reacting to is a political reality that connects the domestic to the national directly. I will argue that the song presents a picture of 'home' life, both in the domestic and the national sense, which destabilizes the common narrative of 'resistance' (queried by Mahmood 2005: 9) because it tells a story about the nation through the everyday politics of homemaking. Therefore, I will present musical evidence that DAM's accomplishment in this provocative song is the self-conscious construction of a reflexive subjectivity that challenges the mainstream representation of strictly vertical power relations prevalent across Palestine scholarship (Sa'di and Abu-Lughod 2007). I will present the case study of the most internationally recognized rap group, often lauded for its resistance stance and support of the Palestinian cause (McDonald 2009b and 2013; Swedenburg 2013) as a way of understanding the delicate political position that 'home' occupies for the '48 Palestinians – citizens of the State of Israel who descend from the Palestinians who were not expelled in the events of 1947–49 (alternative labels are Israeli-Palestinians, Palestinian-Israelis or Israeli Arabs) – and the gender dynamics that support or subvert a resistance framework. The song's critiques reveal uneasiness with the '48 Palestinian positionality in terms of home, belonging and narratives of exclusion.[4] Ultimately, the song's audience objected to the portrayal of a Palestinian woman as a citizen and a victim, when victimhood is chiefly experienced through the lens of and at the hands of the brutality and inconveniences of occupation.

In this chapter, I conduct a close reading of 'If I Could Go Back in Time' in order to establish why audiences reacted with such passion to the song's release. I will argue that Palestinian artists face such pressure to present their material within an exclusively resistant framework that even material that fits within the framework draws negative attention if it is not overtly critical of the occupation. I will further argue that the resistance framework is so ingrained in DAM's work that the song's main subtexts constitute the core themes in Palestinian scholarship of space, time and voice, to which the song's musical, lyrical and gestural characteristics are symbolically allusive references. First, from the gestural/visual imagery in the video, I examine the setting of the young woman's murder in an olive grove. Second, from the lyrical perspective, I discuss the concept of looking back in time, the main theme of the song's chorus, and argue that DAM engages the nostalgic views of the past in the subjunctive mode. And third, from the musical perspective, I mention the interplay of DAM, rapping the song's verses, with female singer Amal Murkus singing the chorus. Finally, I will demonstrate that while the song's national-allegorical connotations are consistent with Palestinian resistance iconography, the song failed to meet an imagined solidarity benchmark because it portrays the private home space as equally violent, despite the absence of state actors.

DAM and the Burden of Over-representation

DAM's critical and commercial achievements are so well documented in the popular press[5] and in scholarship (Massad 2005; McDonald 2009b and 2013; Swedenburg 2013) that they risk overexposure on both fronts. For over a decade, the group have dominated international media depictions of Palestinian performing arts, partly since they are considered a powerful voice of resistance and partly because they are easier to access than performers who live in the Occupied Territories who might not be as media-savvy. DAM's international prominence was further bolstered by the 'Arab Spring',[6] since they have long mediated the Israeli–Palestinian conflict informally. The medium contributes to the ease of circulating DAM's work, since the genre known sometimes as 'global hip-hop' is enjoying scholarly attention as the transnational community-building style of urban youth (Fernandes 2011; Nooshin 2011). In recent years, hip-hop's undercurrent of collective activism has prompted DAM to connect with Palestinians everywhere rather than exclusively with their local population. In short, DAM have served for some time as a symbolic if unexpected figurehead for a resistance movement, the group being especially effective since its members understand Israeli society from the inside.

All three members of DAM are '48 Palestinians, or Palestinians citizens of Israel.[7] There are approximately 1.7 million '48 Palestinians in Israel, where they speak Arabic as a first language and are fluent in Hebrew; they operate a separate school system;[8] and they vote in national elections.[9] This state of affairs, whereby '48 Palestinians participate in the Israeli public sphere but publicly feel ambivalent in relation to the State of Israel's exclusive apparatus, leads to tension with other Palestinians and with the Israeli establishment (Kanaaneh and Nusair 2010: 5).

DAM's three members – brothers Tamer and Suhell Nafar, and friend Mahmoud Jreri – thus belong to a population often characterized, in terms of diaspora, as living on their land but in a foreign state (Rabinowitz and Abu-Baker 2005: 5).[10] That unusual positionality, whereby a minority population lives on the territory of its collective memory and imagination, but under a government that is insufficiently representative, presents a unique counter-example to many of the examples of migrants, pilgrims and diasporas that we find across diaspora literature. Technically, the people that I describe in this chapter live 'at home', although they often identify with the nationalist struggle of their kin in the West Bank, Gaza and abroad (Shulz 2003: 74). '48 Palestinians are sometimes conceptualized as a sort of stepping-stone between Israelis and Palestinians, since they live within internationally recognized boundaries, but paradoxically, the state to which they might openly express loyalty is primarily characterized by its lack of infrastructure and recognition as a political entity. Therefore, the in-between status of '48 Palestinians is the crucial identifying characteristic that renders them liminal figures in both Israeli and Palestinians narratives of home and belonging (Shulz 2003; Rabinowitz and Abu-Baker 2005; Kanaaneh and Nusair 2010).

Whether the in-between status is expressed as a benefit or a challenge most commonly depends on the descriptor's perspective on the Israeli–Palestinian conflict. Plenty of literature has been devoted to the infrastructural prejudices that exclude '48 Palestinians from the Israeli power structure because they are Arab (Shulz 2003; Rabinowitz and Abu-Baker 2005; Sa'di and Abu-Lughod 2007; Kanaaneh and Nusair 2010), and yet '48 Palestinians occasionally find themselves being labelled as collaborators by Palestinian authorities as well (Lang 2005: 79).[11] Meanwhile, in my own fieldwork among ethnic minorities in Tel Aviv-Jaffa since 2008, I have encountered an impulse among certain progressive Israelis and researchers to frame '48 Palestinians not as potential enemy combatants like occupied or exiled Palestinians, but as Israeli ethnic minorities like Ethiopians or Russian-speaking immigrants who inhabit alternative religious spheres and voting blocs in Israeli society.

While holding a recognized travel document provides a degree of security for '48 Palestinians, theirs is a ruptured citizenship. Nafar, Nafar and Jreri grew up in the city of Lydd (Lod in Hebrew), a 'mixed' (Arab/Jewish) city that is fragmented and economically stratified along ethnic lines. As the members of DAM recall (McDonald 2009b; Swedenburg 2013), their neighbourhood growing up was infested with drugs, crime, police harassment and a discriminatory urban planning policy. And yet DAM's members can travel abroad without the hassle and exclusion that refugees experience, and they have access to decent schools and hospitals, resources that set them apart from refugees living across the Levant (Humphries and Khalili 2007; Abu-Lughod 2010: ix). The much-documented second-class status in Israel of '48 Palestinians (see above), on the one hand, and the ambivalence of living under an often-hostile government,[12] on the other, yields a state of being in which daily life is embroiled in the nuance of living in Israel and holding loyalty to the Palestinian cause.

The result of this ambiguous status, a condition of 'necessary politics' (Tawil-Souri 2011: 139), whereby basic aspects of daily life are politicized, manifests itself in the complex web of names applied to '48 Palestinians, and through which one expresses political allegiances. The term '48 Palestinian explicitly frames the events of 1948, the establishment of the State of Israel and the mass expulsion of Palestinians as the central node of group identity (see Khalidi 1997). On the other hand, the term often used by Israelis, 'Israeli Arab', implies an othering of ethnic minorities.[13] A third term sometimes used by academics and progressive Israelis, 'Palestinian-Israeli', implies a fractured collective self through the construction of a binary opposition. The 'necessary politics' that accompanies naming (Rabinowitz and Abu-Baker 2005: 111) reveals the daily experiences of living peacefully under a government in conflict with one's kin group. This necessary politics undercuts the widespread idea that '48 Palestinians are privileged in their ability to participate in the democratic process, providing a vivid contradiction to David McDonald's assessment of the mimetic (affective) versus kinetic (embodied) experience of occupation (2009a).

One reason why scholars and journalists focus so heavily on DAM might be that many aspects of DAM's existence carry this necessary politics that requires political engagement and interpretation. As mentioned frequently in the literature, the name DAM carries multiple meanings, each corresponding to an audience (McDonald 2009b; Swedenburg 2013). The first, in Arabic, means 'eternal', implying a primordial Palestinian connection to the land. The second, in Hebrew, means 'blood', which likewise carries connotations of kinship affiliation, but also an implication of violence. The third, a hip-hop acronym, situates DAM in a global underclass; it stands for 'Da Arabic MC', which draws on the sociolinguistic particularities of hip-hop vernaculars (Terkourafi 2010: 3). Even the name of the town of their origin, Lydd, engages the conflicted dynamic of DAM's status. Referred to in Hebrew as Lod, Lydd is a site of close scrutiny for Israeli historians because of the forced emptying of the town and nearby Ramle in 1948 (Morris 2008: 287), and even the term 'mixed' town exemplifies the institutional neglect of '48 Palestinians in Greater Tel Aviv (see Kassem 2010: 105). In this sense, the basic information that classifies DAM's work and origins requires judgement on '48 Palestinian civic subjectivity and engages life narratives and interpretations of history.

I will not dwell on DAM's past work, which has been covered in detail by David McDonald (2009b and 2013). However, I mention their best-known songs to highlight what I perceive in 'If I Could Go Back in Time' to be a shift towards reflexivity. DAM earned critical attention for the first time in 2002 with the song 'Min Irhabi' ('Who's the Terrorist?').[14] The song focuses on resistance and opposition, with DAM denouncing the methods of the Israeli military by turning the classic Western tropes of Arab terrorism against the Israeli military apparatus. They do this through the imagery of violence and checkpoints, and through their table-turning discourse of 'you're the terrorist'. In their early work, DAM examined problems within Palestinian society as well and have been vocal advocates for women's rights.[15]

Equally, DAM's songs often engage the contact zone between Palestinian and Israeli society, and some of their most exciting songs challenge nationalist narratives, such as the 2004 song 'Born Here'. In 'Kan Noladeti',[16] the song's Hebrew iteration (there is an Arabic version as well, which Eqeiq (2010) and McDonald (2009b) examine in depth), DAM rap in Hebrew and subvert classic Zionist clichés as a way of expressing a subversive bifocal subjectivity that looks both to Israeli and Palestinian society for audiences and critiques. The Hebrew version, commissioned by Shatil, a progressive organization in Jerusalem, makes claims to contested land on the basis of primordial connections. In the Arabic version, DAM employ salty language and imagery of molestation at the hands of the repressive state apparatus, whereas the Hebrew version subverts a classic neo-Zionist Eurovision anthem also known colloquially as 'Born Here'. While the revised song certainly 'resists', perhaps more importantly, it negotiates the liminal space that DAM's core audience inhabits – Palestinians who understand the nuances of Israeli cultural intimacy (Herzfeld 1997; Stokes 2010). DAM's imagination and audacity to perform a song like 'If I Could Go Back in Time' emanate from the understanding of what it means to live 'at home' yet not to feel 'at home'. They are therefore able to transition seamlessly between the domestic space (where they speak Arabic) and the national space (where they often speak Hebrew) as complementary sites of agency.

'If I Could Go Back in Time'

Overall, DAM's early work fits into the popular, though ultimately conventional resistance framework that Swedenburg (2013) criticizes as presenting a monolithic anti-occupation agenda. Swedenburg's criticism makes the important point that Palestinian society's problems might run deeper than the occupation, but a resistance agenda remains the top priority for the Palestinian solidarity movement today. The agenda aligns DAM with the interests of global hip-hop, a movement frequently characterized as a subversive 'oppositional practice' (Rose 1994) that emerged from urban poverty and technological innovation in opposition to state institutions (Durand

2002; Baker 2011; Nooshin 2011). Just as African-American rappers in the 1970s and 1980s opposed the American institutions that discriminate against young black men such as the police (Chang 2007), Palestinian rappers criticize the chief agents of their daily troubles, the Israeli military. The main themes of global hip-hop, and specifically a conscious message of political activism and enfranchisement, all appear in DAM's early work, as do the main indices of global underclass status: resentment of second-class citizenship, a feeling of persecution at the hands of the repressive state apparatus, pressure to demonstrate machismo or protect female kin, and a sense of advocating for a better society rather than dropping out of it or joining a gang (see DAM's earliest work, *Stop Selling Drugs*). In an interview, the widely cited Iranian-British rapper Reveal (Mehryar Golestani; see Nooshin (2011) for a profile of this politically engaged rapper who is heavily involved in the Iranian hip-hop scene) explains that DAM bear this burden of representation whereby audiences expect that they will adhere to a fixed set of political ideologies and communicative strategies:

> When you have extreme conditions of human rights abuse or geographical restrictions, and you have people who seem to be champion of the cause, people, they don't see them as people . . . People will elevate them to an extreme level . . . They see people – DAM – as sort of heroes . . . The false expectation is built on belief and stereotyping. (Interview, London, 12 July 2013)

Reveal makes the point that rappers represent a constituency for whom they are considered spokespeople, and the responsibility of narrating peoples' lives and problems can leave them vulnerable to controversy.

Dabke on the Moon's lead single, 'If I Could Go Back in Time', is framed, as its title implies, as a narrative in reverse of a young woman's life and death. The story is told in three verses, each of which is rapped by a different member of DAM, while the musician/activist Amal Murkus (also a '48 Palestinian) sings the chorus between each verse. The verses narrate, in the third person, the experience of a young woman who is murdered by her father and brother for trying to flee an arranged marriage to her cousin (see Abdo 2004). The discussion in the popular press defines this as an 'honour killing'. In the chorus, Murkus sings, presumably in the voice of the woman, her last thoughts or, based on the video's framing, perhaps from the afterlife, and what she would do if she could live her life over on her own terms. These dual mechanisms in the chorus of time and voice constitute a compelling statement on who has the right to speak for women in general or to tell the Palestinian story in particular (Nusair 2010).

I was especially taken with the accompanying video's visual imagery, which has upset disparate audiences, as inseparable from the song's sonic characteristics. In the video, we find a paradox: Amal Murkus sings a first-person reflection in the chorus of the protagonist's life, but in the video, a young actress plays the story's central character. There is a schism here that, in the video even more than as an audio track, might seem to speak on behalf of an ostensibly voiceless young woman, robbing her of agency and the ability to position herself in the story (Sayigh 2007: 149–50). Whereas in the song's audio renditions she is relegated to the chorus, in the video she is taken out altogether as a participant, left as an observer of her fate, which is especially difficult for some audiences to accept because her fate is death at the hands of her family rather than soldiers (see Humphries and Khalili 2007: 211). Following her death at the song/video's beginning, we watch her life unfold in reverse: the first verse describes the conditions of her murder, the second the circumstances of her unsuccessful escape plan, and the third the context of her upbringing in which she was robbed of personal agency and punished when she tried to assert herself in decisions. As the video ends, the expression 'Freedom for my sisters', the name of another DAM song, flashes across the screen, while the credits state that the video was funded by the organization UN Women.

This brief description contains most of the song's controversial elements. The three main issues that have come out on message boards and in scholarly and activist discussions are the characterization of the framing crime, the voice and agency of the protagonist, and the ironically paternalistic outside funding for the video. These debates can be found easily online, and they briefly overshadowed the release of *Dabke on the Moon* in November and December 2012. The overarching critique was that the trio failed to position themselves as sufficiently committed to resistance, and DAM's liminal, reflexive positionality left some audiences confused. As I examine the song's visual, melodic and gestural imagery, I will argue that the video is especially disruptive, because it engages a seemingly less politicized reading of the lives of '48 Palestinian women than an obvious resistance discourse provides.

The questions of agency that the song raises are especially provocative in the Palestinian context in the wake of the 'Arab Spring', a set of socio-political processes in which hip-hop was credited as a mobilizing agent. Hip-hop around the Arab world today often focuses on the protection of women, reframed in rap terms as disrespect by boyfriends. The group Arabian Knightz's 2011 song 'Sisters'[17] sympathizes with Arab women who are verbally abused by Western men. The song features Shadia Mansour, a London-based Palestinian Christian known as the 'first lady of Arab rap', who, like Amal Murkus, sings beneath the melody in the song rather than rapping. The trope that young Arab women are defiled by outside influences and need the protection of their brothers is widespread in contemporary Arab hip-hop and it is the principle of *sharaf* politics that DAM reject in 'If I Could Go Back in Time'. In both 'Sisters' and DAM's own song 'Freedom for My Sisters' (2006), female protection and emancipation (two seemingly opposing concepts) are equated with ethnic/national protection/emancipation. We recognize in 'Sisters' an impulse to promote ethnic self-confidence rather than female emancipation, while DAM point out in 'Freedom for My Sisters' that women carry the burden of occupation because they experience the physical pain of labour (a resistance activity), linking resistance to women's rights.

Yet whereas 'Freedom for My Sisters' implies the equation of female emancipation with collective political power, political realities collude in the othering of women in subtle ways, even by agents who intend the opposite. For example, considering DAM's work from the same period, one notices a dynamic playing out that sidelines women's issues when self-determination returns to the foreground. The DAM song 'Mah li huriye' ('I Don't Have Freedom') uses a simple pronoun switch to demonstrate that political issues are more often kept separate from women's issues. Contrasting 'I Don't Have Freedom' with 'Freedom for My Sisters' – the narrative 'I' being operatively male – makes the case implicitly that women's voices are frequently abrogated to the resistance struggle. The titles and content of these songs encapsulate a dynamic of gender relations and civil rights in the Palestinian resistance effort (Sayigh 2007: 150),[18] whereby Palestinian men are granted freedom by Israel and women are granted freedom by Palestinian men (Nusair 2010: 81–82). DAM's juxtaposition of civil rights and women's rights as equal concerns in the resistance movement highlights the crucial role that women have played in the Palestinian resistance movement (Rabinowitz and Abu-Baker 2005: 127). So in addition to being chiefly responsible for expanding national borders through procreation (Yuval-Davis 1997: 46) and quantitative nation-building (see Shafir and Peled 2002), women participate in resistance activity frequently (Rabinowitz and Abu-Baker 2005: 112). It is therefore possible that 'If I Could Go Back in Time' upset audiences precisely because the song pointed out to the audience a disparity between political contribution and domestic autonomy. Yet the song connects the political 'I' to the domestic 'she' through a converging of women's bodies and voices, and a portrayal of national space.

Palestinian Women's Voices

In the scholarly literature, Palestinian women are imagined to inhabit multiple sites of occupation (see especially Kanaaneh and Nusair 2010), and DAM's song can be alternately read as sharing the female perspective or co-opting female agency. How one interprets the song depends on how one interprets this set of dynamics in Palestinian life. DAM's promotion of women's causes is well documented, yet a critique of agency and voice is undeniable. In 'If I Could Go Back in Time', the protagonist's story is mediated through the male, third-person voices of Tamer Nafar, Suhell Nafar and Mahmoud Jreri. In an ironic twist, the process of ascribing agency to young women is curtailed, with DAM making the protagonist the object rather than the subject of the story. Moreover, since the narrative content airs the domestic problems of a vulnerable population – domestic problems that have historically manifested themselves politically (Humphries and Khalili 2007: 223) – activists and feminist critics advise that DAM's members are in no position to impose judgement on women's rights and experiences while depriving them of a voice.[19] While this argument's merit seems self-evident in the song's vocals, the protagonist's voice is far from silent in 'If I Can Go Back in Time' and through examining the song's melody, sung by Amal Murkus, I consider the explosive 'necessary politics' of touching on *sharaf* (see Abdo 2004 and Lang 2005), the basis of the song's central event.

When the song was first released, I was surprised by the selectivity of the online critiques by respected luminaries. As already mentioned, activists and bloggers charged DAM with ignoring political realities and depriving women of a voice in the song. This charge emanates from the verses' third-person narration and the ambiguous status of the singer Amal Murkus in the video (the protagonist's role is outsourced to a younger woman whose voice we never hear). But for the moment, it might be useful to focus on the song itself rather than the video, and should we listen to the song without watching the video, we would hear Amal Murkus throughout the entire song.

To remove the song's lyrics from discussion, we can hear several melodic voices through the song. First, Murkus sings the chorus in the first person. Second, the members of DAM rap the verses. Third, beneath DAM's rapping, Amal Murkus sings the main motive (melody) of the song through the verses in an ornamented and melismatic style, sometimes accompanied by an oud and/or a violin. At the risk of reading too much into DAM's intentions, when I listen to Amal Murkus singing the skeletal melody, I interpret the wordless singing as a voice trying to make itself heard (see Humphries and Khalili 2007; Sayigh 2007; or Kassem 2010), which is itself the dynamic that DAM's members intend to replicate in their storyline. It requires only a minor effort to consider what the female voice is doing within the song and why, and Murkus' voice collapses the seemingly stark divide between the male/rapped/past tense verses and the female/sung/present tense chorus, and I am surprised that the song's critics failed to mention it.

At the same time, I was not surprised that the female/first-person/singing voice might be ignored in a rap song, since gendered hierarchies dictate musical production and interpretations (McClary 1990). In a hip-hop song, rapping might be considered the primary (male) activity and singing might be considered a backup (female) activity (Rose 1994). Indeed, DAM employ the technique of male verse rapping alternated with female chorus singing to great acclaim in 'Born Here' with fellow '48 Palestinian musician Abir Zinati. Zinati sings in Arabic, while DAM raps in Hebrew, a code-switching technique that lends itself to novel nuance in its political message (Terkourafi 2010: 3). This formula worked in 'Born Here', so DAM use it again in 'If I Could Go Back in Time', but in this case, their audience cannot accept the song structure because the structure highlights, rather than covers up, the multiple contexts of women's voices being silenced.

It seems that critics have two main problems with the song's gender dynamic that equate to one common issue: first, they say that DAM have robbed the protagonist of her voice; and, second, they argue that DAM presented unfairly a set of domestic practices intended to infuriate those who abhor Arab culture (Abu-Lughod 2002; Shalhoub-Kevorkian 2011). In effect, they object to the conflation of the personal (domestic) with the national (political). In both of these criticisms, commentators ask who has the right to speak on behalf of Palestinian women, whose movement might be controlled by their male family members, who in turn are often denied freedom of movement by state authorities.

While an intensive debate over *sharaf* politics, that is, the politics of disparate domestic disputes that culminate in the planned murder of a female family member or an activity sometimes translated as 'honour killing', is beyond the scope of this discussion, DAM's representation of this set of behaviours is very much at issue among critics (see Abu-Lughod (2002), on the one hand, for an explanation of 'salvation rhetoric', or Lang (2005) for an in-depth discussion of domestic violence that sets aside issues of power relations, on the other hand). Like the vocabulary ascribed to DAM's national origins and hometown, the naming of this set of domestic behaviours reveals a 'necessary politics' agenda. This embodied, symbolic set of domestic behaviours reveals a set of power hierarchies within the Israeli–Palestinian conflict beyond assumptions of occupiers and occupied, with domestic life revealing multiple layers of power and powerlessness.

The domestic behaviour coded as 'honour killing' transpires rarely – among some Palestinians and Druze – when a (usually) male member of a kin group kills a female member in order to preserve the family *sharaf* (honour) (Lang 2005: 57). Sharaf resides in the male members of the kin group, which they maintain through the purity of the female members. Sharaf can be lost, and a family disgraced, when a woman gives birth outside of wedlock, elopes with a member of her religious group or from outside, refuses to marry a person chosen by the family or is defiled through premarital sex or rape (ibid).[20]

The imagery of defilement is applied to the land frequently in Palestinian literature and political speech (Humphries and Khalili 2007: 223), linking the domestic to the political in the case of family possessions. The use of feminine language for women and land, and the pressure on men to preserve the purity of both, makes public and private, or domestic and national, difficult to differentiate. This means that a discussion of sharaf politics on DAM's part subjects them, transitively, to criticism of their credibility as resistants. In this circle of domestic-national linkage, DAM is pressured not to veer far from an excoriating rejection of the occupation. In this light of the ubiquitous blurring of domestic and national language, the charge that 'If I Could Go Back in Time' is apolitical seems to be an unnecessarily narrow interpretation.

DAM's previous work on resistance material focuses on uncovering subaltern voices (Eqeiq 2010: 67) and engaging the oppositional state of being for '48 Palestinians. However, as we see from the particular public debate over 'If I Could Go Back in Time', co-option of the female voice and body has made audiences uncomfortable, in part because the concerns of Palestinian women work in parallel rather than in unison with the resistance effort (Nusair 2010: 91). The complexity and privacy of sharaf politics, the role of women in the resistance movement, the connection between civil rights and gender rights, and the equation of the domestic and the political in nationalist art all make for a song in which discussion of domestic life takes on political connotations (Kanaaneh and Nusair 2010: 12–13), but in which public questioning of domestic norms reads as a betrayal of the resistance cause. However, the gendered language that codes the defilement of land as domestic violence reveals a language of propriety that invokes the domestic and the national equally.

The Concept of Time and the Burden of History

To many activists, resistance is still so much the goal of popular art that developing a subjectivity detached from current affairs is impossible (Abu-Lughod and Sa'di 2007: 7). And yet, the song's title, and its framing device, focused on the concept of time, implies consideration of perhaps the most intractable issue in the Israeli–Palestinian conflict, namely how to interpret and narrate the past. The lyrical focus on time engages with the conflict implicitly, but beyond that, DAM proposes a reflexive engagement with the historical baggage of being a '48 Palestinian.

Palestinian populations, separated by citizenship and borders, tend to self-identify by dates. '48 Palestinians remained within the State of Israel's boundaries after the Nakba (Rabinowitz and Abu-Baker 2005: 3),[21] while '67

Palestinians came under Israeli occupation in the West Bank and Gaza following Arab military defeat (Shulz 2003: 39). Dates define groups in exile as well: 1982 was the defining moment for Palestinian refugees in Beirut (Sayigh 1996: 150),[22] while 1990 marked the dispersal of the refugee population in Kuwait (Shulz 2003: 66).[23] Numbers, particularly dates, and the concept of time most of all, mark a chief form of collective self-reflection for Palestinians because the dates become associated with myths and ethnosymbolic narratives of self-determination (Jayyusi 2007: 109). In DAM's song, the title expression, repeated in each chorus, demonstrates what the young female protagonist would do 'If I could go back in time'. The expressive affect here of nostalgia and regret, expressed in the subjunctive mode, makes a bold statement at the personal or the collective level (Jayyusi 2007: 118). The lyrics repeat across the three choruses:

> Lu araja bez-zaman / Kuntu barsum, baktub / Kuntu barghani
>
> If I could go back/ In time / I'd draw, write/ I'd sing

Amal Murkus sings each subsection for two four-beat measures, and the line of lyrics is embellished (the chorus lasts sixteen measures and we hear it three times). This is not the only explicit reference to 'going back in time', though; in Suhell Nafar's first rapped verse, he explains the mechanism of storytelling in reverse, and in the third verse, Tamer Nafar mentions the young woman looking back on a life in which she never defended herself. Here is a composite picture of a look back that is full not of nostalgia for a better life, but of regret that the young woman's life had been predetermined against her own interests.

This line is sung and repeated in the subjunctive mode, which, as Lena Jayyusi explains, is a widely used device in Palestinian memory to indicate regret (2007: 118). An apparent subtext, and perhaps an undesirably reflexive one for audiences who see Palestinian rap chiefly as a form of resistance, is a querying of historical entanglements. DAM editorializes that the young woman is not at fault in the circumstances leading up to her murder (she is killed for resisting), but she nevertheless considers what she might have done differently. This twist on looking backwards is standard in Palestinian fiction. In the classic stories of the 1970s (roughly what we might consider a Palestinian canon), the protagonist is often an imperfect figure, and a fatal flaw can often be ascribed to the events of 1948 (Abu-Lughod and Sa'di 2007: 13). The narrative tone of DAM's song sounds far more like the remorseful tragedy of Palestinian fiction than the bravado and boasting that determines a rapper's skill and status (Rose 1994).

We might probe further what DAM mean by looking backwards. The story itself goes back to the young woman's birth, which is a familiar literary device, since Palestinian stories commonly use 1948 as a protagonist's year of birth, such as in the classic 'Return to Haifa' by Ghassan Kanafani (1970).[24] Since 1948 is an indelible date for Palestinians, it often serves as an endpoint for a narrator going back in time. Amal Murkus sings that, if given another chance, the protagonist would 'draw, write, sing', with no word about blame or violence. The absence of explicitly political material here is somewhat stark, since it leaves listeners/viewers to draw their own conclusions. The song's lyrical content is so suggestively affective and nostalgic, in contrast to earlier songs like 'Min Irhabi' ('Who's the Terrorist?'), that we might reasonably credit DAM with presenting an alternative perspective on an intractable conflict. In this case, it is understandable why DAM might come under fire to those for whom introspection seems contrary to the urgency of protest. Controversially, DAM engages reflexively in a contested history, and tracking the group's own temporal trajectory engages the 'necessary politics' (Tawil-Souri 2011) of '48 Palestinian life. Yet the mechanisms of going back in time, storytelling in reverse and considering the full lifespan assert persuasively that DAM seek a framework for ascribing agency to Palestinian lives.

The Olive Grove as Political and Liminal Space

When I saw the song's video for the first time, I was, like much of DAM's audience, struck by the poignancy of the violence against the young protagonist. I was equally moved by the location of the murder and the song's first verse. As the story is told backwards, we witness the young woman's murder in an olive grove, where her brother shoots her and her father digs a grave. As we move through the scene, her father and brother drag her from the car trunk and then (as told in reverse) they snatch her from her bed. The complete visual imagery of the first verse therefore comprises the olive grove and the family home. This imagery might immediately resonate with Palestinian and Israeli viewers (see Eqeiq (2010) or Regev and Seroussi (2004) for discussions of imagery in Israeli and Palestinian music). I read this understated imagery of landscape and house to be an apparent expression of Palestinian nationalism (Abu-Lughod and Sa'di 2007: 14).

To set aside the image of the olive grove for a moment, the dual image of land and house is a complementary set of images that pervades both Palestinian and Israeli music and literature. Palestinian poetry and folk music are replete with descriptions of the land and the nation's connection to it, whether in the form of a Zarif-at-tool dabke or a Mahmoud Darwish poem like 'al-Hathihi 'ard' ('On This Land').[25] The primordial impulse of the land 'belonging' to the Palestinian people is supported by an artistic commitment to natural imagery (Humphries and Khalili 2007: 226). Likewise, in Israeli literature and popular songs (see Regev and Seroussi 2004), descriptions of the nation and the family gathered together under the commitment to building a house on the land is a classic nationalist trope. The land-house imagery thus inhabits an exalted symbolic position in the starkly similar nationalist tropes of Israeli and Palestinian self-determination.

Returning to the imagery of the olive grove, DAM present as the opening to this video one of the classic images of both the resistance struggle and the peace process. The olive branch is a widely recognized biblical metaphor for peace that is incorporated today into vernacular speech, but more importantly, the olive tree has come to symbolize the Palestinian resistance in DAM's previous work (see Eqeiq 2010: 58), especially as applied to military conflict. Over the decades of the occupation, the Israeli military has become increasingly bold in its expropriation of Palestinian farmland for ostensibly security-related purposes (Shulz 2003: 107), making agricultural access increasingly strained. As a result, Palestinians often refer to settler and military activity in gendered language of sexual violence, especially the explicit terminology of rape. In this respect, the national space of the olive grove is conflated discursively with the private space of the home, and the olive tree comes to stand in for a mother, daughter or wife. In the West Bank context especially, the olive tree is the home and the nation, in the senses of symbol, metonymy and livelihood.

In addition to the symbolic power of the olive grove in Palestinian land disputes (Bardenstein 1999: 148–57), the location of the young woman's murder represents the imagery of the liminal stage known as the rite of passage. Indeed, not only does Victor Turner (following Arnold van Gennep) invoke the forest as the liminal space where transformative change occurs (Turner 1967; van Gennep 1907), but much of the understanding of how the forest works as liminal space comes from ostensibly familiar landscapes. The Hebrew Bible, and particularly the early books of Genesis and Exodus, is filled with the narrative device of a protagonist in transition fleeing to the forest or desert to experience an epiphany and return to society prepared for leadership.[26] A viewer who has studied the Bible from a literary perspective (as much of DAM's Israeli audience has) would be familiar with this literary device and would recognize it as a multivalent image of transition and personal conflict. DAM no doubt chose the olive grove because of its political and literary meaning in Palestine, but, moreover, the song's imagery draws on the liminal state of being a '48 Palestinian. The video connects with Palestinian narratives of longing for autonomy on the land (Abu-Lughod and Sa'di 2007: 14) and Jewish narratives of the forest as site of personal growth.

All of these images, of the young woman being taken from her home to certain death; of the father digging her grave in an olive grove; and of the family being separated by violence, resonate with Palestinian populations all over the world as representative of recent Palestinian history (Shulz 2003: 2). Indeed, if these images were associated with resistance material, or if the young woman's assailant were an Israeli soldier, the images would carry immediately recognizable national-allegorical connotations (Abu-Lughod and Sa'di 2007: 12-13). However, the category of violence, specifically of domestic violence between Palestinians, increases the affective power of audience objections to DAM's resistance positionality. We might note that the olive grove goes unnoticed in the many critiques online, which take issue with DAM's political positioning.

The dual setting of 'If I Could Go Back in Time' in an olive grove and in the family home indicates a primordialism/kinship theme to the song's narrative tension. The representation of space – an issue that matters above all in the Israeli–Palestinian conflict – indicates that DAM are acutely aware of both the national-allegorical acuity of visual imagery and of the liminal-symbolic power of gestural cues. Suhell Nafar, Jacqueline Reem Salloum and UN Women, the video's producers and directors, have created a video that expresses the multiple layers of vulnerability for '48 Palestinian women so subtly that even well-informed audiences have failed to recognize the video's political agenda. Space – the home and, equally, the olive grove – is a crucial element in articulating the symbolic power of female fertility in Palestinian self-determination. The defiling of the olive grove by family, rather than military violence, is a powerful commentary on the linking of personal tragedy and political disempowerment through the gendered language of sexual violence.

Conclusion

At the moment of its release, 'If I Could Go Back in Time' provoked a reaction that was consensually deemed disproportionate, in part because of the disparate interpretations applied to it. In one, a young woman is murdered by her family without recourse to justice. Another reads the song as an apologia for Western categories of Arab stereotypes whereby history and politics elude fictional accounts of peoples' lives. A third borders on the national-allegorical and puts the song forward as source material for navigating the complex set of living conditions for '48 Palestinians. The central act's location in an olive grove, the nostalgic look at prehistory and the denial of the young woman's ability to procreate and sing for herself present the moral problems facing Palestinian decision-makers about how a future state will deal with land, the complex history of violence leading up to establishment of the state, the expanding population and relations with 'cousins' across the border (see Rabinowitz and Abu-Baker 2005). Indeed, I interpret this song as an ingenious rendering of the national-domestic problems facing Palestinian self-determination.

The song's musical, lyrical and gestural/visual characteristics index the ruptured, oppositional subjectivities that conflict with each other in the context of '48 Palestinian domestic life. Each element addresses the main issues that Palestinians face in their daily lives: negotiating their interpretation of history (Abu-Lughod and Sa'di 2007: 21, Jayyusi 2007: 118), dealing with a troubled/occupied space (Kanaaneh and Nusair 2010) and claiming for themselves a voice that is often ignored (Humphries and Khalili 2007; Sayigh 2007; Abu-Lughod 2010). I argue that the critics of this song, iconoclasts who think that rap doesn't deserve scholarly attention or committed supporters of the resistance movement who argue that it is impossible to decontextualize aspects of Palestinian life from occupation, have overlooked a narrative linking domestic life to nationalist narratives. In the context of a national struggle where land disputes converge with fertility statistics, the house and tree, the backwards narrative momentum and the trapped female voice amount to a perhaps irreconcilable rupture between citizenship, resistance and homemaking.

Over the course of DAM's career, the group have varied the object of their critique, from the State of Israel's military machine, to specific Israeli policies and cultural tropes that deny Palestinian claims to the land, to Palestinian society itself. DAM have disturbed audiences by articulating social problems that decouple domestic life from the occupation. But in a sophisticated reflexivity that is clearly, if perhaps even reductively reliant on a resistance discourse, DAM have shed the identity of a purely oppositional entity and have bound the domestic to the national effectively. DAM have highlighted domestic problems and have perhaps implied that those problems might be an additional obstacle to self-determination. In the process, they have added a layer of complexity to a context of warring essentialist nationalisms. For a population that is torn between supporting the self-determination of one government while living precariously under another (Kanaaneh and Nusair 2010), 'If I Could Go Back in Time' offers a rather spectacular portrait of the constant tug between land, house and nation for a female population doubly demoted in the vertical power relations of Israel-Palestine.

NOTES

1. 'DAM Featuring AMAL MURKUS – If I Could Go Back In Time,' YouTube, accessed 19 December 2017, www.youtube.com.
2. For Abu-Lughod and Mikdashi's article, see: 'DAM featuring AMAL MURKUS - If I Could Go Back In Time,' YouTube, accessed 19 December 2017, www.youtube.com.

For DAM's response, see Tamer Nafar, Suhell Nafar and Mahmoud Jrery (DAM), 'DAM Responds: On Tradition and the Anti-politics of the Machine', *Jadaliyya,* accessed 19 December 2017, www jadaliyya.com.

3.   A great deal of research about the now-secure genre of global hip-hop transpires in online media, and so while DAM do not seem to have suffered a loss of concert audiences (I most recently saw them perform in London in November 2014), the controversy and negative publicity online reveals a trend by which reputation and concert ticket sales offer contradictory evidence of what constitutes critical and commercial success.

4.   Compelling expressions abound that describe adeptly the general state of being for '48 Palestinians, of residing in one nation and identifying with another, such as: 'I'm from here, but I'm not from here' (Kassem 2010: 97) and 'Living and not living in the State of Israel' (Nusair 2010: 76).

5.   The first page of an internet search reveals the following reference in the popular press from the United Arab Emirates and the United States: Alex Ritman. 'Palestinian Rap Group DAM Reach for the Moon,' *The National,* accessed 19 December 2017, www.thenational.ae; 'Pioneering Palestinian Rappers DAM Drop Second Album', *XXL Mag,* accessed 19 December 2017, www.xxl.mag.com.

6.   When the song came out, scholarship about the 'Arab Spring' was still developing, so for lack of extensive analysis, Palestine was often considered the paradigm in the popular media: Ted Swedenburg, 'Hip-Hop of the Revolution (the Sharif Don't Like it)', *Middle East Research and Information Project,* accessed 19 December 2017, www .merip.org.

7.   The majority of this population resides in the Galilee or in Greater Tel Aviv, with residents of East Jerusalem counting as permanent residents, but not citizens. Three small, disparate parties (that sometimes unite on a joint list) represent the population in parliament, although Druze and Bedouin maintain their own separate voting patterns.

8.   This is a characteristic of Israel's fractious population: there are four separate school systems in Israel, broken down along ethnoreligious lines. Ultra-Orthodox, religious Zionist, secular and Arab children all study (and socialize) separately.

9.   Since some '48 Palestinians boycott general elections, their collective political power remains low relative to their demographic power.

10. This will be a common thread throughout this chapter and scholarly literature about being a '48 Palestinian deals with it directly. Individual chapters as well as complete volumes (Kanaaneh and Nusair 2010) examine being 'displaced at home', 'refugees at home' or 'excluded at home'.

11. In contrast to the positive connotation of the term 'collaboration projects' in Israeli music, the term 'collaborator' is undesirable as a label in the Occupied Territories; authorities in the West Bank and Gaza often execute people accused of cooperating with the Israeli government .

12. '48 Palestinians do not serve in the military; the Israeli defense minister ran on a platform of forcing them to sign loyalty oaths to the state in 2009, and the Israeli political right often discusses 'land swaps' or trading Arab villages for Jewish settlements in a final status agreement.

13. However, many Israelis would argue that this is a common type of ethnicity marker for Jewish migrants as well, who are described by their 'Edah' or national origins.

14. 'Min Irhabi-DAM', YouTube, accessed 19 December 2017, www.youtube.com.

15. '48 Palestinian rap is well represented by female rappers, such as Abir Zinati and Safa Hathoot.
16. 'DAM, "Born Here", Hebrew/Arabic with English Subtitles', YouTube, accessed 19 December 2017, www.youtube.com.
17. 'Arabian Knightz – Sisters ft Isam Bachiri and Shadia Mansour', YouTube, accessed 19 December 2017, www.youtube.com.
18. The gender parity mentioned previously is exclusive to '48 Palestinian rappers. Across the Green Line in the West Bank or Gaza, everyone's civil rights, and thus perhaps women's rights all the more so, are far more curtailed.
19. This position is dominant on the internet, even among feminist activists.
20. Isabelle Humphries and Laleh Khalili explain that even threat of rape in 1948 was an effective tool that emptied Palestinian villages; the threat to male kin was strong enough to dictate mass flight (2007: 210).
21. I use the Palestinian terminology here for the sake of expedience and clarity, without engaging in a personal political commentary on the contested interpretations of historical events.
22. See Morris and Black (1991) for an explanation of the Sabra and Shatila massacre, during which time the Israeli military turned a blind eye to the massacre of perhaps several thousand refugees by partisan fighters in the Lebanese civil war (official statistics are generally contested).
23. After Yasser Arafat expressed support for Saddam Hussein in 1990 when the latter invaded Kuwait, the Palestinian population in Kuwait was expelled (Lang 2005: 223, fn 28).
24. In the story, Said and his wife travel to Haifa to visit their old house after the border has been opened in 1967 to allow relative freedom of movement to Palestinians. Said cannot go through with the visit, and when his wife rings the bell, she recoils in horror as she realizes that the baby who was left behind in the chaos of 1948 is fully grown, standing in front of her wearing an Israeli military uniform.
25. Trees, seeds and other plants that grow from the earth dominate Palestinian and Israeli imagery (Humphries and Khalili 2007: 226, fn 21).
26. See Genesis 22 for the liminal motif as applied to Abraham; Genesis 28 as applied to Jacob; and Exodus 3 for Moses.

REFERENCES

Abdo, Nahla. 2004. 'Honour Killing, Patriarchy, and the State: Women in Israel', in Shahrzad Mojab and Nahla Abdo (eds), *Violence in the Name of Honour: Theoretical and Political Challenges.* Istanbul: Istanbul Bilgi University Press, pp. 57–90.
Abu-Lughod, Lila. 2002. 'Do Muslim Women Really Need Saving? Anthropological Reflections on Cultural Relativism and its Others', *American Anthropologist* 104(3): 783–90.
———. 2010. 'Foreword', in Rhoda Ann Kanaaneh and Isis Nuseir (eds), *Displaced at Home: Ethnicity and Gender among Palestinians in Israel.* Albany: State University of New York Press, pp. ix–xiv.
Abu-Lughod, Lila, and Maya Mikdashi. 'Tradition and the Anti-politics Machine: DAM Seduced by the "Honor Crime"', *Jadaliyya.* Retrieved 19 December 2017 from www.jadaliyya.com.

Abu-Lughod, Lila, and Ahmad Sa'di. 2007. 'Introduction: The Claims of Memory', in Ahmad Sa'di and Lila Abu-Lughod (eds), *Nakba: Palestine, 1948, and the Claims of Memory*. New York: Columbia University Press, pp. 1–24.

'Arabian Knightz – Sisters ft Isam Bachiri and Shadia Mansour', YouTube. Retrieved 19 December 2017 from www.youtube.com.

Baker, Geoffrey. 2011. *Buena Vista in the Club: Rap, Reggaetón and Revolution in Havana*. Durham, NC: Duke University Press.

Bardenstein, Carol B. 1999. 'Trees, Forests, and the Shaping of Palestinian and Israeli Collective Memory', in Mieke L. Bal, Jonathan Crewe and Leo Spitzer (eds), *Acts of Memory: Cultural Recall in the Present*. Hanover, NH: University Press of New England, pp. 148–68.

Chang, Jeff. 2007. *Can't Stop Won't Stop: A History of the Hip-Hop Generation*. London: Ebury Press.

'DAM, "Born Here", Hebrew/Arabic with English Subtitles', YouTube. Retrieved 19 December 2017 from www.youtube.com.

'DAM featuring AMAL MURKUS – If I Could Go Back in Time', YouTube. Retrieved 19 December 2017 from www.youtube.com.

Durand, Alain-Philippe (ed.). 2002. *Black, Blanc, Beur: Rap Music and Hip Hop in the Francophone World*. Lanham, MD: Scarecrow Press.

Eqeiq, Amal. 2010. 'Louder than the Blue ID: Palestinian Hip-Hop in Israel', in Rhoda Ann Kanaaneh and Isis Nuseir (eds), *Displaced at Home: Ethnicity and Gender among Palestinians in Israel*. Albany: State University of New York Press, pp. 53–71.

Fernandes, Sujatha. 2011. *Close to the Edge: In Search of the Global Hip Hop Generation*. New York: Verso Press.

Herzfeld, Michael. 1997. *Cultural Intimacy: Social Poetics in the Nation-State*. London: Routledge.

Humphries, Isabelle, and Laleh Khalili. 2007. 'Gender of Nakba Memory', in Ahmad Sa'di and Lila Abu-Lughod (eds), *Nakba: Palestine, 1948, and the Claims of Memory*. New York: Columbia University Press, pp. 207–28.

Jayyusi, Lena. 2007. 'Iterability, Cumulativity, and Presence: The Relational Figures of Palestinian Memory', in Ahmad Sa'di and Lila Abu-Lughod (eds), *Nakba: Palestine, 1948, and the Claims of Memory*. New York: Columbia University Press, pp. 107–34.

Kanaaneh, Roha Ann, and Isis Nusair. 2010. 'Introduction', in Rhoda Ann Kanaaneh and Isis Nuseir (eds), *Displaced at Home: Ethnicity and Gender among Palestinians in Israel*. Albany: State University of New York Press, pp. 1–18.

Kanafani, Ghassan. 1970. 'Return to Haifa', In *Palestine's Children*. London: Heinemann, pp. 149–196.

Kassem, Fatma. 2010. 'Counter-memory: Palestinian Women Naming Historical Events', in Rhoda Ann Kanaaneh and Isis Nuseir (eds), *Displaced at Home: Ethnicity and Gender among Palestinians in Israel*. Albany: State University of New York Press, pp. 93–108.

Khalidi, Rashid. 1997. *Palestinian Identity: the Construction of Modern National Consciousness*. New York: Columbia University Press.

Lang, Sharon. 2005. *Sharaf Politics: Honor and Peacemaking in Israeli-Palestinian Society*. New York: Routledge.

Mahmood, Saba. 2005. *Politics of Piety: The Islamic Revival and the Feminist Subject*. Princeton: Princeton University Press.

Massad, Joseph. 2005. 'Liberating Songs: Palestine Put to Music', in Rebecca L. Stein and Ted Swedenburg (eds), *Palestine, Israel and the Politics of Popular Culture.* Durham, NC: Duke University Press, pp. 175–201.

McClary, Susan. 1990. *Feminine Endings: Music, Gender and Sexuality.* Minneapolis: University of Minnesota Press.

McDonald, David A. 2009a. 'Poetics and the Performance of Violence in Israel/Palestine', *Ethnomusicology* 53(1): 58–85.

——. 2009b. 'Carrying Words Like Weapons: Hip-Hop and the Poetics of Palestinian Identities in Israel', *Min-Ad: Israeli Studies in Musicology* 7(2): 116–30.

——. 2013. *My Voice is My Weapon: Music, Nationalism, and the Poetics of Palestinian Resistance.* Durham, NC: Duke University Press.

'Min Irhabi-DAM', YouTube. Retrieved 19 December 2017 from www.youtube.com.

Morris, Benny. 2008. *1948: A History of the First Arab-Israeli War.* New Haven: Yale University Press.

Morris, Benny, and Ian Black. 1991. *Israel's Secret Wars: The Untold Story of Israeli Intelligence.* London: Hamish Hamilton.

Nafar, Tamer, Suhell Nafar and Mahmoud Jrery (DAM). 'DAM Responds: On Tradition and the Anti-politics of the Machine', *Jadaliyya.* Retrieved 19 December 2017 from www.jadaliyya.com.

Nooshin, Laudan. 2011. 'Hip-Hop Tehran: Migrating Styles, Musical Meanings, Marginalized Voices', in Jason Toynbee and Byron Dueck (eds), *Migrating Music.* London: Routledge, pp. 92–111.

Nusair, Isis. 2010. 'Gendering the Narratives of Three Generations of Palestinian Women in Israel', in Rhoda Ann Kanaaneh and Isis Nuseir (eds), *Displaced at Home: Ethnicity and Gender among Palestinians in Israel.* Albany: State University of New York Press, pp. 75–92.

'Pioneering Palestinian Rappers DAM Drop Second Album', *XXL Mag.* Retrieved 19 December 2017 from www.xxl.mag.com.

Rabinowitz, Dan, and Khawla Abu-Baker. 2005. *Coffins on Our Shoulders: The Experience of the Palestinian Citizens of Israel.* Berkeley: University of California Press.

Regev, Motti, and Edwin Seroussi. 2004. *Popular Music and National Culture in Israel.* Berkeley: University of California Press.

Ritman, Alex. 'Palestinian Rap Group DAM Teach for the Moon', *The National.* Retrieved 19 December 2017 from www.thenational.ae.

Rose, Tricia. 1994. *Black Noise: Rap Music and Black Culture in Contemporary America.* Middletown, CT: Wesleyan University Press.

Sa'di, Ahmad, and Lila Abu-Lughod (eds). 2007. *Nakba: Palestine, 1948, and the Claims of Memory.* New York: Columbia University Press.

Sayigh, Rosemary. 1996. 'Researching Gender in a Palestinian Camp: Political, Theoretical and Methodological Problems', in Deniz Kandiyoti (ed.), *Gendering the Middle East: Emerging Perspectives.* London: I.B. Tauris, pp. 145–67.

——. 2007. 'Women's Nakba Stories: Between Being and Knowing', in Ahmad Sa'di and Lila Abu-Lughod (eds), *Nakba: Palestine, 1948, and the Claims of Memory.* New York: Columbia University Press, pp. 135–60.

Shafir, Gershon, and Yoav Peled. 2002. *Being Israeli: The Dynamics of Multiple Citizenship.* Cambridge: Cambridge University Press.

Shalhoub-Kevorkian, Nadera. 2011. '"It is up to Her": Rape and the Re-victimization of Palestinian Women in Multiple Legal Systems', *Social Difference* 1: 30–45.

Shulz, Helena Lindholm. 2003. *The Palestinian Diaspora: Formation of Identities and Politics of Homeland.* New York: Routledge.

Stokes, Martin. 2010. *The Republic of Love: Cultural Intimacy in Turkish Popular Music.* Chicago: University of Chicago Press.

Swedenburg, Ted. 2013. 'Palestinian Rap: Against the Struggle Paradigm', in Walid El Hamamsy and Mounira Soliman (eds), *Popular Culture in the Middle East and North Africa: A Postcolonial Outlook.* London: Routledge, pp. 17–32.

——. 'Hip-Hop of the Revolution (the Sharif Don't Like it)", *Middle East Research and Information Project.* Retrieved 19 December 2017 from www.merip.org.

Tawil-Souri, Helga. 2011. 'The Necessary Politics of Palestinian Cultural Studies', in Tarik Sabry (ed.), *Arab Cultural Studies: Mapping the Field.* London: I.B. Tauris, pp. 137–61.

Terkourafi, Marina (ed.). 2010. *Languages of Global Hip-Hop.* London: Continuum International Publications Group.

Turner, Victor. 1967. *The Forest of Symbols: Aspects of Ndembu Ritual.* Ithaca, NY: Cornell University Press.

Van Gennep, Arnold. 1907. *The Rites of Passage.* London: Routledge.

Yuval-Davis, Nira. 1997. *Gender & Nation.* London: Sage Publications.

CHAPTER 6

MY MALUKU MANISE

Managing Desire and Despair in the Diaspora

NICOLA FROST

Introduction

One of the purposes of this collection is to begin to disentangle the multiple meanings and implications of 'home' as a commonsense, yet under-investigated term. As other chapters also make clear, understandings of home are multiple, contingent, and socially and historically situated. This is especially evident, and arguably particularly important, for those at a distance from where they consider 'home' to be. This chapter considers the case of a small group of migrants living in Sydney, Australia, who identify with the region of Maluku in eastern Indonesia. Diverse in terms of their age, background, migration history and more, all were living in Sydney in 1999 when fierce ethnoreligious conflict erupted in Maluku. Bloody communal battles pitted Christians against Muslims and indigenous Moluccans against incomers. The violence continued for several years, and left thousands dead and tens of thousands homeless. From being voluntary migrants from a peaceful backwater, Sydney Moluccans became overnight involuntary exiles from a conflict zone. The Maluku they had left, or the one they remembered, had changed suddenly and dramatically in their absence.

This chapter explores aspects of the polarized images of Maluku shared by many Sydney migrants – a memory of Maluku as a peaceful, beautiful idyll, alongside a new narrative of bloodshed, terror and insecurity. In seeking other locations for sentimental images of Maluku, it examines depictions of nostalgia, loss, family and place in the lyrics of traditional Moluccan folk songs. A number of these have been adapted, or simply given new significance, by the recent violence, underlining the parallels between responses to homesickness and physical displacement, and the trauma of bereavement or homelessness as a result of conflict. The chapter also draws on an ethnographic account of an immigration tribunal hearing in Sydney involving a Moluccan family. It details the painful process of objectifying a previously implicit 'home' for the purposes of asylum. The particular history of Maluku and its relationship with the Indonesian state and with others, long before the recent conflict, have an important bearing on how Sydney Moluccans were affected by their change in circumstances. However, there are some more general points to consider. The distinction Eric Hobsbawm delineates between a private, personal 'home' of (migrant) memory and a public 'homeland' of political and historical narrative is useful in this sense.

Maluku, Indonesia and Australia

'Maluku' as referred to here and as used by Moluccans[1] in Sydney denotes an arc of islands in eastern Indonesia between the larger landmasses of Sulawesi to the west and New Guinea to the east. With an area of 850,000 km,[2] 90 per cent of which is sea, it stretches from Makian in the north, near the border with the Philippines, to the southern islands of Tanimbar, just 500 kilometres from the Australian coast. The name 'Maluku' corresponded with the Indonesian provincial boundary until October 1999, when the new province of Maluku Utara (North Maluku) was created, encompassing all the Moluccan islands north of Seram. The name 'Maluku', in its vernacular rather than administrative sense, continues to be used to refer to the region covered by both provinces.

Maluku played a central role in the precolonial history of the region, but especially in the story of European trade and colonization, and the more recent narrative of Indonesian nationalist awakening and struggle. The Spice Islands of European legend, home to valuable clove and nutmeg trees, Maluku has a long and colourful history of contact with outside interests, despite its liminal position within the Indonesian archipelago, a thousand miles from Jakarta (Andaya 1993). The scent of valuable spices wafting across the Banda Sea has attracted Indian, Malay and Arab traders to Maluku for over a millennium (Donkin 2003). The first Europeans to reach the islands were the Portuguese and Spanish, whose ships arrived in Maluku early in the sixteenth century, at a time when Islam was already rapidly spreading throughout the north and central regions. These Catholic adventurers were closely followed by Dutch traders, who established some of the earliest outposts of the Dutch East India Company in the region. Protestant missionaries, following soon after, claimed substantial numbers for their flock, especially in central Maluku. The early years of European involvement in Maluku were extremely oppressive, resulting in some violent clashes over the control of the spice trade (Chauvel 1990: 25).[2] However, Christian Moluccans were given preferential access to Dutch education and generally benefited more from colonial rule than their Muslim neighbours.

Christian Ambonese soldiers were considered excellent and loyal fighters, and were a valued part of the Dutch colonial force KNIL. Roy Ellen describes this as a 'double irony': the very people who had suffered so badly at the hands of the Dutch subsequently became so closely linked with colonial interests that they were considered by other Indonesians as 'no better than hacks and lackeys' (Ellen 1983: 11). In view of this ambivalent relationship with the Dutch colonists, it is hardly surprising that Maluku's relationship with the Indonesian state has also been a troubled one. Although some Moluccans were notably active in the republican movement (van Kaam 1980), many regarded the prospect of forming part of a majority Muslim independent Indonesia with deep suspicion, an unease that resulted in the development of a militant separatist movement. The Republic of South Maluku (Republik Maluku Selatan or RMS) was declared in 1950 by a group largely comprised of ex-KNIL soldiers and was quickly suppressed by nationalist Indonesian forces (Chauvel 1990). The Netherlands today hosts the RMS government-in-exile, which retains a strong separatist following, not least among the now third- and fourth-generation Dutch-Moluccan youth.

Throughout the period of the New Order Maluku, subdued but apparently not forgiven, retreated to the margins of Suharto's Indonesia. Excluded from Suharto's energetic development programme – much of the population continued to rely on subsistence farming and fishing – and dominated by top-down government from Jakarta, Maluku took on an unaccustomed identity as backwater. Heavily centralized government had, until 1999 (when legislation on regional autonomy was passed), ensured that Moluccan people, like many across Indonesia, felt disenfranchised, as local systems of decision-making were dismantled in favour of a countrywide, top-down structure (Pannell 1996). The industry that did exist tended to be extractive and state-controlled from afar, with little space for local intervention (Frost 2001; Laksono 2002). With economic survival reliant to such an extent on state favour, government posts were naturally at a premium. The Muslim population gradually increased in relation to the Christians, thanks to a higher birth rate and migration from other areas (some of it state-initiated). The Southeast Asian economic crisis began to bite, and competition for economic and political resources became severe.

Most commentators see these factors as the underlying source of the recent violence that has gripped Maluku (van Klinken 1999). In early 1999, a simple argument on a bus in Ambon city sparked widespread violence and plunged Maluku into a bloody conflict, pitting Christians against their Muslim neighbours, and autochthonous Moluccans against migrants. Up to 10,000 people died and around 700,000 people – almost a third of the population – fled their homes (International Crisis Group 2002). The violence extended even to outlying islands and remote villages. Although local economic and political issues provided the initial grounds for discontent, it is widely accepted that external elements, among them a Muslim *jihad* force, Christian gang-leaders, and the Indonesian government and security forces themselves, were involved in precipitating and prolonging the conflict. One response from some (largely Christian) quarters was the emergence of a modern version of the RMS movement, the Moluccan Sovereignty Front (Front Kedaulatan Maluku), drawing on a renewed sense of domination and betrayal by the centre, and reawakening memories of the separatist struggle.

Regarding Maluku

There were around sixty people identifying as of Moluccan heritage in Sydney in 2002, all of whom had arrived in Sydney before the conflict began.[3] They were a very diverse group, ranging in age from small children to octogenarians, both Christians and Muslims (though the majority were Christian), some with Australian postgraduate degrees and others with only a basic education and a slight knowledge of English. The migrants had a range of reasons for moving to Australia, though most were either educational or economic. They also had highly varied periods of residency, from a few months to many decades – some had become Australian citizens, while others had no formal immigration status. Importantly, several of those who identified themselves as Moluccan had not lived for any length of time in Maluku; some had never even visited, growing up with Moluccan parents elsewhere in Indonesia and speaking no Moluccan language.

Before the conflict, few of these diverse Moluccans knew each other and even fewer were politically active. Immediately following the initial outbreak of violence in early 1999, a handful of people joined forces to form a formal organization for Sydney-based Moluccans, Ikabema (Ikatan Keluarga Besar Maluku, literally the Association of the Large Family of Maluku), advertising its establishment via one of the Indonesian-language radio stations in the city in order to spread the word to those not already known to the founders. Eventually involving around forty adults, Ikabema was formed partly as a source of mutual support for expatriates, but principally as a – firmly nonpartisan – vehicle for facilitating fundraising to support those affected by the conflict, and for organizing advocacy and awareness-raising of events in Maluku aimed at the Australian authorities and public. Its establishment made possible a series of public demonstrations and representations to parliamentarians, as well as a close working relationship with the Uniting Church, which had a strong humanitarian interest in the conflict in Maluku.

In Sydney, Moluccans talked about Maluku in two sharply contrasting ways. On the one hand, Maluku was a place to be longed for: beautiful, peaceful and essentially innocent. This was the Maluku of childhood memory or family legend. Maluku was a mythical 'land of ease', characterized by beautiful islands, idyllic beaches, plentiful seafood, charming singing and close family, and fragranced by the scent of the cloves and nutmeg that gave the Spice Islands their name. Here, life was simple but wholesome; no one was rich, yet no one was seriously needy either. It was also, crucially, a land of peace, where Muslims and Christians had coexisted harmoniously for centuries. Traditional rules and structures known as *adat,* regulating behaviour and use of natural resources, and organizing local government, were seen as complementing and strengthening the rule of law, and contributing to a sense of stability, even stasis.

To an extent, Sydney Moluccans' nostalgia for a timeless idyll borrows from pre-established traditions. Absence from and homesickness for a peaceful and bounteous land are a recurring theme in Moluccan music, both traditional folk songs and the thriving contemporary pop scene, especially that deriving from Ambon Island itself.[4] This probably owes something to the existence of a substantial and (at least initially) unwilling Moluccan diaspora in the Netherlands, the result of the short-lived Moluccan independence struggle in the 1950s.

A popular traditional song, much covered by contemporary recording artists, is 'Beta Belayar Jauh', or 'I Sailed Far Away'. The lyrics, very loosely translated from Ambonese Malay, are typical of the genre:

> I sailed far away
> Far from Ambon
> When I am in a foreign land, I regret that I left
> Far away from my mother's lap
>
> When will I go back to Ambon?
> Wide seas and high mountains separate us
> Mama come and take me home
> To the land that I love,
> Sweet Ambon.[5]

The 'sweet Ambon' of the final line is a literal translation of the popular Ambonese Malay epithet Ambon or Maluku Manise referred to in the title of this chapter. It is commonly used as a descriptive phrase in song lyrics, in tourist literature, on expatriate websites, etc., and is efficiently expressive of this mood of bittersweet idealizing. In imagining an archipelago of beautiful, coral-ringed islands, supporting harmonious family and community life, Sydney Moluccans were therefore connecting to a powerful, if somewhat sentimental, tradition in folk culture. In 2003 the middle-aged son of one of the earliest Moluccan migrants to Australia, who had never visited Maluku and did not speak Indonesian, wrote a play about the physical longing he felt for this unknown home: 'I want my toes in the sand. I want to walk the village', he told me. His elderly father understood this need for a physical connection, although for him this stemmed from actual experience. He recalled an old Ambonese expression: 'only the *sibu-sibu* [the quiet morning sea breeze] will calm the Ambonese' (known as they are for their hot tempers). 'At that time of day', he said, 'the sea is like glass', and he described a magical memory of being taught to swim by his own father in the still, clear water of Ambon Bay.

Such images intricately merge geographical locations with familial relationships in very personal ways. A similar process is evident in the lyrics of Moluccan folk songs. The 'Mama' in 'Beta Belayah Jauh' is both a loved individual and a cherished island. While clearly there is a common core of sentiment and imagery on which individuals draw, each set of memories and characterizations is personal and particular, referring to objective geographies, but ultimately subjective. It is an understanding of 'home' that refers directly to the external world, but that is given meaning through personal, internal associations.

In contrast to these essentalized, peaceful images, since the conflict began, for Sydney Moluccans, Maluku had become dangerous, lawless, shockingly violent and deeply divided, its innocence apparently irretrievably lost. People talked about the total destruction of villages; how they struggled to imagine, and worried that they would not recognize, a landscape that had 'become forest again'; how the city was now scarred with barricades segregating the population according to religion, so that familiar bus routes, for instance, had become impossible journeys. During this period, physical absence from Maluku was not only highlighted, but for security reasons was also made effectively involuntary. During my stay in Sydney, from 2002 to 2004, no Sydney Moluccan visited Maluku – to my knowledge, no one had made the journey since the conflict had begun. Most claimed that it was unsafe to do so, and some even suggested that relatives had warned that as expatriates who had been active in raising public and political awareness about the conflict, they might be targeted by violent militias. Although it would be inaccurate to suggest visits to Maluku were common for Sydney Moluccans before the conflict, the perceived impossibility of returning 'home' was a dramatic indicator of the devastating changes they envisioned.

I was offered this image of a ruined paradise repeatedly: any suggestion that some of Maluku's previous beauty and charm remained was swiftly rejected.[6] Henny, born and educated in Maluku before heading to university in Java, mentioned a trip she made to Maluku in 1994, as a kind of formal leavetaking before she left Indonesia for Australia. She said she was glad she visited then, before everything was destroyed, in the way that one would be thankful for visiting an elderly relative before their decline into senility. It was as if the old Maluku was dead for her.

The bittersweet pain of physical absence from an idealized Maluku, as exemplified in traditional folk songs like the one quoted above and experienced by Sydney Moluccans, had a dark twin in the powerful sense of loss felt by those affected by the conflict. This too was reflected in the lyrics of songs written or adapted by survivors. In these songs, the images of gentle beauty and innocence have been replaced with depictions of violence and destruction. A direct contrast is often made between a previous paradise and a blood-soaked present. But there are numerous parallels. The songs remain essentially laments for a lost home (whether figurative or concrete) and the suffering that entails. They retain the fluid interaction between person and place. The fact that many of these songs adapt – or simply attribute new meaning to – pre-existing lyrics underlines the parallels, as well as the subtle shifts. One example is a 2001 recording of the well-known Ambonese song 'Sio Mama' ('Oh Mama'), written in Ambonese Malay in 1985 and originally intended as a tribute to a beloved mother. The English translation provided with the recording reads as follows:

Many years ago
When I was still young
I remember back to those days
When my dear Mama carried me

As Mama cooked the sago cakes
She sang me to sleep, caressing me
Even now that I am grown up
I will still never forget Mama

Oh Mama
I long to return home
Oh Mama
Mama you look so frail
I haven't been able to repay you Mama
For all your hard work
Oh all those past years
Oh, Dear Lord Jesus
Please take care of my Mama

Dearest Mama
We were separated for many years

How time flies! It's hard to realize I've grown up
When I think back on my childhood;
Your loving care and protection
Hugging me with your loving embrace
Dearest Mama
Your love could never be repaid
I long to see your face again Mama
Which is growing older
Dearest Mama,
I can only lift my prayers
Dear Lord, please take care of my beloved Mama.

The sleeve notes from the CD (*Hearts of Faith: Songs of the Suffering Church*, produced by an Australian Christian humanitarian organization) claim:

> this song has become an anthem for the hundreds of children who are either orphaned or separated from their parents because of what has happened in Maluku . . . it is particularly special to those from Ambon, who also refer to their home town as Mama Ambon.

A personal lament for a dead mother has therefore apparently become both a collective expression of grief and loss for separated families, and a more general eulogy for a place now transformed so dramatically as to no longer exist in the imagination of its inhabitants.

Another example traces some slightly different shifts between conceptions of home and expressions of loss. 'Goodbye My Village' was based on a poem composed in 1902 by a Dutch missionary, apparently as he prepared to return home to Holland after living in the village of Duma, on the island of Halmahera, in North Maluku. The poem was set to music in the 1950s, at which point presumably it expressed the homesickness of Duma villagers living elsewhere or, more generally, reflected the reflexive mood of a region in the aftermath of unsuccessful separatist struggle. In June 2000, Duma was the site of a violent attack that left at least 200 Christians dead (International Crisis Group 2000). According to the *Hearts of Faith* sleeve notes, the song was performed in Duma by displaced survivors, returning temporarily to bury family members:

Goodbye my village and my beloved homeland
Oh my village – Oh my village
I love you like a mist
Instantly it evaporates, and likewise
I disappear from your sight

Oh my homeland, oh my village
I love you. What a pity today

I leave my greetings
Goodbye my home and my beloved family
Oh my beloved Father and Mother
I am leaving you now
I give my farewell greetings to you
Goodbye everyone
One day we will meet in my Father's home.

All three contexts for this song deal with physical distance to some extent, though clearly its use to mark the trauma and sorrow of a massacre (and therefore the decision by survivors to abandon the village) adds an additional layer of significance. Both traditional nostalgic folk songs, and those given a new context by recent conflict, conflate physical absence and personal loss, to a certain extent, and situate both at the heart of Moluccan culture. Taken together, they also reflect the polarized images of paradise and destruction so apparent in Sydney Moluccans' characterizations. Of course, the experience and perspective of Maluku residents and those of nonresidents should not be confused. As an introductory editorial to an issue of *Public Culture* notes: 'diasporas always leave a trail of collective memory about another place and time and create new maps of desire and of attachment' (The Editors and Editorial Community 1989). Yet the parallels between physical remove and emotional alienation are to an extent revealing.

As the accounts of these songs indicate, changes in perceptions of home are heavily contingent on personal circumstances. The varying ways in which people represent their ideas of home to others is similarly dependent on context. The following section seeks to explore the ways in which the contrasting images of Maluku operate in practice for Moluccans in Sydney, in particular as part of the often-painful process of representing the situation in Maluku to those not closely involved. In this case, the context is a particularly formal and rigid one. It follows a Moluccan family's representations to a refugee review tribunal and examines the effects of the bureaucratic requirement to reconcile emotional attachment with political reality.

Tribunal

It is October 2003. The immigration tribunal is held in a bright modern building in the central business district of Sydney. Win Liemena has arrived early. She sits outside in the sunshine and smiles a greeting, but her face is shining with tears. Her family joins her and we travel up in the lift to level 29, admiring the view of the sparkling harbour but saying little. Win and her young son came to Australia from Maluku in 1997 with her husband Harry. A talented computer scientist and university lecturer in Maluku, Harry had won a scholarship to study for a Master's degree in Sydney. With a degree in soil science, but at that time rather uncertain English, Win concentrated on raising her son, planning to return to her career when their stay in Australia was over.

In April 1998, Harry was involved in an appalling road accident. He survived, but was seriously brain damaged and was left epileptic, partially paralysed, and requiring constant care and specialist medication. He was in hospital for months: 'everything changed', Win explained. At that time pregnant with their second child, she suddenly had to take charge of the family's affairs, find work and deal with the immigration authorities. The family remained in Australia on Harry's student visa until it expired, then applied for leave to remain on medical grounds, without success. Since Maluku was by this time a conflict zone, the Liemenas then filed an asylum claim, on the basis of having become refugees 'sur place' during their absence.[7] This initial application was unsuccessful, but the family had appealed. The Refugee Review Tribunal hearing that was about to take place was, barring ministerial intervention, the final stage of appeal.

We are ushered into the hearing room and are joined by the Liemenas' friend, Helena Marchant. Helena was born and grew up in Maluku, and is married to an Australian. She has not visited Maluku since she left Indonesia some thirty years ago, but keeps in close contact with her family there, in particular her sister, with whom she lost touch for six anxious months at the height of the conflict. Helena is here to testify as a witness to conditions in Maluku. Waving away the offer of an interpreter, she explains about her sister's experience, displaced by the fighting and still, more than four years after the violence began, unable to return home. She brandishes a sheaf of foreign travel advisories from the Australian and U.K. governments (recommending their citizens avoid all travel to Maluku) and a clutch of newspaper articles, which, she says, demonstrate how unstable Maluku continues to be. Indeed, she claims, since the Bali bombings in October 2002, nowhere in Indonesia is safe. The atmosphere is very tense and most people are crying. Harry rocks to and fro, and uses handfuls of tissues. Win kicks him distractedly under the table. The children look upset and cuddle each other.

Win does not have much to add – all the detailed information is already in the files. 'If Ambon was like when we left I'd go home tomorrow', she had told me earlier. But the Liemenas' house on Pattimura University campus in Ambon was destroyed in the violence, and the university itself, heavily targeted by rioters and looters, is barely functioning. She also notes that ethnic differences have become the focus of violent and discriminatory behaviour in Maluku; the fact that Harry is of Chinese descent, while Win is an indigenous central Moluccan and that therefore theirs is a 'mixed' marriage, could also now prove difficult. Besides, the family's own circumstances have of course changed dramatically. Harry is dependent on medication to control his epilepsy that Win says cannot be reliably obtained in Ambon. Added to this, she suggests, mental disability is not viewed sympathetically in Indonesia and Harry could be subject to discrimination for that reason.

The member hearing the case sums up the relevant details. He emphasizes Harry's medical condition and the potential grounds for asylum on the basis of the lack of medical care available in Indonesia as a whole, and of the discrimination someone as disabled as Harry could face. A decision is postponed for a month pending further details of the facilities available in Indonesia and an updated medical report for Harry.[8] As we stand to leave, the member turns to Helena and says that he visited Ambon once in the 1980s; he was in the armed forces and was visiting the Allied War Cemetery there. 'It's a very beautiful island', he remembers. Helena says quickly, blinking away tears: 'It used to be beautiful, it's true, but not now. Now everything is destroyed.'

* * *

The tribunal hearing described above threw into relief some of the different ways in which the idea of home resonated for Helena, the Liemenas and other Moluccans in Sydney during the conflict. Indeed, 'home' is here notable by its absence from the narrative. Both Helena and Win are largely silent about what home means to them, how much they love it and miss it, and how devastated they are by its destruction. The format of the tribunal hearing, and the grounds on which an appeal may be judged successful, require participants to emphasize the objective deficiencies of Maluku, while omitting the more subjective, emotionally charged story of (be)longing and exile. This process of disconnection is *in itself* a painful and difficult one, but it does at least provide some kind of emotional protection. Once the formal business is completed, the member hearing the case tries to leaven the atmosphere with a brighter comment – Ambon is a beautiful island. But Helena refused to accept this shift into a more personal register; it used to be beautiful, but now it is all destroyed, she insists.

Theorizing Home and Homeland

Writing about the relationship of diasporic Croatians in Canada with a newly independent Croatia, Daphne Winland focuses on the tensions inherent in a shift between victimhood and citizenship, and between exile and émigré (Winland 2002). She describes the ambivalence felt by many of her diasporic informants at a move from self-characterization as displaced victims of conflict to reimagining themselves as citizens of a new and not entirely blameless Croatian state. Looking beyond a static triad of home, host and diaspora, she examines emerging tensions and discord within and across these boundaries. She describes the difficulties of this changing relationship with 'home' in terms of oscillation between desire and disdain. As she is careful to point out, different people might lean more heavily towards one or the other, and the balance might shift according to the context.

Moluccans in Sydney similarly experienced a dramatic change in the political situation at 'home' during their time in Australia. For many of them, the shift was between voluntary (and often temporary) migration from a much-loved home, and involuntary and apparently indefinite exile from a place destroyed by violence, segregation and distrust. For those who had more distant links with Maluku as a physical location, but who considered being Moluccan an important aspect of their identity, the sense of destruction, of dismantling of constants, existed more in the imagination. For both of these groups, in contrast with the Croatian example, rather than desire and disdain, the poles were perhaps more properly desire and despair, so comprehensive was the sense of annihilation and transformation following the conflict.

However, it is not correct to suggest that one impression (despair) has simply replaced the other (desire). In one sense, obviously, the Maluku of death, destruction and terror was more immediate in the years following the outbreak of violence, dominating any political action and, of course, asylum claims like the Liemenas'. And yet the Maluku of sparkling seas and fragrant spices remained a current and powerful narrative that was shared and reinvigorated at social gatherings, through preparing traditional food, or playing and singing folk songs like the ones described earlier. One young man, living in Melbourne, was an energetic campaigner and fundraiser during the conflict, drawing wider public attention to the political situation in Maluku while helping support victims. As part of this work, he maintained a website with news reports and data on the conflict, which was intended as an archive project for future researchers. He was therefore more fully aware than most of the terror and destruction spreading across the region. Even when it had become safe to do so, he explained that he was unwilling to return to Maluku to visit, saying that he wanted to preserve the image he had in his head, not dislodged after months of gruesome news reports, of Maluku as a peaceful and beautiful place.

For this young man, a peaceful, beautiful Maluku could in some sense coexist alongside extensive exposure to a violent, chaotic one. The 'Maluku as peaceful paradise' and 'Maluku as lawless hellhole' narratives apparently belong to different registers, appearing both to coincide and contradict. In a similar way, Winland notes that, however disaffected members of the diaspora became with homeland Croatians, this did not interrupt the continued romanticization of Croatia the country, with its glorious heritage and beautiful landscape. In an introduction to a journal issue on forms of exile, Eric Hobsbawm draws an important distinction between private memory and social category, differentiating between a private, individual Home (Heim) and a collective Homeland (Heimat):

> home in the literal sense, Heim, chez soi, is essentially private. Home in the wider sense, Heimat, is essentially public . . . Heim belongs to me and mine and nobody else. Anyone who has been burglarized knows the feeling of intrusion, of a private space violated. (Hobsbawm 1991: 67)

Home is linked to location, certainly, but is fundamentally relational, framed by personal memory and family history. For Helena, who we met at the tribunal earlier, home was an Ambon of which she had had no direct experience in many decades, but that burned brightly in her consciousness through memories of her childhood, and through the strong connection with her sister and other relatives. Helena claimed descent from Martha Christina Tiahahu, a celebrated Moluccan heroine who fought bravely against the Dutch colonists in the early nineteenth century. This was where she got her fierce love of Maluku: 'it's in the blood', she said. Home in this sense is of course firmly subjective, existing in the imagination. It echoes the interlacing of kin relations with physical location that we saw in the Moluccan folk music tradition.

The idea of homeland (or Heimat), by contrast, has far broader frames of reference: it is shared by many more people and is therefore necessarily objectified – dislocated from the elements that make meaning for individuals. As Hobsbawm has it:

> Heimat is by definition collective. It cannot belong to us as individuals. We belong to it because we don't want to be alone. Moreover, it doesn't need us. It goes on quite well without us, which is the tragedy of political exile. (Hobsbawm 1991: 67)

Homelands are defined to a greater extent than is 'home' by external, geographical boundaries – as Nicole Constable puts it, they are objective places rather than situated spaces (Constable 2002). Family lore and personal memory make way for collective histories and narratives of origin, sovereignty and struggle. In the case of Maluku, these narratives include understandings of traditional *adat* authority, accounts of Maluku's relationship with its colonial masters, and its struggle for recognition vis-à-vis emergent Indonesian nationalism. Identification with a distant homeland can have a more socially or politically derived basis than a personal evocation of home and therefore can encompass a range of subjectivities. Sydney Moluccans from very different backgrounds therefore found ways to engage with the idea of a Moluccan homeland.

Before the conflict, everyone who identified as 'Moluccan' in Sydney had of course a firm – if largely implicit – impression of a personal home, composed of private memories, family stories, ethnic heritage and experience of localities. The idea of 'being Moluccan' in any public sense in Sydney had not seemed relevant until the formation of Ikabema; although some individuals knew each other, often through family connections that pre-dated migration, these relationships remained personal and essentially private. Throughout the conflict and its aftermath, Ikabema has provided a public, collective focus for individuals' sense of commitment to and responsibility for action to alleviate the crisis in Maluku.

The conflict therefore brought people together in a way that facilitated political and humanitarian action. Crucially, however, it also engendered a more self-conscious collective identification with Maluku-as-homeland. Those for whom being Moluccan was a family issue, without broader political or ethnic resonance, began to make connections between contemporary events and their own position with regard, for example, to the revived question of Moluccan independence. For Yopie Latul, for example, with significant figures from both sides of the debate in his family, the conflict prompted something of a political awakening, during which he researched the history of the separatist struggle and came down on the side of the secessionists. This new Moluccan identity was crystallized *through* the conflict and produced an awareness of the homeland that was distinct from individual images of home.

Hobsbawm's characterization of Heim and Heimat in terms of sentiment, and in particular his use of those terms, now overburdened with additional significance, recalls the nineteenth-century Romantic understanding of Heimat as an unspoiled rural idyll, as a contrast with or a haven from an urbanising, modernizing world.[9] This has some resonance with regard to Maluku, which has been at certain points in history both a unique and globally significant centre, and the ultimate periphery, the quintessential place of exile (Ellen 1983; Frost 2005). Even during the height of the spice trade, the islands' remoteness contributed to the exoticism of the spices growing there, as well as to their value. The Moluccan islands continued to be considered by the Javanese establishment not only as geographically distant, but also as sufficiently culturally alien that exile there represented complete disconnection from civilization. In some cases this was characterized simply as a vacuum – an absence of political sensibility. Before Indonesia achieved independence, the young nationalist agitators Sutan Sjahrir and Mohammad Hatta, 'whose political passions the Dutch thought might be balmed by the serenity of the scene and the lovely climate' (Hanna 1978), were banished to the Banda

Islands between 1936 and 1942. In others, there was a sense that Maluku epitomized a certain brutality born of remoteness and a lack of refinement. The majority of the 2,000 graves in the Allied War Cemetery in Ambon are those of Australian servicemen who died in Japanese prisoner-of-war camps in Maluku after Japan occupied Indonesia in 1942. The novelist Pramoedya Ananta Toer is only the most celebrated of the inhabitants of the New Order penal camp on the central Moluccan island of Buru in the 1960s and 1970s.

In one sense, then, narratives of chaos and savagery during the recent conflict in Maluku chime with this impression of the region being beyond the pale. In another, however, they act to reconnect Maluku with the wider (contemporary, political) world in a way that reflects the temporal contrast between premodern rural idyll and modernizing urban centre. Characterized as a place of remove, of exile, there is a sense that Maluku's remoteness is matched with a degree of timelessness, of being outside history, effectively insulated from events in the rest of Indonesia or further afield. Certainly, living in Southeast Maluku during the widespread rioting that preceded the fall of President Suharto in 1998, I was repeatedly told 'this won't happen in Maluku, not here'. The violence that erupted just a few months later and, in particular, the direct connection that was quickly made with organized Islamic extremism throughout the region dramatically disrupted this sense of isolation from broader concerns. Obviously, the impact of the conflict was incomparably greater for Maluku residents than for those outside the region. Yet the shock of confronting Maluku's reconfiguration with relation to economic crisis, militant Islam, would-be secessionism, etc. is arguably more jarring for those comparing current reality with nostalgia-tinged memories. More than once, a Sydney Moluccan's lament for the lost innocence of pre-conflict Maluku was followed by a complaint about the amount of traffic in Ambon City nowadays. Arguably, then, the conflict could be seen less as an aberrant event and more as a particularly acute focus for a more general process of migrant mourning for a home that no longer exists.

Conclusion

For Sydney Moluccans, reconciling significant personal memories and relationships with a more objective perspective was not easy, particularly when these images diverged so sharply. The immigration tribunal hearing was a striking illustration of this. In accordance with the strictures of a legal process, Win and Helena painted a uniformly bleak picture of destruction, violence and discrimination, without mention of music, family, food and tradition. Such an occasion was bound to be emotional, but it was particularly painful to articulate the 'despair', while suppressing the 'desire'; as Arien Mack points out, home is supposed to be a place of comfort and refuge (Mack 1991).

Sydney Moluccans hold multiple, contrary and at times contradictory understandings of home. Thinking about these contrasts in terms of home and homeland provides one way to examine the effects of the conflict on this migrant group. The examples discussed here show that while the conflict had dramatic and profound effects on Sydney Moluccans' sense of identity, those effects were not unrelated to other, more commonly experienced processes of nostalgia and longing for a home distant both in time and space.

Acknowledgements

This chapter is based on fieldwork conducted in Sydney between 2002 and 2004. It was funded through an Economic and Social Research Council Research Studentship (Award number R42200134193) and a fieldwork grant from the Emslie Horniman Fund. Deep thanks are due to Ikabema members, and to Aretha Kakerissa.

Nicola Frost has a Ph.D. in Social Anthropology from Goldsmiths, University of London. She has conducted fieldwork in Indonesia, Australia and the United Kingdom, working on community organization, multiculturalism, and the cultural politics of food and festivals. She has held postdoctoral fellowships at City University London and SOAS. She recently travelled home to Devon and now works for the Devon Community Foundation, doing research, data analysis and evaluation.

NOTES

1. I use the local term Maluku rather than the colonial Moluccas, but the adjectival form Moluccan, as this reads more naturally in English.
2. See, for example, Hanna (1978) on the massacre of 1621 in Banda, Central Maluku, when Dutch troops exacted bloody retaliation following decades of resistance to colonial control. See also Zerner (1994) on the punitive *hongi* raids, aimed at protecting the nutmeg monopoly through the destruction of 'unofficial' plantations. In 1817, the celebrated Moluccan hero Pattimura led an unsuccessful rebellion against Dutch domination.
3. As official statistics obviously do not differentiate between Indonesians and Moluccans, and only consider identity based on citizenship and birthplace, this is necessarily an anecdotal estimate.
4. In some colloquial contexts, 'Ambonese' can refer more broadly to the islands and people of Central Maluku. It is sometimes used interchangeably with 'Moluccan', most often by Central Moluccans themselves. Those from other parts of Maluku will

quickly, and rightly, point out the significant cultural, linguistic, topographical and other differences in such a scattered archipelago.

5. Translated by Aretha Kakerissa.
6. I had actually visited Ambon and some of the islands in Southeast Maluku briefly in early 2001, far more recently than any of the Sydney Moluccans, but my observations did not alter the picture of total destruction and alienation.
7. *Handbook on Procedures and Criteria for Determining Refugee Status under the 1951 Convention and the 1967 Protocol relating to the Status of Refugees,* Geneva, 1979, Part One, Chapter II, paragraphs 94–96.
8. The appeal was successful and the Liemenas secured leave to remain in Australia as refugees.
9. Following this, the co-option of the term for use in Nazi ideology has lent it an essentialist, totalitarian association, despite considerable efforts to rehabilitate the concept in postwar Germany.

REFERENCES

Andaya, L. 1993. *The World of Maluku: Eastern Indonesia in the Early Modern Period.* Honolulu: University of Hawaii Press.

Chauvel, R. 1990. *Nationalists, Soldiers and Separatists: The Ambonese Islands from Colonialism to Revolt 1880–1950.* Leiden: KITLV.

Constable, N. 2002. 'At Home But Not at Home: Filipina Narratives of Ambivalent Returns', in F.V. Aguilar Jr. (ed.), *Filipinos in Global Migrations: At Home in the World?* Quezon City: Philippine Migration Research Network and Philippine Social Science Council, pp. 380–412.

Donkin, R.A. 2003. *Between East and West: The Moluccans and the Traffic in Spices up to the Arrival of Europeans.* Philadelphia: American Philosophical Society.

The Editors and Editorial Community (1989). 'Editors' Comment: On Moving Targets', *Public Culture* 2(1): i–iv.

Ellen, R.F. 1983. 'The Centre in the Periphery: Moluccan Culture in an Indonesian State', *Indonesia Circle* 31: 3–15.

Frost, N. 2001. Enabling Fictions: Politics, Representation, and the Environment in Maluku, Indonesia, Goldsmiths Anthropology Research Paper No. 5, London: Anthropology Department, Goldsmiths College.

Frost, N. 2005. 'Revisiting Centre and Periphery: Maluku in the World', *Masyarakat Indonesia* XXXI(1): 113–25.

Hanna, W.A. 1978. *Indonesian Banda: Colonialism and its Aftermath in the Nutmeg Islands.* Philadelphia: Institute for the Study of Human Issues.

Hobsbawm, E. 1991. Introduction', *Social Research* 58(1): 65–68.

International Crisis Group. 2000. *Indonesia: Overcoming Murder and Chaos in Maluku.* Jakarta/Brussels: International Crisis Group.

———. 2002. *Indonesia: The Search for Peace in Maluku.* Jakarta/Brussels: International Crisis Group.

Laksono, P.M. 2002. *The Common Ground in the Kei Islands.* Yogyakarta: Galang Press.

Mack, A. 1991. 'Editor's Introduction', *Social Research* 58(1): 311–12.

Pannell, S. 1996. PKK: The Construction of Women as Corporate Bodies and National Symbols', in D. Mearns and C. Healey (eds), *Remaking Maluku: Social Transforma-*

tion in Eastern Indonesia. Darwin: Centre for Southeast Asian Studies, Northern Territory University Press, pp. 140–155.

Svasek, M. 2002. 'Narratives of "Home" and "Homeland": The Symbolic Construction and Appropriation of the Sudeten German Heimat', *Identities: Global Studies in Culture and Power* 9(4): 495–518.

Van Kaam, B. 1980. *The South Moluccans: Background to the Train Hijackings.* London: Hurst & Co.

Van Klinken, G. 1999. 'Towards a Mapping of "at Risk" Ethnic, Religious and Political Groups in Indonesia', *Inside Indonesia Digest* 86.

Winland, D. 2002. 'The Politics of Desire and Disdain: Croatian Identity between "Home" and "Homeland"', *American Ethnologist* 29(3): 693–718.

Zerner, C. 1994. 'Through a Green Lens: The Construction of Customary Environmental Law and Community in Indonesia's Maluku Islands'. *Law & Society Review* 28(5): 1079–1121.

CHAPTER 7

ANECDOTES OF MOVEMENT AND BELONGING

Intertwining Strands of the Professional and the Personal

COLIN MURRAY

Framework

The themes of migration, home, loss and identity can be analysed professionally through observation of the lives of other people. They are also intensely personal, in that they pervade our own lives. We all move about; our ideas of 'home' are variable over time and highly subjective; we all experience loss, in one form or another; the question of who we 'really' are often troubles us, and sometimes it troubles other people also. For me, these themes illustrate the absurdity of any presumption that it is desirable or indeed possible to separate the professional and the personal in their analysis. Accordingly, I see this chapter as an opportunity to reflect on the intertwining strands over forty years of my experience of them in my own working life and my professional study of other people's experience of them. Inevitably, there is much (selective) autobiography here, but I write it not in a spirit of self-indulgence, but in the conviction that everyone's story is interesting in its particulars, everyone's story is different and I can only properly write about my own.

This objective was prompted by a moment of coincidence in May 2012. One evening, I received two emails that define for me the beginning of the trail – in the early 1970s, the extended family histories of people far away in southern Africa; and the end of the trail (for the time being) – in the early

2010s, the extended family histories of a number of people from the past who have shared with me a strong attachment to a very particular small place in southwest Scotland.

One email was from my nephew Morobi, in Brakpan, east of Johannesburg, who was getting back in touch after some years and seeking my help in reconstructing the Pitse family tree, rooted in a village in the northern Leribe district of Lesotho. He attached photographs of the family graves, newly refurbished by his maternal uncles, my brothers. Himself approaching forty, Morobi is the son of my sister Ntebaleng. She is the daughter of Semahla Pitse, the man who in late July 1972 generously received me, then a total stranger, in his home village of Pitse's Nek, took me under his wing and settled me on a patch of ground below his own homestead. This was my home for two and a half years of concentrated anthropological fieldwork until December 1974 and I shall always remember it with affection in the gracious Sesotho idiom *moo ba nkamohetseng ke le ngoana lapeng,* 'where they received me as a child of the house'. It was sufficient explanation of my sometimes-intrusive presence. I was easily absorbed into the genealogy and despite the passing of the generations, I remain known there, on my short and now very intermittent visits to Pitse's Nek, as Thabo Pitse.

The other email was from my elderly aunt Vonca in Kelso, in the Scottish Borders. She forwarded the Dropbox containing her cousin John Greenhouse's (in Canada) painstaking transcription of more than 460 pages of the letters written home to his family in Cheshire by his father Frank Greenhouse as a soldier in India and Mesopotamia before and during World War I. Frank was one of the many siblings of Hilda Greenhouse (1888–1993), who was my step-grandmother and the mother of my aunt Vonca. Hilda was the wife of the second 'house' – to use an African idiom – of my grandfather John Murray (1893–1981), and thus no blood relation to me, but I knew her throughout my own life until her death. The reason my aunt forwarded the Greenhouse letters to me was that I had been drawn during 2009–10, in the evening of my own life, as my father predicted I would be, to pursuit of our own (Murray) family history. I had written a manuscript and distributed it around our extended family, including cousins in Canada and Australia.

The coincidence of emails serves briefly to introduce two discrete sets of relatives, belonging to entirely different worlds. In 1972–74, on anthropological fieldwork, I studied the lives of many people who were compelled, for want of employment in Lesotho, to engage in repeated contracts of migrant labour in neighbouring South Africa, in the mines and elsewhere – away from their homes and families for up to a year at a time. They were subject to the routine harassment of the pass laws, and the great majority remained aliens in the apartheid state. Only a few of them were able to establish permanent homes in South Africa. Many of my fellow-villagers were largely illiterate and the stories they told me about their family histories had very little authority in written sources. The extended Pitse family, to which I came to belong, was a large one in the village, and I recorded in my field diaries its many complex wrangles of the past and their reverberations in the (then) present. I published my analysis of them in *Families Divided* (1981). In doing so, because some of the disputes were sensitive and controversial in that place and at that time, I adopted pseudonyms throughout the book. It was a decision I have come to regret, because it arbitrarily cut off members of the family two generations 'down' from substantial parts of their own family history. Of course, I recorded privately a long list of correspondence between the pseudonyms and the real names, but these columns must now be painstakingly copied and cross-referred to the genealogical diagrams published in the book for my nephew Morobi to make any sense of it in relation to the real lives of his antecedents. On the basis of two and a half years of intensive oral fieldwork in 1972–74, then, I emerged – for a much younger generation of the family that had all but lost touch with its original 'home' village in Lesotho – as an authority of sorts on Pitse family history. I also became keeper of a gate I had myself unwittingly erected, through which interested members of the family must now pass to discover their ancestors, to place them in a larger genealogy and to understand some of the intricacies of their lives.

I am sure this is a not-unfamiliar situation for an elderly anthropologist to find himself/herself in, but it has left me with a sceptical view of the habit that then prevailed by which, when we wrote about people in faraway places, we often disguised their identities, nominally to protect our informants. It has also left me with a keen sense of the curious contingencies through which the ancestors reassert themselves long after their own lives have drawn to a close. Late in his own life, my father, John Murray (1919–1999) – a practical farmer, an amateur engineer and a keen sailor – discovered this for himself. Preoccupied in his retirement with identifying an ancestor in the late seventeenth century and placing him in a known genealogy, he knew that the Murray patriline was rooted in the Scottish Borders for about three hundred years from the mid seventeenth century to the mid twentieth century. The trails led him all over the south of Scotland, the Borders region in particular, and to the realization that 'Fam Hist', as he put it, is a stimulating route into 'Hist'. Thus, an ostensibly narrow preoccupation with rooting 'our' missing ancestor in a recorded genealogy turned into intensive reading on the dramatic events and the rapidly shifting religious and political loyalties and antagonisms of the mid to late seventeenth century in Scotland. Aware that his obsession sometimes sorely tried the patience of his family, he remarked wryly in a letter to me that 'ancestors acquire reverence only when you are about to join them'. By December 1987, he was writing: 'I may be wrong but I suspect that you may find my present pursuit of ancestors irresistible by the time you are my age.' And so it came to pass. Much of the manuscript I wrote in 2010 outlined the lives of five generations of my antecedents in the patriline, from the early nineteenth century to the mid twentieth century, and those of two successive generations in the matriline of my great-grand-father. For me, the fascination of the exercise lay not in 'mere genealogy', but in detailed and painstaking reconstruction of the historical circumstances of their lives.

My intellectual roots were in Cambridge anthropology as it was in the late 1960s and the early 1970s. I absorbed the department's keen interest in 'kin-ship'. Its slippery intricacies intrigued me and they suited my temperamental habits of persistent curiosity, close attention to detail and single-minded in-tensity – a combination I have found to be a mixed blessing in the conduct of everyday life. The intricacies have intrigued me throughout my professional life. However, for years now, my definition of my abiding preoccupation has been 'family history', not 'kinship'. The distinction may seem a slight one, but it conveys what now seems to me a paradigmatic shift in the foci of my intellectual interests. In Pitse's Nek in the early 1970s and in much of anthro-pology at the time, there was rather little 'history'. Now I cannot do without it. The decisive fieldwork experience that defines this shift for me and that on reflection significantly shaped the trajectory of my life thereafter took place in 1980 and is outlined below. Part of my overall reflection, in reviewing my own history before and after that date, relates to what I have found in Britain to be a broadly inverse relationship between intellectual comfort with strong interdisciplinary aspiration, on the one hand, and formal progress within the boundaries of conventionally defined academic departments, on the other hand.

The 1970s: Cambridge Anthropology, Conventional Fieldwork and Political Economy

The root of my experience in Africa was a year on VSO (Voluntary Service Overseas) in southwestern Uganda in 1966–67, when I was eighteen, teach-ing maths and English in a new bush secondary school near Rwashamaire in Ankole. The setting was a romantic one: the landscape was hilly, open and undulating; Ankole cattle blocked the roads with the dramatic span of their horns; herders often stood on one leg, carrying a spear. I was supposed to be mugging up on Thucydides and Homer and Virgil in order to read Classics at Cambridge. The appeal of this rapidly palled. I was seduced instead, in the old cliché, by the waters of the Nile, and within three weeks of my first term at Cambridge, I changed from Classics to Archaeology and Anthropology. I became engrossed in all sorts of literature, much of it relating to the comparative study of African societies. I had a brief initiation into fieldwork at Easter 1969 in the Essex village of Elmdon, the anthropologist Audrey Richards' home village, on a small local and family history project that she directed over a number of years, and returned to Ankole in the summer vacation of 1969 to undertake a small study of the inverse relation between family cattle holdings and levels of schooling attained. In 1969–70, the last year of my undergraduate degree in Social Anthropology, some of us chose as a specialist option a course on 'The Southern Bantu', based on a series of the classic ethnographies of the 1930s, 1940s and 1950s. They included Audrey Richards on the Bemba, Monica Wilson on the Nyakyusa, Clyde Mitchell on the Yao, Eileen Krige on the Lovedu and Hilda Kuper on the Swazi. I remember writing an exam answer on the esoteric subject of cross-cousin marriage amongst the Lovedu. The 'unit of study' defined in ethnic terms then seemed unproblematic. All that changed later.

I planned fieldwork in Ankole towards a Ph.D. However, when I graduated in June 1970, I set off hitchhiking with a friend from Nairobi to Durban, South Africa, where I spent three months working for the South African Institute of Race Relations in poor Indian and 'Coloured' townships, and three months teaching in a north Durban white high school. The first experience sharply opened my eyes to some of the realities of racial segregation and extreme inequality in the apartheid state. The second gave me an unhappy insight into the mindset of loutish white teenage boys. Stranded somewhat by shortage of money, I postponed my return to Britain for the Ph.D. (The delay rightly aggrieved Meyer Fortes, who had been my patron for an SSRC [Social Science Research Council] award that was lost to the department as a result.) Following Idi Amin's coup in Uganda in January 1971, it became clear quite quickly that a return to Ankole for fieldwork was not going to be feasible. I applied instead to Monica Wilson, Professor of Anthropology in Cape Town, for a job in her department, and duly emerged at the age of twenty-two as Junior Lecturer in Anthropology.

My focus of prospective fieldwork changed accordingly. Without funding now, I began to explore Lesotho as a possible site. By a stroke of fortune, Monica Wilson's family retreat in the Hogsback in the Eastern Cape adjoined that of the Secretary of the Chairman's Fund of the Anglo American Corporation. Through her influence, I was given a generous grant from the fund in late 1971 for two years of fieldwork in Lesotho in 1972–74 (subsequently extended by six months). The Fund took a broad view of its philanthropic terms of reference. To its credit, there was no attempt to influence or to limit the ways in which I defined my project, and no attempt to inhibit criticism in due course of some of the practices of the mining industry.

So, towards the end of three weeks in July 1972 exploring the mountains of Lesotho in a Land Rover, traversing alone a bitterly cold and partly

snow-covered landscape, I came by chance to be received and settled at
Pitse's Nek. My hut was rebuilt from a tumbled-down state. I embarked on
fieldwork (supervised by Monica Wilson) amongst my new relatives and
my neighbours, for the most part poor people largely dependent on the
remittances of household members working as migrant labourers in South
Africa. The dominant substance of my fieldwork became observation and
analysis relating to the mundane but fundamentally important particulars
of how people lived. I built up genealogies of many families and carried out
successive household surveys, since demographic turnover was high and
absent members of households made critically important contributions to
daily livelihoods. It was obvious, then, that writing up my material towards a
Ph.D. at the end of fieldwork required a macro-framework that allowed me
to interpret almost every parochial activity or 'work' of custom in relation
to a regional system of the exploitation of black labour with a distinctive
history and a pervasive reach. This history was central to an understanding
of industrial development in South Africa and, politically and socially, to its
passage from Segregation to *Apartheid* in the twentieth century.

In 1975–76, back in Cambridge, I explored strands of literature that
opened up such a possibility. A broad framework of radical political economy was developing at the time that sought to relate the extreme inequalities
of class and race in South Africa to the dynamics of capitalist accumulation.
It was in part rooted in a critique of the liberal historiography exemplified in
the two-volume *Oxford History of South Africa* (1969, 1971). More broadly, it
reflected the influence of an all-too-brief ferment of revival of Marxist analysis that swept the academies of Western Europe and America in those years,
in several different disciplines. Strands of social history 'from below' flow-
ered alongside and as part of this ferment.

I completed the Ph.D. at Cambridge in 1976 and found a temporary teaching post in the Department of Anthropology at the London School of Economics (LSE). It was a mixed experience, but was happily the occasion of a
friendship with Tom Selwyn that has persisted intermittently through the
decades since. Neither of us was appointed on a longer-term basis, I have
suspected since because neither of us could quite be relied upon not to be
subversive. Through the mid to late 1970s, for me, the stimulation of expanding my intellectual horizons in favour of political economy and social history was accompanied by a creeping partial disillusionment with prevailing
paradigms in anthropology. My wrestling with these tensions is reflected in
articles on bridewealth (1977) and on customary conciliation of the ancestors that required substantial material resources, derived principally from
earning from migrant mine labour (1979). The sharpest tension for me was
induced by an invitation to collaborate with a liberal historian, William Lye,
in writing the second volume of a new series on 'The People of Southern

Africa' published by David Philip in Cape Town. Our volume was to be on the Tswana and Southern Sotho. We were unable to reach a mutual under-standing on ways of integrating liberal historiography with radical political economy, so that the volume emerged a little uncomfortably with separate chapters clearly identified as his work and my work respectively. I argued strongly for a title that shifted the centre of gravity of the overall enterprise away from the ethnic focus that inspired it. Thus, a book provisionally en-titled *The Tswana and the Southern Sotho* became *Transformations on the Highveld* (1980) and, somewhat to my public embarrassment and my private satisfaction, it killed off the series as originally conceived.

Meanwhile, there was a tightening squeeze in the late 1970s on Africanist jobs in British universities. Two years at the LSE in 1976–78 proved to be my first and last employment in a department of anthropology in Britain. How-ever, I was fortunate in being offered a three-year Research Fellowship in Sociology at Liverpool University. The head of the Sociology Department, John Peel, specifically welcomed a further infusion of Africanist interests; then and subsequently, he proved to be my sole intellectual patron in the pursuit of employment.

By the end of the 1970s, writing my half of *Transformations on the High-veld,* I had disclaimed an anthropological approach to the subcontinent that was rooted in the convention that anthropologists studied 'tribes'. The great ethnographers of the past acknowledged, of necessity, that significant 'social change' had taken place. For me, understanding the 'social change' in ques-tion was itself the central intellectual enterprise, hence the macro-framework of regional political economy. Thus, for example, a routine preoccupation in the transaction of family life in Lesotho, that of bridewealth, based on the customary premise that *ngoana ke oa likhomo* ('the child belongs to the cattle'), had to be understood in relation not only to individual lifecycles and extended family interests, but also in relation to the opportunities and constraints of mine employment in South Africa, far beyond the confines of the ethnic group.

The book that arose directly from my extended fieldwork in the early 1970s, *Families Divided* (1981), was fairly conventional in form, but it also re-flected this shift of intellectual interest. I followed up the original fieldwork with a further period of fieldwork in Lesotho in 1978, which was intended to analyse the local impact of significant changes relating to mine employment that had taken place in the mid 1970s, above all those of 'internalization' (an increasing proportion of mineworkers recruited from within South Africa itself) and 'stabilization' (a structural shift towards mine labour as a 'career' for smaller numbers of more skilled workers). Both changes threatened a sharp increase in structural unemployment amongst young men in Leso-tho, and so it turned out. Subsequently, I was awarded an SSRC grant for a longer period of fieldwork in the first half of 1980 to pursue the implications of this.

However, in March 1980, I was shocked by the 'discovery' of two new concentrations in different parts of the Orange Free State (OFS) of very large numbers of people who had been displaced from white-owned farms and large and small towns in the province within the broad terms of the most insidiously destructive aspect of the infrastructure of apartheid, that of the mass forced removal of 'redundant' Africans from their homes in 'white' South Africa. One of these concentrations was the large rural slum then known as Onverwacht – it later became Botshabelo ('place of refuge') – outside Thaba Nchu in the eastern part of the province. The other was Qwaqwa, a small African reserve in the northeastern corner of the OFS, bordering Lesotho and Natal, whose population had increased by several hundred thousand during the 1970s. The original intention of my research was abruptly overtaken by what seemed to me then to be a more immediate priority: to investigate these places. This led to awkward negotiations with the SSRC over the terms of reference of their support. They were concerned, naturally enough, by the obvious fact that I could obtain no official permission in South Africa to conduct such research. From my old home base in Pitse's Nek, I carried out a series of brief and intensive forays over the following months to Onverwacht and Qwaqwa. I recorded many varieties of human misery embodied in the experiences of the inhabitants of the new rural slums, often expressed to me with vigorous indignation and sometimes unnerving for me to listen to. In *Black Mountain* (1992), I have analysed at length some of the detail of the stories told to me by people of Onverwacht/ Botshabelo. For my purposes here, I describe my experience of fieldwork in Qwaqwa in the same period, a very different experience from that of earlier 'settled' fieldwork in Lesotho.

Qwaqwa, 1980: A Pivotal Moment

I first visited Qwaqwa in December 1970, on a journey first by car and then on foot up past the Sentinel to the magnificent frowning precipices of the Drakensberg, which at that point form the boundary between Lesotho, KwaZulu-Natal and the Free State. Phuthaditjhaba ('gathering of the nations') was a small cluster of municipal boxes that contrasted starkly with the still-rural atmosphere of the rest of the old Witzieshoek reserve. Ten years later, in 1980, I came to Qwaqwa to investigate the appalling scale and the hideous experience of mass forced relocation. Through the 1970s, the population of this small and barren enclave, tucked up against the Drakensberg by a protruding ridge that gave the place its name today, had increased from 24,000 to approximately 300,000. It had been declared the 'homeland' of the Basotho, and Chief Minister Tshiame Kenneth Mopeli, who won his second election for the Dikwankwetla Party in March 1980, immediately preceding my visit, had summoned 'his people' from the further reaches of the southern Transvaal, the northern and western OFS and the northern Transkei. The 'push' forces, then, were the political exclusion of black South Africans from any future in 'white' South Africa and the gathering pace of farm evictions, whether direct or indirect, from the white-owned countryside. The 'pull' forces were Mopeli's campaign to bring 'his people' 'home' and the desperate need for a secure place to live that was felt by hundreds of thousands of people chased off farms and out of the old locations of the larger towns of magisterial districts throughout the OFS.

My black-and-white photographs of that period show a haphazard sprawl across the former countryside of Witzieshoek/Qwaqwa of new mud-brick shacks with corrugated sheeting roofs. My fieldwork diary records: 'Phuthaditjhaba an enormous box plain with hive of dust, industrial sites. Cast in the peculiar dull light of an oncoming storm, down from the escarpment.' There was a large school, a shopping centre, a long central road, a turning up to the office of the Employment Bureau of Africa (TEBA), where men were recruited in already diminishing numbers for the mines. In 1979, there was a much higher proportion of 'Specials' (with bonus certificates) than there had been in earlier years, which was cited by the office manager as evidence of the Chamber of Mines' new policy of retaining skilled workers. 'But often the mines report they are full up', he conceded, 'and they are not taking anyone except Specials at the moment.'

Everything, I discovered, was connected to everything else, even in this remote enclave of Qwaqwa. More skilled employment at higher wages for fewer men was the other side of the predicament of acute structural unemployment for a whole generation of youth in Lesotho and to a lesser extent in the OFS. A booming gold price in the early 1980s followed the second OPEC oil price hike of 1979, but the United States simultaneously imposed high interest rates in order to finance its budget and trade deficits, and thence effectively exported economic recession around the world. Thus, the boom in the gold price gave only temporary relief from the longer-term trend of declining mine employment. For their part, South African farmers shivered in the cold wind of a decisive shift from negative to positive real interest rates; their escalating debt, alongside drought and increasingly adverse terms of trade, precipitated a further wave of farm evictions. Thus, the tidal waves of international macro-economic change washed swiftly into every nook and cranny of the regional economy of the eastern OFS.

I had an abortive visit to the magistrate, van Vieren, who discovered I was British and advised me to apply for a research permit to Pretoria. He knew as well as I did that this would take months and was wholly unlikely to be granted to a foreigner. Meanwhile, deviation from the main road was not permitted. As I emerged from the magistrate's office, I was besieged by a cluster of men seeking work, any sort of work. It's the first time we've seen a place like this, they said, without anything, without jobs or money or fields or cattle. Their momentary quickening of expectation died in disappointment when they discovered I was a vagrant sociologist, not a potential employer of labour. 'You can see the fear in people's eyes and whole demeanour', I recorded in my diary, 'there is no joy in children's faces amid the hunger.' For me, then, Qwaqwa in 1980 was the most dramatic physical example of the grotesque social engineering of the apartheid state by which structural unemployment and poverty and black political aspirations were exported and confined to remote 'rural' areas of the country. It was a place of dust and bleakness and fear and hunger. The bar of the Qwaqwa Hotel in Phuthaditjhaba was sub-Graham Greene in its unwitting parody of garish style and seedy incompetence. A motley succession of confidential wide boys sidled up to this foreign white man, ill at ease as I was in a place of dismal unwelcome. In implicit invitation to explain myself, it seemed, they offered me semi-plausible but contradictory accounts of the chicaneries of the 'other lot', whoever they might be: South African security police, Qwaqwa government spies, disappointed notables of the local political opposition or Lesotho government spies.

In May 1980, I returned to Qwaqwa and carried out some detailed interviews in Tseki, one of the new settlements. The schools were on strike. The police moved in, closed the schools and arrested 'troublemakers' who invariably, a trader told me, turned out to be boarders from Gauteng (Johannesburg and its environs, the Place of Gold). One good thing about Mopeli, the same trader said, was that he would stand for no nonsense. By default, at the time, I was the OFS representative of the Surplus People Project (SPP), convened by Laurine Platzky and Cherryl Walker to investigate and report on the nature and extent of forced relocation throughout the country. Chaos prevailed both in Onverwacht/Botshabelo and in Qwaqwa. However, whereas Onverwacht had sprung up on the bare veld and a white foreigner without papers could get lost in the sprawl of new settlement as construction engineers and typhoid inspectors drove furiously about, Qwaqwa was 'orderly' in the sense that at least 250,000 new immigrants were absorbed into the established infrastructure of tribal authorities, headmen and spies. Even as chiefs and headmen watched their fields and grazing land being converted into sprawling shack settlements, the political subordination of many more people meant the extension of their own patronage.

A large group of us connected with the SPP met on the Natal South Coast for a weekend in mid June 1980 for an intensive two-day meeting to share information and to develop strategy in the light of our findings. On the Saturday afternoon, we were interrupted by three men in loud t-shirts and thigh-tight shorts, who turned out to be security police and who wanted to know what we were doing. It was 14 June, immediately before the anniversary on 16 June of the schoolchildren's revolt in 1976 that went into history as 'Soweto' – a time when the authorities were especially jittery. I was singled out, and invited outside, as the only foreigner in the group, and Lieutenant Ferreira impressed me with his long memory. They obviously had a file on me. He asked me whether I had been living in Greyville, Durban, in the latter part of 1970, ten years earlier. Yes, I said. And they could answer my question too, since they carried radios. It was the afternoon of the British Lions game against the Springboks at Bloemfontein, and the match hung in the balance. My interest in the outcome, already intensely partisan, was quickened by their infuriating fusion of the virility of the Springboks with the security of white supremacy. (Alas, the Lions lost.)

Four days later, on 18 June 1980, immediately on my return to Qwaqwa from the Natal South Coast, and midway through an interview in Tseki, I was apprehended courteously but firmly by a blue-uniformed policeman. He turned out to be 'under the chieftainship'; finding no papers on me, he informed me that it was 'God's law' that blacks should 'respect' (*hlompha*, i.e. socially avoid) whites; he advised me to go to the magistrate for permission to visit people in Qwaqwa. Otherwise my behaviour was illegal. There followed a tediously protracted scramble for some transient legitimacy in Qwaqwa. I was taken to the Minister of Health, Motebang Mopeli, who was also chief of the Kwena tribal domain, then to the Minister of the Interior and then briefly to Chief Minister T.K. Mopeli himself, outside the Qwaqwa Parliament. Rotund, avuncular and unbending, he referred me to the (new) magistrate, Wolmarans, who discovered that I had studied anthropology and swiftly inferred that we had something in common, since he had studied ethnology (*volkekunde*) at university as part of his training in Bantu Administration. This proved to be the only possible terrain of mutual understanding, and I duly emerged with a four-day permit to study 'whether customs of Sotho in Qwaqwa differ much from that in Lesotho'. The usual conditions applied: I must not lodge with blacks and I must refrain from interfering in the domestic affairs of blacks. Further, in my dealings with blacks, 'if any', I must behave in a dignified manner and refrain from criticism of the administration of the government. I was given a supporting letter from the Basotho-Qwaqwa Government Service, which requested chiefs and headmen in the Mopeli domain to cooperate with me.

During those few intensive days, several people cooperated with me to a great extent. They introduced me to their families, recalled their experiences of relocation (forcible or otherwise) and told me other stories of their lives and labours in the tentacles of apartheid's manifold embrace: in the towns, down the mines, on the farms and elsewhere in the countryside.

The 1980s: Late Apartheid, Unconventional Fieldwork, Institutional Marginality

As a consequence of my encounter with the security police in June 1980 described above, it turned out in late 1981, when I was detained at Jan Smuts Airport in Johannesburg, in transit (or so I thought) to Lesotho, that my visa exemption status as a British citizen had been withdrawn and that I had no permit to be in South Africa. It remained withdrawn for ten years, until 1991, when the political climate had greatly relaxed and I nagged the Department of Home Affairs through the London Embassy until it was restored. The result of the ban was a habit of subterfuge, honed over the years for a decade, by which I would fly on from Johannesburg to Maseru, the capital of Lesotho, take a combi/taxi up to Ficksburg bridge, one of the principal crossing points from northern Lesotho into the OFS, and walk across the road bridge connecting the two. I would engage the immigration officials in casual conversation and hope – in those days prior to computer registration – that they would not reach over their shoulders for the printed list of prohibited persons, but would let me pass without hindrance. This strategy let me down only once, when I was forced instead to make a long detour south and cross the border into the Herschel district of the Transkei (the first 'independent African homeland' in the grand apartheid strategy) and thence into 'white' South Africa without passing an immigration post, so that I did not on that occasion have an entry stamp in my passport. This caused a hiccup when I came to leave the country, but the official was sufficiently ignorant of geography to confuse the Herschel district of Transkei with Botswana. I had to sustain a constant wariness on every field trip through this period lest the *konstabels* take an interest in my presence here or there. This was tedious. It was also tedious for these ten years to incur the odium both of the South African immigration authorities for going to South Africa and of the anti-apartheid movement in Liverpool for going to South Africa.

Fieldwork was utterly different, then, before 1980 and after 1980. Prior to that date, it was largely a conventional anthropological experience of settled and protracted 'immersion' in the lives of small communities in Lesotho, in all of which my presence was officially negotiated and approved. From early 1980 onwards, my intermittent bouts of fieldwork were fast and intensive and were undertaken in many different places in the Free State and elsewhere, in short periods of, typically, only three weeks at a time, and often on several different projects in parallel. In almost all of these places, for a decade, my presence was technically illegal and officially disapproved. This made me all the more stubborn. Reasonably good fluency in Sesotho was of course a necessary condition of effective work in such circumstances, and frissons of insecurity inevitably accompanied it. There was a quite different circumstance, this time a very happy one, which greatly constrained both the frequency and the duration of fieldwork trips to southern Africa. Our home was in Liverpool throughout this period and my two daughters were born in 1982 and 1985.

In retrospect, it is clear that my fieldwork in the first half of 1980 – variously at Onverwacht/Botshabelo in the eastern OFS, in Qwaqwa in the northeastern OFS and in Lesotho itself – was the decisive 'moment' in my shift from the paradigms of anthropology to those of political economy and social history. I have written in depth in *Black Mountain* about the place of Onverwacht/Botshabelo in the regional political economy of the eastern OFS. I explained that there the ways in which, and the reasons why, a project that began as an investigation of the experience of mass forced relocation both contracted in space and deepened in time. It emerged as a detailed study of the social history of one district of the OFS over a period of one hundred years.

For much of the 1980s, I also had spasms of professional insecurity. The Liverpool research fellowship came to an end in 1981 and, since we were committed for the time being to a home life in that city, I did not find it easy to find further employment. I had judged it politic to develop an alternative arm of my teaching portfolio, in Race and Community Relations in Britain, and for a temporary year was employed by Edge Hill College in Ormskirk. There followed various temporary stints, some of them part-time, again at Edge Hill in Afro-Asian Studies, at the Open University and the Liverpool Institute of Higher Education, the Liverpool Institute of Public Administration (LIPAM) and the Sociology Department at Liverpool University. From early 1987, already having a foot in the door, I was offered a longer-term contract at LIPAM and taught there until 1994. It was the period of my career that most stretched the credibility gap between my experience and intellectual interests on the one hand and my various teaching commitments on the other. I had no evident qualifications or aptitude in public administration and management. The saving grace was that many of the students were 'international' – some of the most industrious were from Africa (for whom sources of financial support later dried up) – and most of them were interested in 'development', broadly construed. While, on the whole, it was possible to bend my teaching obligations so that they were more intellectually congenial than otherwise would have been the case, it remained a jarring experience to juggle these obligations and the writing of *Black Mountain*. Fortunately, I was invited to Yale for one semester in 1988 to participate in its

Southern Africa Research Program, and this enabled me to break the back of the writing. Fortunately too, my sense of being a fish out of water at LIPAM was counterbalanced by long-term membership of the editorial board of the *Journal of Southern African Studies* – a thoroughly congenial association.

The 1990s: Land Reform, Public Policy and Social History

A dramatic change in the political climate took place from 1990, with the release from jail of Nelson Mandela and the revocation of the ban on the African National Congress and other political organizations. For the first time in a decade, I could pursue fieldwork in South Africa 'in the open', and new research opportunities opened up as the political transformation took shape and the outlines of future policy began to emerge. William Beinart and I carried out a study of agrarian change in the eastern Free State (1995), in which he interviewed white farmers and I explored the predicament of black farm labourers who were, for the most part, already ex-farm labourers. White farmers were at the time, as one of them explained to me, 'farming backwards at a hell of a speed'. The trends of the 1980s – heavy indebtedness, positive real interest rates and adverse trade terms – had worsened for them, partly as a result of the withdrawal of state subsidies that had historically favoured 'white' farming. The immediate consequence for many farm la-bourers and their families was a further wave of evictions from white-owned farms. From the late 1980s, following the repeal of the pass laws, many such people moved to the new shack peripheries of small district towns through-out the province. In the early 1990s, therefore, the experience of structural unemployment in the 'white' countryside was best investigated through fieldwork in small towns.

Otherwise, as a result of my disparate work in the Free State in the 1980s, I became involved with the new structures of the Department of Land Affairs, the Free State provincial administration and various regional non-governmental organizations (NGOs) committed to an emerging land reform policy. All this was new to me: working explicitly with official structures and no longer covertly against them, with the political tide and not against it. I contributed substantially to the Free State pilot study, with detailed field-work here and there myself and analytical and editorial coordination of the contributions of others. In the following years, through regular field trips in the period 1995–98, I was able to investigate progress in the implementa-tion of the several complex elements of land reform: restitution of land from which Africans had been forcibly removed in earlier decades; redistribution of state and private land; and efforts to resolve insecurity of land tenure in 'communal' areas. During this period, I directed a small project on the specific comparative experience of restitution, published in 1998, subtitled *A Long Way Home*.

By 1994, in Britain, following the distress of marital separation but sharing a continuing commitment to full parenthood, we had ourselves moved from Liverpool to Manchester. I took the risk of taking time off from my employment at Liverpool University to take up a one-year research fellowship at Manchester University, which to my great relief turned into an appointment as a University Senior Research Fellow for the five years 1995–2000. I was affiliated to the Institute for Development Policy and Management (IDPM) and (loosely) to the Department of Sociology. The opportunity was of course accompanied by responsibility, in this case not least to raise outside funding for research. I applied to the Department for International Development (DfID) with Elizabeth Francis of the LSE and gained support for a project entitled Multiple Livelihoods and Social Change, involving the comparison of two particular areas: Qwaqwa in the Free State and Ditsobotla in the North-West Province, from 1998 to 2002. The project employed one researcher, Rachel Slater.

The project gave me a glimpse of an inevitable trade-off, not altogether happily realized, between managing a project, on the one hand, on which someone else was employed to undertake the principal fieldwork, and striving to sustain a much-diminished opportunity, on the other hand, for bits and pieces of first-hand fieldwork myself that were always for me the lifeblood of any one research project. Thus, for example, eighteen years after my mini-household survey in Qwaqwa in June 1980, in January and November 1998 I looked for the key individuals again, this time without the need to dissimulate to officials, and sought rapidly to understand how their lives had changed. (In the course of the November research visit, in Phuthaditjhaba together with Rachel Slater, we were swiftly mugged and I was stabbed in the shoulder. Qwaqwa has not been my favourite place of fieldwork.)

I have always liked the ways in which different research projects grow out of small adventitious conjunctions. I have especially valued for this reason, for example, my correspondence and friendship with Miriam Basner, whom I knew for the last twenty years of her life until her death in 2003. She was the widow of H.M. (Hymie) Basner (1905–77), a Jewish lawyer of Latvian family origin who had immigrated to South Africa at an early age and cut his teeth in the 1930s on the politically demoralizing but often individually successful defence of Africans prosecuted for contravention of the pass laws, brewing and selling illegal liquor, etc. Miriam Basner herself wrote with Chief A.S. Mopeli-Paulus of Witzieshoek a novel, *Turn to the Dark* (1956), on the theme of chieftaincy and medicine murder, and composed with him a manuscript of his autobiography. Our first phase of correspondence, in 1983–84, had to do with my fieldwork in Qwaqwa in 1980, described above, and the analysis of rural slums that arose out of it, thirty years after her own experience with Basner in Witzieshoek (Qwaqwa).

Our second phase of correspondence and meetings, concentrated in the period 1995–98, arose out of her having put together light reminiscences of her own life in southern Africa, including material relevant to the cases of Chiefs Gabashane and Bereng. Her enquiry drew an approach to her from the private secretary of the King of Lesotho, Moshoeshoe II. (The reason for this approach remained elusive, following the King's death in a car crash in March 1996.) Intrigued, I started my own threads of enquiry on the sources available. She put me in touch with Peter Sanders, a historian who had been one of the last generation of colonial officers in Lesotho in the early 1960s. She referred to us as her 'two young men'. It became obvious that we should pool our efforts, and the outcome of a happy collaboration over the following years was a jointly authored book (Murray and Sanders 2005). Most of the book concentrated on the twenty-year period from the 1940s to the 1960s, when medicine murder reverberated politically and socially throughout the country. It was based on extensive archival sources at the Public Record Office in London and the Lesotho National Archives and primary fieldwork in some of the villages concerned. My own first file on medicine murder had been opened in 1971, when my interest was stirred by meeting Thabo Rust, a storekeeper at Phamong in Chief Bereng's domain in southern Lesotho. (He was the uncle – another adventitious connection – of Joni Mcgregor, who I met in Durban in 1970 on my first visit to South Africa and who remains a close friend forty years later.) Thabo Rust told me that his father Lud Rust was convinced that Chief Bereng was innocent of the crime for which he was convicted. My first file then languished for twenty-five years, until Sanders and I picked up the threads in 1996. Miriam Basner told me in 1995 that her husband had been convinced that Chief Gabashane was innocent of the same crime.

An accidental sideline of the investigation of medicine murder, for me, was stimulated by obscure footnote references here and there in the reports on medicine murder written in the late 1940s by Hugh Ashton, the ethnographer of the Basotho, and in 1951 by G.I. Jones, the officially commissioned investigator for the Commonwealth Relations Office in London (who had lectured me in economic anthropology at Cambridge in the late 1960s). The references were to a lurking suspicion that Solomon Lion (1908–87), the leader of a well-known African independent church, based at Maboloka to the northwest of Pretoria, was involved in medicine murder himself. Solomon Lion was a close friend of Chief Gabashane, and, in the next generation, the former's son married the latter's daughter. I had encountered the name of Solomon Lion much earlier, through newspaper reports of violent confrontation in 1976–77 at Maboloka, then incorporated into the Moretele-Odi district of Bophuthatswana. In part caused by Solomon Lion's virulent talent for stoking acrimony, the conflict arose out of the absurd reification of ethnic boundaries promoted by the dogma of 'separate development'. It turned out that Miriam Basner knew him long before, in the early 1940s, when he was on the committee for Basner's election as Senator for Africans. Basner defended him in 1948–49 on a series of charges of multiple rape and murder. Solomon Lion traversed the South African Highveld and Lesotho in colourful and controversial ways, and systematically abused the daughters of his followers and dissidents in his community (see Murray 1999). Thus, Miriam Basner personified for me the links, through her direct experience here and there in southern Africa and the writing interests she developed in retirement in Wales, between several quite different projects that engaged much of my own attention.

In the late 1990s, my research was rather sharply divided between projects relating to 'development' and 'policy-making' in the 'new' South Africa, and projects relating to deep social history in the region. However, fieldwork trips embraced all of them. My field diaries of the time reflect both the stimulation and the stresses of pursuing, on any one short and intensive visit, a number of different projects requiring disparate sorts of fieldwork. I felt some similar tension within the institution in Manchester (the IDPM) to which I was formally affiliated. The first set of activities fell clearly within my public terms of reference: fundraising from external sources for research of a 'policy-relevant' kind. The second set fell outside those terms of reference and, despite my strong intellectual engagement with the projects concerned, I felt to some degree that they were private indulgences.

The last phase of my employment in Manchester University, ending with early retirement in 2002, was affiliation to the Sociology Department, with principal responsibility for the MA in Development Studies and joint responsibility for research training across the Faculty. Again, however, I had some sense of leading a 'double life' in respect of finding the time for the sustained concentration that it required through that period in order to bring the very large medicine murder book to fruition.

I have a general sense of being somewhat at odds, ever since 1981, with the directions of change in British universities. Intellectually, I was often uncomfortable with the prevailing paradigms in whichever academic department saw fit to employ me, especially from the point in the 1980s when postmodernist discourse swept sociology and anthropology and other fields of enquiry, while I remained committed to fundamental questions of a mundane kind, such as how people made a living. Institutionally, I was never comfortable with criteria of advancement that seemed to me in more recent times to subordinate the pursuit of an approximately common intellectual endeavour between colleagues to the manifestly more important question of how much money those colleagues individually brought in.

From 2005: Coming 'Home'

In northern Lesotho in the early 1970s, through the hot and arid summer months of December and January, and in those moments of ennui that afflict all long-term fieldwork, I dreamed of soft driving rain in a small place that has been since childhood very close to my heart. It is a small and uninhabited tidal island in Galloway in southwest Scotland. My family has had the great good fortune, by courtesy of three generations of the family of the local laird who owns it, to have had use of the island cottage for a few weeks in the summer since 1956. I was then eight years old. We quickly came to love it and its primitive conditions of daily life. More than half a century later, my younger daughter retains the habit today, with a group of friends, of an annual occupation.

After the large medicine murder book was 'put to bed' with the publisher in late 2004, I found myself through much of the calendar year of 2005 in a fretful mood, for want of an intellectual project. I had retired early for health reasons in 2002. In July and August 2005, crossing over to the island with my wife Jane and our frisky eight-month-old puppy Mac, there occurred in swift succession two chance encounters. One was with the wife of a well-known retired local undertaker, who it turned out had a cache of family photographs of the island taken in the early 1920s, when his grandfather rented the cottage for the summer for several years. The other was with a visiting Londoner, the grandson of a well-known local man, Fred Heron (1874–1954), who had lived and worked on the island with his family from 1908 to 1919. He had been employed by Harry Glover (1867–1945), a doctor who spent his working life on tea estates in Assam, but also rented the island cottage between 1907 and 1921.

There were other moments of serendipity also. Over the decades, for me, they have repeatedly been an important stimulation of first-hand fieldwork, and they also survive as part of the later frisson of thinking and writing. One thing led to another. In this case, these moments and the trails they sparked induced the gestation of what I have loosely called the Island Project. As I gradually developed my pursuit of the connections of different families with the island, principally in the first part of the twentieth century, it became clearer to me what I wanted to do: first, to identify 'key' individuals who had, like me, known it very well and loved it; and, second, to pursue their extended family histories, spread around the world as they were. One of these extended family histories is, of course, my own. The trigger for detailed pursuit of that was an involuntary ten-day stay in hospital at Easter 2009. I was able to turn it into an accidental opportunity to relieve my intense boredom there by starting to disentangle a heap of miscellaneous bits and pieces left over from the past that were kindly sent to me by my aunt Vonca, who was referred to at the beginning of this narrative. This related deviation took me a year and a half until mid 2010, since when I have intermittently resumed the writing of the Island Project.

I developed a 'core' diagram showing the diverse connections of these five or six families with the island over time. Most chapters of the manuscript contain a variation of it. The diagram explains why I adopted the absurd conceit for my purpose that a small uninhabited tidal island in Galloway is the centre of the world. The unifying theme at the micro-level is that the 'key' individuals knew the island well and loved it. The unifying theme at the macro-level is that so many of them – or their antecedents in the first or second generations above them – were variously engaged on the frontiers of and at the heart of the British Empire. Many intriguing interconnections may be traced in the passage from the one level to the other. It is possible that they are of historical interest, at least to the descendants of the families concerned, although they may carry no historical significance. There is of course no limit in principle to the extension of such trails; it is merely one of time and interest and energy and resources.

So my professional life has come 'home'. For forty years, through many different research projects, two themes have remained constant: the preoccupation with family history and the intellectual commitment to sustaining a creative tension between micro-level detail and macro-level context. My methodological habits have also remained consistent: first-hand fieldwork and the integration of disparate archival and oral sources of evidence. One of the outcomes of the Island Project that I have greatly relished is the haphazard contingencies that connect 'island families' with parts of my own past in ways that have nothing to do with the island. Two specific illustrations come to mind. One is that a number of young men who belonged to island families joined the British Army in South Africa in 1900, following its first few disastrous months in the Boer War in late 1899. Several of them passed through the Thaba Nchu district of the eastern OFS in the course of the campaign. This is terrain that I know very well. As related above, my primary fieldwork and my research time through the 1980s were largely taken up with a detailed study of the distinctive history of the Thaba Nchu district over one hundred years from the late nineteenth to the late twentieth centuries. One chapter of *Black Mountain* is devoted to the experience and the local aftermath of the Boer War.

Another set of haphazard contingencies is that Harry Glover, the doctor who rented the island cottage, had a close friend called William Townsend

Smith (1861–1937), a tea plantation manager who worked with him in southern Assam and who visited him once on the island in Galloway for a few days in late January 1914. He spent his working life in Assam, but of all his experiences, it was his three martial adventures about which he reminisced with slow animation amid the pipe-smoke of his later years, especially the active combat of the first two: the Manipur campaign of 1891; South Africa in 1900 (I have tramped the quiet and lonely hillside northeast of Bloemfontein that was his 'baptism of fire' with Lumsden's Horse); and Mesopotamia in 1916–18, in the later stages of World War I. Although Townsend Smith had only a fleeting connection with the island, and that at one 'remove', out of curiosity I also pursued his extended family. He emerged as the third brother of ten siblings in a very distinguished Scots family with close connections to India, the Church and the academy. The Smiths and many of their spouses' families are identified by Noel Annan as classic members of the British 'intellectual aristocracy' that he traced from the early nineteenth century into the first half of the twentieth century. Their story appears as an appendix to the Island Project because it proved an irresistible fascination to explore some of the many trails that were laid down in public places by the numerous members of the intellectual aristocracy to whom Townsend Smith was related in one way or another. It is their deposits, both published and unpublished, that help me to bring an awkward and reclusive man out of the shadow of his illustrious siblings. William Townsend Smith's youngest sister, for example, married Montagu Butler (1873–1952), who became Governor of the Central Provinces of India and, in retirement, Master of Pembroke College, Cambridge. (They were the parents of R.A. Butler, Chancellor of the Exchequer at the time Annan was writing; Townsend Smith was thus an uncle to 'Rab' Butler.) Montagu Butler's younger sister Isabel was the mother of Audrey Richards (1899–1984), formerly of the LSE and Wits University and first director of the East African Institute of Social Research at Makerere in the early 1950s, whose work on the Bemba of Zambia I read as an undergraduate. She was a close friend of my Ph.D. supervisor in Cape Town, Monica Wilson (1908–82). Monica Wilson's father-in-law was the Shakespearian scholar John Dover Wilson (1881–1969), who knew well William Townsend Smith's eldest brother, the Old Testament theologian George Adam Smith (1856–1942), when he and his wife lived in retirement in Balerno outside Edinburgh. And so it goes on. Wheels come full circle. 'Kinship' and 'family history' again converge.

I grew up variously in the Scottish Borders, Aberdeenshire and rural Suffolk. I have never been confused about being Scots. In the early 1970s, a long way from home in southern Africa, I found another home in northern Lesotho and lived amongst people many of whose family members were away from home as migrant workers across the border in South Africa. In the

1980s, much of my fieldwork was taken up with tracing the lives of people here and there in the OFS who had never had a secure home of their own. Under the perverse pressures of grand apartheid, they eventually found one in one or other remote and desolate rural slum, reflecting in part the state's rigid imposition of apparently immutable ethnic identities. In the 1990s, under the perverse pressures of 'new times' in the South African country-side – farmers facing acute financial difficulty and anticipating a loss of the degree of freedom to dispose of 'surplus' labour they had under apartheid, further mass evictions took place of black farmworkers and their families. Again, they had to seek some security elsewhere, many in the new shack pe-ripheries of small towns across the Highveld. In the mid to late 2000s, after retirement, I became absorbed in pursuit of the extended family histories around the world of a few people who like me had known and loved a small uninhabited tidal island in Galloway. On the island I now have a keen sense of ghosts jostling from the past. It isn't my home and I have no rights to it, but it is the place that evokes for me the strongest sentiment of belonging. Accordingly, it is the place where my nearest and dearest are instructed to dispose what remains of me in due course to the wind and the rain there. Just so, in the fullness of time, the ancestors come home.

Afterword

by Tom Selwyn

When I first invited Colin to the conference at SOAS (coordinated by Par-vati Raman and myself on behalf of the Centre for Migration Studies and MA in travel, tourism, and pilgrimage respectively), on ideas of home and homecoming – one of the ancestors of this volume – he was hesitant on the grounds that he did not feel as conversant as he would have liked with current anthropological literature in the field. However, he decided – with his char-acteristically graceful enthusiasm – to give a keynote paper, after we agreed that his contribution would weave together reflections on the interrelation-ships between the ways in which his own life's personal and professional tra-jectories had interacted with the places, ideas and feelings of attachment and loss that he directly and indirectly shared with others, including interlocu-tors in his ethnographic field (in Lesotho), his family members both there and here in Britain, together with friends, students, and colleagues. Colin died on 14 October 2013. His essay appears here as a powerful and lasting conclusion to our volume expressing the view that, ultimately, the idea of 'home' may be found in the spaces in which the multiple overlapping rela-tions between the intimate and global, emotional and intellectual, self and other come together.

Colin Murray was born in 1948 and died in October 2013. Much of his intellectual and emotional life is described in his chapter in this book as well as in the obituaries indicated in the links below. Suffice it briefly to make the following points in this paragraph. His intellectual roots, branching out as they did throughout his life, lay in late 1960s Cambridge Anthropology and led to his becoming one of the most distinguished anthropologists of the latter half of the twentieth century. Two of his most distinctive and mutually reinforcing achievements were, first, to push anthropology into the arms of history and political economy and, second, to seal the definitive departure from and abandonment of the then tendency for anthropologists to view their African subjects in terms of ethnic and/or tribal groupings. His extensive publications on economy and society in southern Africa included the books *Transformations on the Highveld* (1980), *Families Divided* (1981) and *Black Mountain* (1992) – the latter two of which have become classic reading for contemporary students of anthropology, sociology and history – and (with Peter Sanders) *Medicine Murder in Colonial Lesotho: The Anatomy of a Moral Crisis.* His teaching career included periods at the LSE, as well as Liverpool and Manchester Universities. For many years, he was joint editor of the *Journal of Southern African Studies,* a post he always spoke of with warmth and enthusiasm. Further biographical details can be found at:

https://www.theguardian.com/science/2013/dec/22/colin-murray-obituary

and:

https://www.scotsman.com/news/obituaries/obituary-colin-murray-anthropologist-and-author-1-3252393.

References

Murray, Colin. 1977. 'High Bridewealth, Migrant Labour, and the Position of Women in Lesotho', *Journal of African Law* 21: 79–96.

———. 1979. 'The Work of Men, Women and the Ancestors: Social Reproduction in the Periphery of Southern Africa', in S. Wallman (ed.), *The Social Anthropology of Work.* London: Academic Press, pp. 337–63.

———. 1981. *Families Divided: The Impact of Migrant Labour in Lesotho.* New York: Raven Press.

———. 1992. *Black Mountain.* Edinburgh: Edinburgh University Press.

———. 1999. The Father, the Son and the Holy Spirit: Resistance and Abuse in the Life of Solomon Lion (1908–1987)', *Journal of Religion in Africa* 29(3): 341–86.

Murray, Colin, and William Beinart. 1995. *Agrarian Change, Population Movements and Land Reform in the Free State.* Working Paper no. 51, Land and Agriculture Policy Centre, Johannesburg.

Murray, Colin, Marj Brown, Justin Erasmus, Rosalie Kingwill and Monty Roodt. 1998. *Land Restitution in South Africa: A Long Way Home.* Cape Town: IDASA.

Murray, Colin, and William F. Lye. 1980. *Transformations on the Highveld: The Tswana and Southern Sotho.* Cape Town: David Philip.

Murray, Colin, and Peter Sanders. 2005. *Medicine Murder in Colonial Lesotho: The Anatomy of a Moral Crisis.* Edinburgh: Edinburgh University Press.

AFTERWORD

TOM SELWYN

What can we learn from our authors? How does their ethnographic and theoretical work direct us towards further understanding of micro (intimate, personal, individual and familial) and macro (global, political and economic) processes involved in travelling towards home? What intellectual traditions do they tap into and build upon? What political implications are there?

Taking our chapters in turn in the order they have appeared in this volume will enable us to take an overview of the collection as a whole.

Chand Starin Basi and Kaveri Qureshi demonstrate how collective senses of sexual identity and solidarity amongst gay South Asian men in London challenge and rebalance many of the assumptions about the primacy of national and ethnic identity held by their parents. Their canvas is necessarily broad: the authors show how the social and cultural processes they describe involve us looking across wide geographical and generational spaces to explore ideas and practices in a small community in a London borough in which 'coming out' is in a certain sense also 'coming home'. Exploring home within this context is at once a macro affair and an intensely personal and familial one.

Shuhua Chen's analysis of the building of a more-or-less 'permanent temporary home' in an industrial city draws together observations on the convulsions of the rapidly transforming the Chinese economy with a quintessentially domestic ethnography. Chen explores her interlocutor's identity work in her new home (which includes consideration of the relationship with her landlady) with a skilful blend of spatial and emotional analysis.

For the Ukrainian families described by Marina Sapritsky as they retrace their steps back from Israel to Odessa, the tension between global geopolitical processes and personal life courses is particularly marked. Sapritsky notes how such apparently prosaic and pragmatic considerations as childcare networks, job opportunities, comfortable living arrangements and avoidance of the dangers of political turbulence in the Middle East shaped decisions to 'return home'. These are presented in striking contrast with ideological pressures, such as those associated with notions of *aliyah* or 'ascent' to the national homeland.

When home is claimed simultaneously by different groups very revealing sparks can fly. Yuko Shioji's exploration of the ideas and values of 'incoming' migrants from English cities to Chipping Campden points to the ways in which these intersect with and have an effect on the lives and spaces of long-established local families. Shioji's work is contextualized by such changing features of the British economy as the decline of rural employment, austerity and low wages in the English countryside vis-à-vis relative prosperity in London, and their effects on rural populations. Shifting economic patterns disrupt local families' residency patterns; an urge to preserve local 'heritage' has an unintended consequence of making homes for some while unmaking them for others.

Unlike as the initial settings appear, parallel phenomena are apparent within the political and economic context of Ilana Webster-Kogan's reading of the Israeli/Palestinian rap group DAM. Israel/Palestine may be shaped by war, violence and the creation of refugees in ways that the Cotswold town is definitely not, yet the simultaneous placing of some in the spaces of displaced others seems strikingly similar. Also comparable (although expressed in completely different ways) are particular elements of sociocultural self-examination in both places. Does not the apparently unchanging 'heritage'-based culture of Chipping Camden resemble in some way the generally understood apparently unchanging traditions (which DAM's lyrics suggest include honour killing) of occupied Palestine?

The refugees from Maluku who Nicola Frost describes in Sydney are haunted by an insistently passionate desire to return both spatially and temporally to their 'homeland paradise' in the Spice Islands, recently disfigured by conflict. Remembered and/or imagined 'home as paradise' is a thematic thread that may be traced throughout several of our chapters. Another thread binds Frost's interlocutors with those of Sapritsky. Both authors take care to point out that in the face of ideology (linked to emotional and nostalgic desire for return in the former case and *aliyah* in the latter), an essential pragmatism is evident in both homemaking contexts.

Colin's Murray's chapter combines the two main underlying themes of this book, displacement and reconstruction, in more than one way. His ethnographic field in Lesotho was structured by the political violence of the South African apartheid system. But his care and close observation of the families amongst whom he worked made him a specialist in the history of those families. Changing regional politics eventually allowed former workers displaced by apartheid to 'come home' to South Africa. Here we are fortunate to have an example of anthropological work being an essential part of homecoming itself. Murray himself was deeply involved with reconstructing the family memories and histories of those with whom he worked. In so doing, he made a lasting contribution to those returning home to South Africa following the demise of apartheid.

Additionally, and uniquely in this volume, Murray tells us a *second* story, profoundly linked as this is to his African work, namely how he reconstructed his own family in the course of carrying out his 'island project' in the Scottish Borders. Working in his characteristically methodical way through the archives of those of his family and friends who had been touched by their contact with a small Hebridean island that he repeatedly visited on holiday, he allows us to glimpse how his *own* 'travel towards home' was accomplished in the part physical, part imaginary reassembling of both the living and ancestral voices of his family from across the world to his island.

We may now draw together some common threads. The chapters in this volume are concerned in distinctive yet comparable ways by transformations of persons, families and communities as a result of global, regional and local politico-economic processes. Taken together, all the chapters are underpinned by two dialectically related themes, namely displacement from and creative reconstruction of home.

All our chapters, in one way or another, suggest that a theoretically coherent lens through which to view processes of displacement and reconstruction of home is composed of at least four features.

The first anchors all the cases described here to a 'world systems' jigsaw. All our authors directly or indirectly place their case studies within global and regional structures and processes. For example, the life of an asylum seeker in Sydney is inexorably linked to conflicts and war in the Spice Islands. More generally, and as referred to in our Introduction, asylum seeking in the United Kingdom and parts of Europe is clearly part of the continuing history of wars and political conflict in Asia, Africa and the Levant.

The second is found in questions of identity and formation of the self. Such questions are obviously and inevitably part of homemaking and homecoming processes. Thus, gay Asian youth in London find and creatively construct their identity from collectively celebrating their sexuality, whilst, surrounded, as they are, by flower gardens, tea sets and Tudor beams, the citizens of Chipping Camden take part in dialogues about identity within politico-economic and sociocultural contexts in which cosy settlement into a version of traditional England for some coincides, and in certain ways is dependent upon, austerity and difficulty in finding appropriate homes for others.

The third concerns the symbolic uses of objects, including the human body, to think about homemaking: Chen's courtyard rubbish, Shioji's tea-pots, Murray's island, and Starin Basi and Qureshi's bodies of their young informants. Here, careful ethnography demands an anchoring in the personal and domestic, exploring the everyday expression of homemaking practices.

The fourth element of our lens, revealed throughout the collection of chapters in this volume, concerns the discourse used in the street and by voices in the media about those who are travelling towards home and the social relations they encounter and engender as they do so. Media reports about those leaving the United Kingdom following 'Brexit discourse' and about those who have successfully constructed their homes in the United Kingdom over the same period illustrate our point effectively (see below).

In addition to their uniformly clear ethnographic work, all our authors have explored the variety of intellectual lineages that have given rise to their own chapters. There is very little for us to add here in this postlude except to offer the lightest of confirmatory observations about theoretical traditions that underlie the collection as a whole. The relevance and pertinence of both ideas and authors are probably very familiar to our readers already. Nevertheless, it seems worthwhile to us to set them out. We will stay with the four elements of our lens.

First of all, each chapter bears the intellectual imprint of 'world systems' approaches pioneered by Immanuel Wallerstein (2015). Second, and equally clearly, each chapter is simultaneously concerned with the formation of community, personal and intimate identities. Here, the work of Ed Mayo and Henrietta Moore (2002) as well as Nicholas Long and Moore (2013) seem actively present. Recent works by these authors appear as intellectual companions of our own authors in insisting that the adoption of 'world systems' approaches can give birth to, rather than contradict, exploration of the social self. Third, there has recently been an explosion of anthropological work on objects, object relations and the centrality of objects to creative social life. This tradition is well established in anthropology, going back at least to Marcel Mauss, articulated more recently by Daniel Miller (1997) and most recently by the several authors engaged in the ethnographic studies gathered together in Bloomsbury's (from 2015 and continuing) excellent series on the role of objects in everyday life.

The fourth aspect of our lens consists of the role of discourse – as found within, and employed by, the many tracks and traces of both popular and scholarly media (from print to painting to music and all points in-between) in processes of home and homemaking. We may return briefly to our Introduction, and allow ourselves, as coeditors, a moment to reflect about one significant part of our own context as we write this postlude. The unfolding evidence of 'Brexit rhetoric' reveals that some citizens of the United Kingdom, who have come from the European Union, feel disquiet and distress. A mounting number are leaving the United Kingdom.

The intellectual tradition of discursively breaking identities into fragments, in the process dividing populations into 'us' and 'them', is very familiar. Edward Said (1978) demonstrated how this was done in the productions by the various Orientalist authors and painters he explored. More recently, the work of such well-known authors as Noam Chomsky (2015) and Amin Ma'alouf (2011), whose image of unpeeling fruit as a metaphor for rhetorically peeling identities, join our authors in theoretical solidarity.

Finally, as to the political implications of our book, we suggest it lies at the centre of a project that is both anthropological and political, namely the continuing tradition of work that combines three fundamental elements: space, identity work and discussions about what Mayo and Moore (2002) have termed the 'mutual state', that is, the plurality of governance institutions in a state that allow and encourage homemaking and homecoming. In a fragmenting world in which travellers of all kinds, including all of those described here, are 'travelling towards home', our politics and policy-making need to deliver spaces and places where sociality and conviviality can flourish (Coleman and Collins 2006; Crouch 2010; Kousis, Selwyn and Clark 2011; Nieuwenhuis and Crouch 2017), where identities can be creatively explored and transformed in landscapes free from walls and hard borders (Derrida 2000; Baker 2013) and where states, together with their planners, architects, and policy-makers generally, place homemaking at the very centre of their activities (Obordo 2017; Yates 2017). In this view, home and homemaking in the uncertain contemporary world described by our authors echo John Donne's (2010 [1620]) aphorisms in one of the more famous poems in the English language:

> No man is an island, entire of itself;
> every man is a piece of the continent, a part of the main.
> If a clod be washed away by the sea, Europe is the less,
> as well as if a promontory were.
> As well as if a manor of thy friend's or of thine own were.
> Any man's death diminishes me, because I am involved in mankind;
> and therefore never send to know for whom the bell tolls;
> It tolls for thee.

Tom Selwyn is Professorial Research Associate in the department of anthropology at SOAS, University of London, and visiting professor at Breda University, the Netherlands, and Bethlehem University, Palestine. He was awarded an Emeritus Fellowship in 2014 by the Leverhulme Foundation. He is widely published (including six edited/coedited volumes) in the field of the Anthropology of Travel/Tourism/Pilgrimage (ATTP) and has directed/codirected five multinational research and development projects in the Mediterranean and Balkan regions for the European Commission, as well as projects for other international agencies elsewhere, including Ethiopia. He was Honorary Librarian and council member for the Royal Anthropological Institute for ten years and was awarded the RAI's Lucy Mair medal in 2009.

REFERENCES

Baker, G. (ed.). 2013. *Hospitality and World Politics.* New York: Palgrave Macmillan.

Chomsky, N. 2014. *Hospitality and Hostility in World Politics.* Lecture at Boston College, Massachusetts. Retrieved 9 April 2018 from https://www.youtube.com/watch?v=-NGQ9INMnq0.

Coleman, S., and P. Collins (eds). 2006. *Space, Place, and Context in Anthropology.* Oxford: Berg.

Crouch, D. 2010. *Flirting with Space: Journeys and Creativity.* Farnham: Ashgate.

Derrida, J. 2000. *Of Hospitality.* Stanford: Stanford University Press.

Donne, J. 2010 [1620]. *The Complete Poems of John Donne.* Harlow: Longman.

Kousis, M., T. Selwyn and D. Clark (eds). 2011. *Contested Mediterranean Spaces: Ethnographic Essays in Honour of Charles Tilly.* Oxford: Berghahn Books.

Long, N.J., and H. Moore (eds). 2013. *Sociality: New Directions.* Oxford: Berghahn Books.

Ma'aluf, A. 2011. *On Identity.* London: Vintage Digital.

Mayo, E. and H. Moore (eds). 2002. *Building the Mutual State: Findings from the Virtual Think Tank.* London: New Economics Foundation.

Miller, D. 1997. *Material Cultures: Why Some Things Matter.* London: University College Press.

Nieuwenhuis, M., and D. Crouch. 2017. *The Question of Space.* Lanham, MD: Rowman & Littlefield.

Obordo, R. 2017. 'Brexit was the Tipping Point: EU Nationals on Why They Left the UK'. *The Guardian,* 7 December. Retrieved 9 April 2018 from https://www.theguardian.com/uk-news/2017/dec/07/brexit-tipping-point-eu-nationals-left-uk.

Said, E.W. 1978. *Orientalism.* London: Routledge & Kegan Paul.

Wallerstein, I.M. 2015. *Uncertain Worlds: World Systems in Changing Times.* London: Routledge.

Yates, K. 2017. 'Our Safe Haven: How We Made Ourselves at Home in Britain'. *The Guardian,* 26 November. Retrieved 9 April 2018 from https:// www.theguardian.com/lifeandstyle/2017/nov/26/our-safe-haven-immigrants-at-home-in-britain-cultural.

Index

www.ingramcontent.com/pod-product-compliance
Lightning Source LLC
Chambersburg PA
CBHW070930030426
42336CB00014BA/2614